TERROR AND CONSENSUS

Contributors

Jean-Marie Apostolidès

Marc Augé

Barbara Cassin

Françoise Gaillard

Maurice Godelier

Jean-Joseph Goux

Françoise Lionnet

Jean-François Lyotard

Mark Poster

Pierre Saint-Amand

Susan Rubin Suleiman

Philip R. Wood

TERROR AND CONSENSUS

VICISSITUDES OF FRENCH THOUGHT

Edited by Jean-Joseph Goux and Philip R. Wood

STANFORD UNIVERSITY PRESS

STANFORD, CALIFORNIA

1998

Stanford University Press
Stanford, California

© 1998 by the Board of Trustees of the
Leland Stanford Junior University

Printed in the United States of America

CIP data appear at the end of the book

Acknowledgments

Most of the contributions to this volume were originally delivered as papers at a conference organized at Rice University in April 1993 to mark the inauguration of a new, expanded, and interdisciplinary department of French Studies. We gratefully acknowledge the generous financial support this conference received from the Florence Gould Foundation, the former Dean of Humanities at Rice University (Allen Matusow), the Rice Center for Cultural Studies and its Continental Theory Workshop, the Collège International de Philosophie, and the Services Culturels Français près du Consulat de France à Houston. We are also grateful to the current Dean of Humanities at Rice University, Judith Brown, for financial help with translations and editing.

We would like to thank the editor of *RISS* for permission to publish Maurice Godelier's "Is the West the Universal Model for Humanity?" and the editor of *Eighteenth-Century Studies* for permission to publish a revised version of Pierre Saint-Amand's "Hostile Enlightenment," the editor of *Les études philosophiques* for permission to publish an English translation of Barbara Cassin's "Speak, If You Are a Man, or The Transcendental Exclusion," the editor of *Contemporary French Civilization* for permission to publish a substantially modified version of Philip R. Wood's "'Democracy' and 'Totalitarianism' in Contemporary French Thought," and Johns Hopkins University Press for permission to reprint Mark Poster's "Postmodernity and the Politics of Multiculturalism." An early version of the essay by Susan Rubin Suleiman first appeared in French in *Les cahiers naturalistes*.

We thank Jennifer Gage for her work as translator, and gratefully acknowledge the help with translations and editing we received from Graham Harris, Shelley Hagen, and Gunnar Person.

We owe thanks to our departmental coordinators, Allene Biehle Korinek and Somarine Diep, for their invaluable administrative assistance.

J.-J.G.
P.R.W

Contents

Mission and Limits of the Enlightenment

Reference Matter

Contributors

Jean-Marie Apostolidès

Jean-Marie Apostolidès is William Bonsall Professor of French and Professor of Drama at Stanford University. He is the author of *Le roi-machine* (Minuit, 1981) and *Le roi sacrifié* (Minuit, 1987). His latest book is *L'Affaire unabomber* (Pauvert, 1996). His most recent mise-en-scène was Genet's *The Maids* at Stanford's Little Theater.

Marc Augé

Marc Augé is Directeur d'Etudes at the Ecole des Hautes Etudes en Sciences Sociales. His most recent works include *Non-Lieux* (Seuil, 1992), which appeared in English as *Non-Places* (Verso, 1995), *Le sens des autres* (Fayard, 1994), translated as *A Sense for the Other* (Stanford University Press, 1998), and *Pour une anthropologie des mondes contemporains* (Aubier, 1994), also in translation with Stanford University Press.

Barbara Cassin

Barbara Cassin is a researcher at the Centre National de la Recherche Scientifique in Paris and codirector of the collection L'Ordre philosophique at Editions du Seuil. She is the editor of *Si Parménide* (Press Universitaire de Lille, 1980) and the author of *L'Effet sophistique* (Gallimard, 1995) and, with Michel Narcy, *La décision du sens* (Vrin, 1989). She is currently at work on a dictionary of untranslatables in philosophy.

Françoise Gaillard

Françoise Gaillard teaches at the University of Paris VII. She has published numerous articles and is a member of the editorial boards of *Crises* and *Esprit*. She is presently working on a book entitled *Romans et savoirs au tournant du siècle*.

Maurice Godelier

Maurice Godelier is Directeur d'Etudes at the Ecole des Hautes Etudes en Sciences Sociales in Paris. His many publications include *Sur les sociétés précapitalistes* (Editions Sociales, 1970), *La production des grands hommes: Pouvoir et domination masculine chez les Baruya de Nouvelle-Guinée* (1982), and *L'Idéel et le matériel: Pensée, économies, sociétés* (Fayard, 1984). In 1990 he was awarded the Humboldt Prize in the social sciences.

Jean-Joseph Goux

Jean-Joseph Goux is Lawrence H. Favrot Professor of French Studies at Rice University. His most recent books translated into English are *Symbolic Economies* (Cornell University Press, 1990), *Oedipus, Philosopher* (Stanford University Press, 1993), and *The Coiners of Language* (University of Oklahoma Press, 1994).

Françoise Lionnet

Françoise Lionnet is Associate Professor of French at Northwestern University. She is the author of *Autobiographical Voices: Race, Gender, Self-Portraiture* (Cornell University Press, 1989) and *Postcolonial Representations: Women, Literature, Identity* (Cornell University Press, 1995).

Jean-François Lyotard

Jean-François Lyotard is Woodruff Professor of French and Philosophy at Emory University. His many books include *La condition postmoderne* (Minuit, 1979), *Le différend* (Minuit, 1983), and *Tombeau de l'intellectuel* (Galilée, 1984).

Mark Poster

Mark Poster is Professor of History at the University of California, Irvine. Among his many books are *Existential Marxism in Postwar France: From Sartre to Althusser* (Princeton University Press, 1976), *Critical Theory and Poststructuralism: In Search of a Context* (Cornell University Press, 1989), and *The Mode of Information* (University of Chicago Press, 1991).

Pierre Saint-Amand

Pierre Saint-Amand is Professor of French and Comparative Literature at Brown University. He has published *Diderot: Le labyrinthe de la relation* (1984), *Les lois de l'hostilité: La politique à l'âge des Lumières* (1992), and *The Libertine Progress: Seduction in the Eighteenth-Century Novel* (1984). He was named the Walter H. Annenberg Distinguished Professor of the Year in 1995.

Susan Rubin Suleiman

Susan Rubin Suleiman is the C. Douglas Dillon Professor of the Civilization of France and Professor of Comparative Literature at Harvard University. Her books include *Authoritarian Fictions: The Ideological Novel as a Literary Genre* (Columbia University Press, 1980), *Subversive Intent: Gender, Politics, and the Avant-Garde* (Harvard University Press, 1990), *Risking Who One Is: Encounters With Contemporary Art and Literature* (Harvard University Press, 1994), and a memoir, *Budapest Diary: In Search of the Motherbook* (University of Nebraska Press, 1996).

Philip R. Wood

Philip R. Wood is Associate Professor of French Studies at Rice University. He is the author of *Jean-Paul Sartre* (University of South Carolina Press, 1990), and is completing a two-volume work on French philosophy and literature since the 1930's for Stanford University Press.

TERROR AND CONSENSUS

JEAN-JOSEPH GOUX AND PHILIP R. WOOD

Introduction

The papers assembled here comprise contributions to a conference entitled "Terror and Consensus: The Cultural Singularity of French Thought?" held at Rice University in 1993, the bicentenary of the Great Terror of the French Revolution, and other contributions solicited subsequently. Like the conference itself, this volume addresses two issues: first, those historical and cultural determinants that have given rise to what frequently has been described as "the French exception," that unusually conflictual French political process inherited from the revolutionary past in the eighteenth and nineteenth centuries and its accompanying avant-gardism in artistic, literary, and philosophical practice, both of which distinguish France from other European countries; and second, the exhaustion of this tradition in recent years—noted in prominent places on the occasion of the celebration of the bicentennial of the Revolution (e.g., by François Furet et al.)— in a progressive "normalization" of French society that has been the final outcome of the liquidation of the colonial empire, the collapse of Marxism as a social force, and the integration of France into the European Union. This normalization has been characterized by the "consensus" that has emerged around the fundamental values of "the West"—democracy, liberal capitalism, and human rights. This process has included the attenuation of the avant-garde in the arts, the decline of the kind of intellectual figure exemplified by Sartre, and a systematic assault on the last representatives of the philosophical avant-garde (Derrida, Foucault, Lyotard, and

1

company)—"*la pensée '68*"—by an aggressive constituency of neoliberal thinkers and conservatives.

The result of these developments is that we currently find ourselves in a paradoxical state of affairs. At the very moment when French thought has, in recent decades, achieved a visibility and presence in the humanities and the social sciences outside of France without precedent, the historical conditions of possibility for this presence—that is, the French exception—are on the wane, and we may be faced therefore, according to some, with the exhaustion of the revolutionary heritage that had made French thought distinctive.

The situation is complicated by the fact that the members of the philosophical avant-garde themselves have continued, often vociferously, the *remise en question* of the contributions of humanist modernity undertaken by their philosophical forefathers, Nietzsche and Heidegger. What is this modernity whose values of freedom, individualism, rationality, universality, and emancipation are apparently now globally celebrated—let alone the attributes that *Homo economicus* owes to modernity? We would seem to have entered a new period, a period of deep crisis—a generalized crisis—of the dominant values of modernity that terms like "postmodernity" attempt with more or less felicity to characterize. There are significant, diverse intellectual constituencies today that suspect that the contemporary broad consensus on the values of democracy and the so-called "Rights of Man"—indeed, the entire heritage of the French Enlightenment and the Revolution of 1789—in fact conceals new conflicts, new forms of oppression, that are the products of the very weight of that consensus as the ne plus ultra of modernity itself. Is, for example, a Western universalism that subordinates local cultures to the increasingly constrictive imperatives of the global capitalist market simply a more pacific, insidious form of imperialism than its colonial predecessor, or is it instead a ferment of planetary liberation, as our political masters would have us believe? Is that cult of the "goddess Reason," which Robespierre wanted to found in 1793, reasonable? Is it perhaps terroristic? Are we not currently witnessing a crisis of identities (national, ethnic, religious, sexual) that would seem to call into question the dream of a humanity that might at last realize its unity despite the existence of different cultures?

Such are the ethical dimensions of this crisis of humanism that has shaken French thought. These and other problems are now in the forefront of both French and American culture in a manner all the more acute to the extent that the ideals of the Enlightenment were more important for the founding of French and American modernity than for any other nation. When modernity is contested, how is one to manage what Lyotard has called "the differend," those conflicts for which no shared system of values or adjudication can be found to appeal to for arbitration? How are exclusions and segregations going to be lived, and in the name of what can they be denounced? How are the margins and alterities of our societies to make themselves heard? Terror and consensus: two poles of social, political, and esthetic existence that organize the play of understanding and incomprehension, the play of violence and dialogue, agreement and disagreement, norm and dissidence.

These two ambiguous poles have played a preeminent role in the changing fortunes of French thought, as if a historical primitive scene was still being played out after two hundred years. It is not, however, the purely historical or commemorative dimension of this conflict that interests us in this volume, but the conceptual framework that has been its legacy and that enables us to problematize the most diverse aspects of our contemporary world.

Our first group of essays, under the rubric of "Parameters of an Ongoing Crisis," frames these issues in a more comprehensive manner. We have chosen to open the collection with a paper by Barbara Cassin because of the exemplary fashion in which it traces the history of the fundamental oppositions in this debate from Aristotle down to our contemporaries— Heidegger, Lyotard, Habermas, Apel, Rorty. In "Speak, If You Are a Man, or The Transcendental Exclusion," Cassin demonstrates how Aristotle, in the course of settling accounts with the Sophists, condemns to exclusion any discursive regime other than what makes "the transcendental demand of meaning," that is, consensus. Tracing the history of this gesture down to our present moment, Cassin concludes that not much has changed since Aristotle's founding text of Western metaphysics.

By contrast, Jean-François Lyotard, in a polemical piece, "Terror on the Run," plunges us directly into our contemporary context, in which the philosophical and artistic avant-garde are on the defensive, having been negatively portrayed—in what is perhaps the dominant (bourgeois, liberal) use of the term "terror"—by the neoliberals, Manfred Frank, Jürgen Habermas, and others—as "terroristic" and "irrational." Academics in this country familiar with the currently embattled condition of French thought will recognize a familiar gesture here. Lyotard is careful to point to the pluralistic flexibility of what he calls the consensus of "the system" (i.e., a triumphant liberal, imperialist capitalism): in a remark that is not without resonance in some of the other contributions (perhaps as a helpful corrective), he points out that this system solicits and promotes differences: thus, multiculturalism, for example, presents the system with no difficulties as long as it bows to the consensus on the rules of disagreement.

In "Subversion and Consensus: Proletarians, Women, Artists," Jean-Joseph Goux reaffirms that the commensurability of all human activities with money, while it liberates the social bond from ancestral despotisms and allows one to define the equality and freedom of individual forms of thought as separate and independent, nonetheless is also at the source of the permanent destruction of the social bond. It was with a view to reconstituting this bond against the claims of political economy that sociology was born in the figure of Auguste Comte. The latter had argued as early as 1847 that three agents of the reconstruction of *socialité* were conceivable: proletarians, women, and artists. Comte thus enumerated from the outset the three possibilities of subversion that in separate ways (Marx, Flora Tristan, and Rimbaud) or simultaneously (surrealism, and above all May '68) have been at work in modernity. Goux affirms that the simultaneous critique of capital, of the father, and of logos (that is to say, of the principal forms of "numismatic" mediation) expresses the combined protests of proletarians, women, and artists. He wonders, however, what becomes of this subversion when the mediation by the circulating general equivalent (having become a pure symbol)—the autonomy of the medium—seems an accepted fait accompli, an ontological truth rendering illusory any "reappropriation." Postmodernity, in the final analysis, would be such a moment, the anesthesia of all utopias by the prevalence of the autonomous medium over what it mediates. But the consensus this establishes may be more fragile than the aestheticization of political economy, which today organizes the spectacle of the social bond, would have us believe.

With our second group of essays—"Situations of Current French Thought: The End of 'The French Exception'?"—we have assembled discussions of the putative demise of the French exception in France itself, as well as critical engagements with French "theory" in fresh contexts (in the United States academy and in the global economy at large). Interestingly, with their recognizably more "American" concerns, the papers of Lionnet and Poster both suggest that the exportation of "theory" from France seems to have had, among its many consequences, both the recognition of its special contribution and, simultaneously, the *remise en question*, if not the dissolution, of any French cultural specificity, as French thought has been annexed to the new global thought of "multiculturalism."

Marc Augé, in "The French Exception: End or Continuation?" takes as his point of departure the current debate in France in which "consensus" has been a key buzzword. Addressing the evolution that has culminated in Right and Left no longer existing as "an irreducible conflict between principles," but as "the necessary coexistence of opposites"—in short, the widely trumpeted end of "the French exception" of which so much has been made in the debate over "French identity"—Augé chooses to shift the debate from identity to two terms he equates: "otherness" and "ambiguity." Instead of making an issue of affiliation, Augé chooses to emphasize the question of relationships between people. In this domain Augé locates "a crisis of otherness" consequent upon a severance of the symbolic social bond by a liberal, capitalist order that is simultaneously homogenizing and atomizing people: "because we are unable to think of the other as other (he or she who is neither like me nor unlike me, and who therefore is related to me), we make the other a stranger." Repudiating the *évidence* of consensus—dangerously compromised by its allegiance to notions of identity—Augé sees the future of the French exception in the problematization of such notions.

In "The Terror of Consensus," Françoise Gaillard aggressively attacks the contemporary consensus that, she maintains, has substituted a cosmetic vision of society for a conflictual one. The term "consensus," Gaillard argues, originally was physiological in meaning and presupposes a belief in a natural and organic order aptly named "the body politic." It is this natural harmony—which functions more as a regulatory idea for conservative thought than as a sociological reality—that some people would have us take for the realization of democracy in its essence. By contrast, the Greeks knew full well that if there is something miraculous about democracies, it is not consensus, but the balanced living together with conflict that they recognized as the basis of politics. If this is acknowledged, and if one understands by the term something more than the mere exercise of power, then does not politics consist in managing disagreements without denying their existence, that is, without harmonizing them? Following this reasoning, Gaillard concludes, it becomes obvious that a consensus, which appears by definition as the negation of conflicts in the interests of the search for a common sensibility, is one of the most insidious forms of the negation of the democratic exercise of politics and announces the end of politics. If, therefore, there exists a form of terror today—however flabby it appears to be—it is consensus.

Philip R. Wood, in "'Democracy' and 'Totalitarianism' in Contemporary French Thought: Neoliberalism, the Heidegger Scandal, and Ethics in Post-Structuralism," examines our problematic in the context of the "*affaire* Heidegger" and the attacks on post-structuralism that have been mounted since the early 1980's, which he situates within the successful alignment of France with the new transnational global economy dominated by liberal, capitalist democracies. In the course of these controversies, neoliberals and others have maintained that Heidegger and his French philosophical progeny have sought to undermine the autonomous critical subject of modernity, which they hold to be the principle bulwark of democracy, thereby displaying a complicity with totalitarian terror. Wood examines these complaints in close detail, specifically within the context of Heidegger's involvement with Nazism, arguing that while Heidegger's hostility to the humanism of modernity is undeniable (and well founded in his view), it is incorrect to assert that Heidegger's, or Derrida's, position entails the abolition of human choice and agency and, *a fortiori*, an abdication to totalitarian political arrangements under the guise of *Gelassenheit* or "serenity" (notwithstanding the choices Heidegger himself made during the fascist period). Without wishing to mitigate the exceptionally ugly circumstances of Heidegger's work, Wood invokes Walter Benjamin's seventh Thesis on the Philosophy of History to argue that the *affaire* is exemplary for the questions we should be raising about all thought. With regard to the charge frequently leveled at post-structuralism, that it is unable to generate an ethics, Wood seeks to clarify the notion of *différance* in relation to the Hegelian system, and he suggests that it implies an attitude of compassion for all beings and a novel attitude, in modernity, toward the biosphere.

Mark Poster, in "Postmodernity and the Politics of Multiculturalism: The Lyotard-Habermas Debate over Social Theory," lays out the fundamental differences opposing Habermas and the French post-structuralists, attributing them to rival conceptions of the relation of language to the subject in the era of electronically mediated communication. Poster makes no bones about which side of the debate he is on. He frankly opts for the post-structuralists' position that Habermas's theory of communicative action constitutes a terroristic subordination of concept and meaning to instrumentality, a denial of the unrepresentable and of differences of class, culture, and gender. On the other hand, addressing the current context of furious controversy over "multiculturalism" in the United States—which he says exists in a "troubled" alliance with post-structuralism—Poster asserts that French postmodern writers may not be up to providing a theoretical space for non-Western cultures that is anything better than an "empty alterity," devoid of specificity.

Like Poster, Françoise Lionnet, in "Performative Universalism and Cultural Diversity: French Thought and American Contexts," chooses to question the place of post-structuralism in multicultural debates in the United States. In these debates, post-structuralism has been simultaneously expropriated, exploited as a commodity, and repudiated (often by the very same people), a paradoxical condition that Lionnet sees as revelatory of the intensity of the identity crisis characterizing French studies today. She places post-structuralism in the historical context of decolonization (as the event that showed up the provincialism of French pretensions to cultural universality), stressing its hybridized and *métisse* origins and character. She also places it in the context of cultural diversity both in the United States and France and in our transnational global economy. These developments notwithstanding, Lionnet concludes with a discussion of a contemporary form of "terror"—which she argues was unleashed, originally, not in 1793, but in the fourteenth century. It was then that the first proposals were made to impose the king's language on the whole country, a practice that continues to be virulent, as evinced by statutes and pronouncements delivered by the French government to this day, and in response to which the innumerable efforts to *parler autrement* are a constant attempt at deterritorialization. As this notion implies, however, this struggle cannot and should not assume identical forms in the very different French and American multicultural academies.

In our final section, "Mission and Limits of the Enlightenment," we have gathered a group of essays that span the historical trajectory of modernity, on the one hand illuminating our current context through excavations of the historical crucible of the notions of terror and consensus—the Enlightenment and the Revolution—and, on the other, interrogating a speculative future from within our postmodern moment. Thus, Jean-Marie Apostolidès, in "Theater and Terror: *Le jugement dernier des rois*," returns to the great Terror of 1793 itself in order to investigate the connections between political terror and its spectacle (in the sense employed by Guy Debord and the Situationists). Apostolidès analyzes closely one of the plays sponsored by the Committee of Public Safety during the Revolution, Sylvain Maréchal's *Le jugement dernier des rois*, a play that was staged throughout France and that was widely disseminated in print at the expense of the government. He sees this play as the earliest of those revolutionary French literary manifestos that would culminate in Dada and surrealism. Breaking aggressively with eighteenth-century theatrical tradition, Maréchal saw his work as "a fictive space [that] must almost exactly reproduce social space." In the course of harmonizing the emotions onstage with those of the street, that is, with the will of the people, consensus is achieved. In this fashion, the people come to occupy the imaginary position of the king and achieve sovereignty. Apostolidès concludes from Maréchal's play—which he describes as, like the guillotine, both fascinating and repulsive—that "terror can engender a consensus only by moving from social space to symbolic space. It must be deployed as a symbol."

In contrast with one kind of reading of Enlightenment ideology—which placed its emphasis upon peaceful "universal reciprocity," benevolence, progress beyond warfare, and its replacement by the rule of law—Pierre Saint-Amand, in "Hostile Enlightenment," chooses to highlight the ambivalence of reciprocity, relying for this purpose on Marcel Mauss and other anthropological references. He focuses principally on vengeance as a model of violent reciprocity that the Enlightenment thinkers had refused to consider. Thus, contrary to the mainstream figures like Montesquieu or Rousseau, who postulated humanity's sociability, Sade made the apology of vengeance as a form of natural justice that ought to be restored to its rightful place. Without endorsing all the authoritarian consequences of such an extreme position, Saint-Amand argues the need to recognize that the philosophies of dissensus (including those of Simon-Nicolas-Henri Linguet, Nietzsche, and, more recently, Carl Schmitt) provide us with a more complex approach to social phenomena than their optimistic counterparts, which obliterate the violent side of humanity.

Susan Suleiman, in "The Intellectual Sublime: Zola as Archetype of a Cultural Myth," discusses the current status and future of one of the most prominent (and now contested) legacies of the philosophes: the figure of the intellectual. She investigates the originary gestures of precisely the kind of intellectual whose demise contemporary opinion has celebrated and proclaimed to be definitive. In the course of close examination of both Zola's own self-representation and the mythic representation of his role in the Dreyfus affair in subsequent cinematic and television versions of the latter, Suleiman sketches the fabrication of the engaged universal intellectual whom a figure like Sartre already saw as problematic, a figure he would both emulate and ridicule. In response to prominent and divergent meditations on this figure—by Sartre, Foucault, Lyotard, and Blanchot—Suleiman chooses to buck what she sees as the dominant recent trend and declares that there is still a role for the engaged intellectual to play in the disturbance of the easy consensus of mass hysteria and the terrorism of conformist stupidity.

Finally, in "Is the West the Model for Humanity? The Baruya of New Guinea Between Change and Decay," Maurice Godelier examines the global phenomenon of Westernization. He detects three fundamental components of the West: capitalism, parliamentary democracy, and Christianity—three elements combined quite recently into a cultural unity that seems today, despite contradictions, to be endowed with an irresistible power of assimilation perfectly in line with the universalizing project of the Enlightenment. In the course of evoking the culture of a tribal society exemplified by the Baruya of New Guinea, Godelier examines the rapid process of violent disintegration brought about by colonialization, religious conversion, and a monetary economy. Godelier raises the question whether these processes are irreversible and whether they will extend to the whole world. With regret, he concludes that this scenario is the most likely, even if all the elements of the West are not always necessarily present in the process of Westernization (as the case of non-Christian Japan demonstrates). Godelier refuses to conclude, however, that we are obliged to resign ourselves to this predictable hegemony by accepting that there is only one universal model for humanity, a planetary consensus to which we have to commit ourselves.

One can only endorse this implicit plea for diversity on the part of Godelier and so many other contributors to this volume—a plea for differences that would constitute not the mere multivalency that any system necessarily incorporates and even foments (a significant part of contemporary feminism and multiculturalism, for example), but what some have called "radical alterities." The current outlook in global geopolitical terms is bleak indeed, with the seemingly unstoppable investment of populations and psyches by a triumphant liberal capitalism. If the contributions to this volume are any indication, however, debates of these issues are far from over, and to this extent, there is perhaps some glimmer of hope that, if battles have been lost, perhaps the war is not quite yet done.

Parameters of an Ongoing Crisis

BARBARA CASSIN

Speak, If You Are a Man, or The Transcendental Exclusion

> For people who are puzzled to know whether one ought to honour the gods and love one's parents or not need punishment, while those who are puzzled to know whether snow is white or not need perception.
>
> —Aristotle, *Topics*, book 1, 105a5–72

How does the ethical enter into language? The answer given from Aristotle's time up to our own would seem to be: with the requirement of meaning or sense.[1] Ever since the originary scene set up in the *Gamma* book of Aristotle's *Metaphysics* as a war machine against the ancient Sophists, those plantlike pseudomen who claim to speak for the sake of (the pleasure of) speaking, the same structure—sense, consensus, exclusion—appears to have been repeating itself over and over again; the repetition continues right through the philosophies of consensus, ethics of communication, and pragmatics of conversation developed by Karl-Otto Apel, Jürgen Habermas, and Richard Rorty, whose diminishing demands for language nevertheless entail the same type of undesirable others to be excluded, to be forced to exclude themselves from humanity. Thus, meaning, understood as a transcendental necessity, that is, as a condition of possibility of human language, is supported by, and only by, an exclusion no less transcendental than the necessity itself. Or simply: common sense, being both sense and common, produces non-sense and senseless agents, noncommonality and inhumanity.

The Originary Scene

Aristotle has just articulated the first principle of the science of being as being, which posterity has tagged the principle of noncontradiction. Such a principle, the "firmest of all," is also the "most intelligible" and, like Plato's

Good, is dependent on nothing else.[2] There are, however, those who deny it by asserting, and asserting their support for, the claim "that it is possible for the same thing to be and not to be" (*Gamma* 4, 1005b35–1006a1): these ill-bred boors oblige Aristotle to demonstrate a principle despite the fact that it is doubly impossible to demonstrate: both because it is formally first, and because it contains the very possibility of all demonstrations.

Nevertheless, Aristotle complies:

> But even this can be demonstrated to be impossible, in the manner of a refutation, if only the disputant says something. If he says nothing, it is ridiculous to look what to say to one who does not say anything, in so far as he says nothing; such a person, in so far as he is such, is similar to a vegetable. By "demonstrating in the manner of a refutation" I mean something different from demonstrating, because in demonstrating one might be thought to beg the original [question], but if someone else is cause of such a thing it must be refutation and not demonstration. In response to every case of that kind the original [step] is not to ask him to say that something either is or is not (for that might well be believed to beg what was originally at issue), but at least to signify something both to himself and to someone else; for that is necessary if he is to say anything. For if he does not, there would be no speech for such a person, either in response to himself or to anyone else. But if he does offer this, there will be demonstration, for there will already be something definite. But the cause is not he who demonstrates but he who submits; for destroying speech he submits to speech.
>
> (*Gamma* 4, 1006a11–26)[3]

Aristotle's strategy consists of replacing the impossible demonstration with another type of demonstration that—unable to avoid begging the question—places all the responsibility upon the other. The demonstration becomes a refutation: showing that the opponent himself, by rejecting the principle, always already has presupposed it, the demonstration deduces the principle of its own negation through the claim "You said it."

Two insufficiently radical scenarios are to be rejected. Refutation is not, as is most often the case with Plato, the bringing to light of a logical self-contradiction by applying the thesis to itself; of course, if the same is and is not, is both true and false, by the admission of the one making the claim, this thesis is no less false than true. But then this scarcely matters, since the opponent claims the right to contradiction. Nor does refutation function solely through pragmatic self-contradiction. Of course, as soon as the opponent agrees to take a thesis and defend it, he is pragmatically begging the principle he is trying to combat, but he can once again refuse to read his defeat as a contradiction, even between theory and practice; or worse, he can simply refuse to enter into the dialectical game.

The weakness of both of these scenarios lies in the failure to give full consideration to the warning Aristotle pronounces at the start: "the original [step] is not to ask him to say something either is or is not . . . but at least to signify something both to himself and to someone else."[4] In other words, since dialectic, which nevertheless constitutes the very element of refutation, itself already begs the principle, we must envisage a passage to the limit: something like a refutation at degree zero of dialectic that—because it entails conditions of possibility for dialogue and for language itself—we may call "transcendental refutation."

This entire refutation consists of a series of equivalences that take us from "saying something" (*Gamma* 1006a3, 22) to "signifying something both to himself and to someone else" (*Gamma* 1006a21). By this means, the injunction to speak ("Say 'Hi!'") can serve as the ultimate weapon: either the opponent shuts up, refusing to live up to the trait proper to man, who is endowed with the faculty of speech and thus counts neither as opponent nor as alter ego, or else he speaks, therefore he signifies, and thereby rejects the possibility of denying the principle, for the principle of noncontradiction is proven and instantiated only in the impossibility of the same (word) simultaneously having and not having the same (sense). Sense or meaning is thus the first experienced or experienceable entity that cannot tolerate contradiction. The refutation that serves to demonstrate the principle of noncontradiction implies if not that the world is structured like language, at least that beings are constructed as sense, as meaning.

The Responsibility of Thought: Heidegger

At the other end of the temporal chain, Heidegger's appropriation of Aristotle's principle confirms this reading: Heidegger repeats, with modifica-

tions, this relegation of contradictory man. He discusses the question that
Nietzsche asks concerning the principle of noncontradiction: if this is indeed the supreme principle, we must ask ourselves all the more "what sorts
of assertions it already fundamentally *presupposes*."[5] "The question that
Nietzsche demands that we ask here," Heidegger continues, "has long since
been answered—indeed by Aristotle—so decisively that what Nietzsche is
asking about constitutes the sole content of this law for Aristotle." The exegesis of this singular answer combines two features. First, "something essential about beings as such: that every absence is foreign to presence," or
in other words, "*The essence of being consists in the constant absence of
contradiction*" (Heidegger's emphasis). But also, something essential about
man, for the man who contradicts himself is not only failing to reach being, he is lacking in himself: "Through contradictory assertions, which
man can freely make about the same thing, he displaces himself from his
essence into nonessence: he dissolves his relation to beings as such."[6]

The passage immediately following shows clearly that, rather than
maintaining an interpretive distance here, Heidegger takes sides: "This fall
into the nonessence of himself is uncanny in that it always seems harm-
less, in that business and pleasure go on just as before, in that it doesn't
seem so important at all what and how one thinks; until one day the catastrophe is there—a day that needs perhaps centuries to rise from the night
of increasing thoughtlessness."[7]

Let us add that the very paradigm of "idle talk" as "a mode of being of
Dasein" (which Heidegger discusses under the heading "Falling as a basic
movement of Dasein") is the colloquium or congress, where "one is of the
opinion that the cumulation of this lack of understanding will nevertheless
eventually generate an understanding." The whole litany of notions bearing the prefix Ver- (*Verdeckung*, "covering up," *Verstellen*, "disguising,"
Verkehrung, "inversion," *Verfallen*, "falling") inevitably recalls the Sophistic *pseudos*: "Ancient sophistry was nothing but this in its essential
structure, although it was perhaps shrewder in certain ways."[8]

The diagnosis remains the same, then, and so would the condemnation,
if Heidegger were not more Christian than Aristotle: failure, falling, and
inauthenticity do not mean the person who claims to uphold the contradiction is a vegetable. Rather, he or she remains a person whose essence is,

essentially, also nonessence. This intelligence of difference thus makes difference a self-difference proper to each person in virtue of being human, rather than a difference among individuals. Philosophies of consensus appear to lack this at least theoretical cautiousness.

The Reiteration of Structure: Karl-Otto Apel

Apel, Habermas, and probably Rorty have in common a desire to rescue ethics from irrationalism when Kantian autonomy no longer seems sufficient to do so. Against the impasses of formalism, they seek universality in the regulation of language conceived as communication: a rational foundation for ethics includes the discovery of the fact that logic presupposes an ethics. Apel thus speaks of a "transformation of philosophy." I particularly wish to draw attention to identical points common to decision in the Aristotelian sense and to the a priori of the communication community.

What enjoins Apel from receiving, and even from understanding, the question is first of all his classical, neo-Hegelian–Heideggerian conception of the history of philosophy. As is well known, for Apel, philosophy obeys three paradigms in succession. First, the ontological paradigm, which addresses the question of beings or of the being of beings, "l'être de l'étant," and defines truth using the classical theory of correspondence. This paradigm is shared by Plato and Aristotle and its canonical definition is even found in the *Gamma*: "to say that that which is is not or that which is not is, is a falsehood; and to say that that which is is and that which is not is not, is true" (*Gamma* 7, 1011b25–27). The second paradigm, that of Descartes, Kant, and Husserl, has to do with reflexivity of consciousness and with the transcendental subject, defining truth as what is evident. Finally, the third paradigm—that of Karl-Otto Apel himself, following Wittgenstein and Peirce—takes into account the linguistic turn: "The third paradigm is the paradigm in which the first question is not that of the conditions of knowledge, but that of the conditions of possibility of meaningful discourse (*sinnvollen Redens*) or of meaningful argumentation (*sinvollen Argumentierens*). This is for me the most radical question at this time."[9] The theory of truth that corresponds to this paradigm is a consensual one, which presupposes a shared interpretation of the world. As Apel writes in his essay "The *A Priori* of the Communication Community and the Foundations of Ethics," the ethics of logic "is sought in the reconstructive recourse to the *transcendental-pragmatic* preconditions for the possibility of logic and thus of science—namely in the *a priori* of the communication community."[10]

This third paradigm, rather than overtaking the other two, seems to me to hark back—precisely in what is most Apelian about it—to the Aristotelian gesture inscribed in *Gamma*. I propose to isolate four analogous points.

PROBLEMATIZATION OF THE NOTION OF AN ULTIMATE FOUNDATION

The double bind of an ultimate foundation is that there must be at once foundation and an end to foundation. Münchhausen's trilemma leaves us the choice of infinite regression, circular logic, or an unfounded interruption of the process of foundation. Apel freely acknowledges that Aristotle was conscious of the aporia: to the very extent that the principle of non-contradiction cannot be contested without self-contradiction or founded without begging the principle, "the foundation of the principle of noncontradiction by Aristotle can serve as an illustration of the classical problem of the ultimate foundation."[11]

RESOLUTION OF THE APORIA

This is where Apel, by his own account, diverges from Aristotle, but to my view he repeats Aristotle, and doubly so: both in the foundational gesture (of a transcendental nature) and in the contents of the foundation, that is, the requirement of meaning. Indeed, in Apel's eyes, Aristotle is "the artisan of the apodictic," that is to say, of an "organon of argumentation purged of any potentially disturbing elements of pragmatism." Because he differentiates philosophy, which is geared to the relation between discourse and things, from poetics and rhetoric, which are oriented toward the relation to the listener, Aristotle is even considered the initiator of the "sophism of abstraction"—abstraction from the pragmatic dimension upon which rests the contemporary logic of science, entirely oriented toward syntax and semantics. Instead, Apel himself proposes a "transcendental pragmatics," or "reflection upon the conditions of possibility of a verbally formulated knowledge, that is, a knowledge virtually valid from an intersubjective viewpoint" (p. 903).

This strikes a less conventional reader of the *Gamma* as none other than the Aristotelian procedure. We have seen Aristotle replace the impossible demonstration with the refutation, whose unique, necessary, and sufficient condition is that the adversary speak / say something / signify something for himself and for the other. It is in the univocity that constitutes meaning—the "something"—that the principle is begged. It is now inevitable, in the sense that no one can avoid it. Taking a step backward that can quite adequately be designated as a transcendental search for the conditions of possibility of human logos, Aristotle's achievement is thus to convert the element of controversy itself into a ground that he already has conquered in advance: *sinnvollen Reden* or *Argumentieren* is to "say something," to "signify something, both to himself and to someone else."

ADMINISTRATION OF THE PROOF

For Apel and for Aristotle alike, adversaries contradict each other not only with regard to the logical and formal, and not solely with respect to the pragmatic and empirical. When Apel argues against Karl Popper's decisionism, according to which "irrationalism can be upheld without contradiction because one can refuse to accept arguments," he echoes the specific mechanism of Aristotelian refutation: the rules of the transcendental game are "rules whose validity has always already been implicitly recognized" (pp. 926–27), or as Aristotle says: "for destroying speech [*logos*] he submits to speech" (*Gamma* 4, 1006a26,).[12]

THE RELATION TO UNIVERSALITY AND THE STATUS OF THE EXCEPTION

Alongside myself and all the other "me's" that are animals endowed with logos, two categories of bad others can be delineated: the assimilatable bad other and the radical bad other. The assimilatable category consists of those who, saying what they want, nevertheless conform to the obligation to "subject themselves to argument" (*hupekhein logon*, *Gamma* 6, 1011a22,), for they belong de facto to the community of those who signify and argue. This is the "Devil" of Apel's article "The *A Priori* of the

Communication Community and the Foundations of Ethics": contrary to popular belief, the Devil does not constitute an exception to the universal; indeed, an objection to the universality of ethical foundation is that "even the Devil, given an instrumentalist reservation—such as the improvement of his art of persuasion or the mastery of the 'know-how' of scientific technology—could participate in Lorenzen's dialogue game for grounding logic and thus take part in the community of argumentation without abandoning his evil will. To state it in Kant's terms: he can behave 'dutifully' without acting 'out of a sense of duty.'" But one need only reply as follows: "It is not Kant's argument—that even devils who can use their intellect *can*, in principle, behave 'dutifully'—which is relevant, but rather the argument that even devils *must* behave dutifully if they wish to partake of the truth. . . . This means that the Devil, inasmuch as he desired to be a member of the community of argumentation, would for ever more have to behave towards its members (i.e. all rational beings) as if he had overcome egoism and, consequently, himself."[13] In other words, the Devil's or the Sophist's evil intent to speak falsely and to deceive—their egoism—can function only if it is always already caught up in the universality of meaning.

But even more diabolical than the Devil is the man who refuses to sustain his discourse or even to act as if he wanted to say something. In this case, "persuasion" is of no avail; only "constraint" can be used: "the remedy is to refute what is said in the sounds of the voices and in the words" (*Gamma* 5, 1009a21–22). However, as Aristotle himself acknowledges, this constraint is "impossible," for those who speak in this manner "think that they *can* say contraries, as soon as they *do* say contraries" (*Gamma* 6, 1011a15–16).[14] There remains only exclusion, which consigns a whole swath of speech to silence and deprives of speech those who speak without signifying. In Apel's terms, "the human being can be separated from the institution" that is the transcendental game of language—the "meta-institution of all possible human institutions"—"only by sacrificing the identity of the self as an agent of sense: through suicide, existential despair, or the loss of the self caused by the pathological process of autistic paranoia."[15] When it is not a death sentence, this is a life sentence: vegetables that speak are dispatched either to the morgue or to the asylum.

Reliance on meaning as the transcendental condition of logos, the elaboration of meaning through consensus ("both to himself and to someone else," *Gamma* 4, 1006a22), the passage to the universal by reducing the exception to the positive void that is inhumanity: the structure of philosophical consensus in the mode of Aristotle and Apel is entirely bound up with the problematics of meaning. "Sense and nonsense have a specific relation which cannot copy that of the true and false":[16] sense has no opposite; its nature is such that something either makes sense or else simply *is* not; someone either is an agent of sense or else is not human.

What Is at Stake in the Everyday: Habermas

Both Habermas and Rorty, each in his own way, retreat from the transcendental necessity at the root of consensus. The backward step that Habermas quite explicitly takes in his critique of Apel consists in refusing to see a foundation in the rules of the transcendental language game: if sense and consensus impose their necessity, it is simply because there is no replacement rule. They can be acknowledged or obtained only through and in discussion. In Aristotelian terms, and hewing squarely to Aristotelian doctrine, Habermas does not admit that a refutation ever may constitute a demonstration. Thus, with every Sophist, every time someone refuses to admit the ethical a prioris, the effort must be made to demonstrate that by the same token he contradicts himself and betrays the intention of his discourse, which is to convince and to reach an intersubjective agreement. Instead of a foundation, we come finally to definitions: a discussion aims at consensus or it is not a discussion; every instance of communication is ethical, or else it is not communication.

But such an approach only renders more formidable the problem of the exception to the universal. At this point, the topos of exclusion is strictly unaltered. This time, the most diabolical of all is the *"consistent skeptic,"* who "will deprive the transcendental pragmatist of a basis for his argument. He may, for example, take the attitude of an ethnologist vis-à-vis his own culture, shaking his head over philosophical argumentation as though he were witnessing the unintelligible rites of a strange tribe. Nietzsche perfected this way of looking at philosophical matters, and Foucault has now rehabilitated it." The height of strangeness is, of course, that he chooses to remain silent, and that "through his behavior the skeptic voluntarily terminates his membership in the community of beings who argue." Habermas, it seems, does not see how Apel's theory could accommodate this silence. However, in his own treatment of the recalcitrant one, he merely repeats—using Apel's very terms—the exclusion invented by Aristotle: one who refuses argumentation "may reject morality, but he cannot reject the ethical substance (*Sittlichkeit*) of the life circumstances in which he spends his waking hours, not unless he is willing to take refuge in suicide or serious mental illness."[17]

Here, the characteristic schism of the senseless is no longer found in the domain of language, but rather in the dimension of behavior, of everyday authenticity, echoing Aristotle's assertion that the "something" of "to signify something"—the identity required by language and noncontradiction—does not differ from the "something" necessary to the "rather than," from the identity required by practical choice and by the principle of reason. For Aristotle as well, it is clear that the adversary cannot do what he says (or doesn't say), nor can he behave as his discourse/silence require him to: "Why does he not proceed one morning straight into a well or over a precipice, if there is one about: instead of evidently taking care to avoid doing so, as one who does not consider that falling in is equally a good thing and not a good thing?" (*Gamma* 4, 1008b15–17; cf. 5, 1010b9–11, and 6, 1011a10–11). Here Habermas simply ups the ante: "As long as he is still alive *at all*, a Robinson Crusoe existence through which the skeptic demonstrates mutely and impressively that he has dropped out of communicative action is inconceivable, even as a thought experiment."[18]

In order to be truly consistent with himself, Cratylus—a true Heraclitean, who, unable to make his discourse conform to the flux of phenomena, was content merely to wiggle his finger (either in silence or whistling furiously)—would have had to let himself die. As Habermas correctly emphasizes, not only the argumentation of reason, but also all of everyday life is pervaded with the ethical, and one is subject to sense not just as soon as one opens one's mouth, but as soon as one is alive. This is true to such an extent that the reverse of this necessity must finally be more than a relegation. It is a liquidation.

Socrates, or Conversation According to Rorty

The backward step taken by Rorty is apparently so big that he might as well take it all the way back to a Sophistic position—and indeed, he is sometimes refuted with the scorn usually reserved for Sophists.

Rorty's watchword is "conversation," as prized in his American usage as idle talk is denigrated in Heidegger's German. Rorty's definition of pragmatism hinges on the notion of conversation: "pragmatism . . . is the doctrine that there are no constraints on inquiry save conversational ones."[19] Such a definition has the merit of introducing "a renewed sense of community" to compensate for the loss of "metaphysical comfort" associated with essentialism. Straightaway, such pragmatists are "relativists" in the sense that they believe that "our culture, or purpose, or intuitions cannot be supported except conversationally."[20]

For Rorty, conversation—unlike Apel's argumentation or Habermas's discussion—has neither foundation nor finality beyond itself. Thus, Habermas is by definition an anti-pragmatist insofar as he believes "that conversation necessarily aims at agreement and at rational consensus, that we converse in order to make further conversation unnecessary."[21] In contrast, the only aim of pragmatic conversation is itself, rather than any goal of sense or consensus: this conversation for conversation's sake ought to be placed alongside the "speaking for the sake of speaking" that Aristotle ascribes to Sophistic vegetables.

And yet such is by no means the case. It is as if, unable to produce the topos of exclusion from within the system, Rorty de facto reproduced the same exclusive impulses, which now have the force of mere commonplaces. Indeed, all he comes up with is "the prolepsis of the moral subject," to borrow Jacques Poulain's terms.[22] He quite explicitly takes Socrates as his model—not the complex, shades-of-gray Socrates of Plato's dialogues, but a postcard Socrates, at odds with the Sophists, who are too caricatural ever to have existed. "This is the issue between Socrates on the one hand and the tyrants on the other—the issue between lovers of conversation and lovers of self-deceptive rhetoric. For my purposes, it is the issue about whether we can be pragmatists without betraying Socrates, without falling into irrationalism."[23]

The clinical profile of the bad other hardly has altered: tyranny and irrationalism are the effects of "self-deceptive rhetoric," the *apatê*, or deception, about which Gorgias said, conversely, that "someone who proffers it is more just than one who does not, and someone who suffers it is wiser than one who does not."[24] Rorty's response is to unabashedly assimilate the Socratic virtues (goodwill applied to speaking and listening to the other, to weighing the consequences of one's acts for others) to the virtues of conversation, and the virtues of conversation, quite simply, to the ethical virtues.[25]

Socrates and conversation: a rather unexpected pairing for the reader of Plato's dialogues in their concrete unfolding, since the interlocutor is regularly, and often summarily, reduced to acquiescent monosyllables. What authorizes Plato's Socrates, in contrast to Rorty's, to eschew true dialogue is that his constantly proclaimed goal is not the love of conversation, nor words themselves, but rather the search for the true and the good—the things themselves. The conversation lovers described by Rorty as if he were dizzy even at this remove from the ancient parapets are still and always the lovers of wisdom. Thus, speaking for the sake of speaking becomes, like saying what occurs to one, the final metamorphosis of the moral constraint of sense.

Examining Apel, Habermas, and Rorty in sequence makes it obvious that less and less is required in order to escape the condition of a vegetable: to enter into the transcendental game of language, to survive, to speak for the sake of speaking. The world of sense constantly swallows up what is outside it. But the exclusion retains its litigious dimension: this is the obligation to confront alterity and nothingness. In Jean-François Lyotard's terms, this contentiousness is even a paradigm of the differend; for undoubtedly it can be said that the semantic regime does harm to all other discursive regimes by depriving them of the means to prove this harm: every other regime is inaudible, unnamable, foreclosed.

TRANSLATED FROM THE FRENCH BY JENNIFER CURTISS GAGE

JEAN-FRANÇOIS LYOTARD

Terror on the Run

The contemporary world presents the picture of liberal, imperialist capitalism after it has triumphed over its last two challengers, fascism and communism: this is what Marxism would say, if it weren't dead—a posthumous critique that the system is not concerned about in the least. It is simply called the system. It does not promise peace—it guarantees security through competition. It does not promise progress—it guarantees development by the same means. It has no others. It creates disparities, it solicits differences. Multiculturalism suits it, as long as it agrees on the rules of disagreement. This is called "consensus." The intrinsic structure of the system is not subject to radical upheaval, only to revision. Radicalism is rare these days, as is any search for origins. In politics, alternation is a rule, alternatives are excluded. Globally, the system functions according to the rules of a multiplayer game. These rules determine the elements and operations allowed in each domain. The object of the game is always to win. There is complete strategic freedom within the framework of the rules. You are not allowed to kill your opponent.

The system is continually being revised by integrating winning strategies in the various domains: we say that it builds itself. Its complexification permits it to control and exploit forces that previously had been dissipative, "natural" or "human." "Health is the silence of the organs," René Leriche, surgeon of pain, used to say. The system silences noises; or at least it watches over them.

In politics and war in modernity, two principles of legitimacy were in confrontation; God and the Republic, Race and Universal Man, the Proletarian and the Citizen. This struggle for legitimacy, whether national or international, always took the form of a civil or total war. Postmodern politics are strategies of management, wars are police actions. The goal of the latter is not to delegitimize the opponent, but to force him to negotiate his integration into the system according to the rules. If he is too poor to put anything else into play, he can at least play upon his indebtedness. As for the legitimacy of the system itself, it lies in its ability to construct itself. There result, from this law based simply on fact, a few difficulties—in administering justice for example, or in determining the purpose of education. And national frontiers are abstractions from the point of view of the exigencies of development.

Confronted with such banal, obvious facts, geonoetics seems outdated. The latter dates from a time when thought, *noesis*, believed that it could establish its authority on the basis of a land and its name: German philosophy, the American dream, French thought, "English spectacles [*lunettes*]," said Rosa Luxemburg. Or else it was the other way around: the "spirit" of a particular people became for a while the repository and witness of the founding Idea: freedom in Athens, Philadelphia, or Paris; imperial peace in Rome, in London; the race as savior in Berlin or Tokyo. Each of these, even the bastard ones—a racial *Reich*, a republican empire—was meant for war.

We say today that the most suitable system for development was being sought through these conflicts of ideals domesticated beneath proper names. What was really being evaluated was the capacity of each one of them to mobilize and organize the available forces in the demographic and geographic areas whose name it proudly bore. Shortly after the defeat of the German Empire in 1920, Ernst Jünger appraised the success of the Allies in these cynically thermodynamic terms: a community of citizens who believe themselves to be free is more suitable for "total mobilization" than the hierarchical body of Wilhelm II's subjects. This diagnosis was confirmed with the outcome of World War II and that of the Cold War. The superiority of capitalist democracy is no longer contested. Under the perfectly neutral name of "system," it prevails, in truth, after thousands of years spent trying all sorts of forms of community organization. Human history was but natural selection of the most successful—by means of competition, of course—among forms springing up at random: that is, the aforementioned system. It is from this henceforth incontestable fact that the world in its present form draws its prestige, or its authority. It is to this system that we (the French included) give our consent: consensus stems from this obvious fact.

Do I need to elaborate? Respect for human rights, the duty of humanitarian aid, the right to interference (as in Somalia), the status of immigrants and refugees, the protection of minority cultures, the right to work and to have shelter, aid for the sick and elderly, respect for the person in biological and medical experimentation, the right to an education, respect for the person in the justice and penal system, the rights of choice for women, the duty to give financial and technical help to populations left destitute after the dissolution of the colonial and Soviet empires—these are just some problems among many others that need to be resolved, questions that need to be debated, and sometimes urgently. But always within the rules of the game, within the consensus of the system.

Should this unanimity be called humanist? Certainly, if by humanist we mean that the system must have consideration for the human beings that it is made up of, but without neglecting the fact that in return, the system requires of the said humans that they bend before the exigencies of its development. For example, to be precise, people need to accept that there is certainly no longer work for everyone in the current conditions of production in the manufacturing and service sectors. If this is humanism, we must not, except by imposture, understand it to be the humanism of the Enlightenment, whose purpose ideally was a community of equal, enlightened citizens able to deliberate freely on the decisions to be made in communal affairs. Humanism today is a pragmatism, less contractualist than utilitarian, in which utility is calculated according to the supposed needs of individuals and those of the system. I say "supposed," because games within the system are always based upon "partial information," as we used to say in the days of Von Neumann and Rappoport: whatever we expect to find out from polls, statistics, and espionage for better situating our adversary or partner (which are the same from now on), there remains a certain area of uncertainty about which we can do nothing. (Unless I am mistaken, isn't the "veil of ignorance" in whose pathos John Rawls drapes his theory of justice just this same old "incomplete information"?) But the system favors this uncertainty because it is not closed.

I did not bring up these platitudes to suggest that the world in which we live no longer offers food for thought and grounds for intervention. On the contrary, many things need to be said and done—as we have seen—proposed in that very margin of uncertainty that, precisely, the system leaves to reflective thought. Who among us does not work with some sort of local, national, or international association that aims to help solve such and such a problem, sometimes serious, like those I have mentioned, or others, and who among us does not publish under our own name the reasons that we have for choosing and implementing a certain solution? We participate in debates, we enlist ourselves in combats, no less than our forebears—the Voltaires, Deweys, Zolas, and Russells—did for two centuries.

But we do this under completely different auspices, at an entirely different cost. Their fight laid claim to an ideal—the People, Freedom, the Person—Humanity, in short—that was not accepted in the system at the time, or, even if it was in principle, was violated in practice. In both cases, they exposed themselves to censure, judicial action, prison, exile, to some form of death, in fact, not of their bodies, but of their expression. Because their expression was insurrectional. As for us, whatever our intervention may be, we know before speaking or acting that it will be taken into account by the system as a possible contribution to its being perfected. It's not that the system is totalitarian, as was thought for a long time. Sartre still thought so, Foucault as well, perhaps, much to their dismay, because they weren't prosecuted. On the contrary, this margin of uncertainty is rather broad. We can't help being thankful for that leeway, but we must also take the measure of the price that thought and writing, which are our lot, must pay for this consideration.

This price was explicitly set in the programmatic article that Pierre Nora, one of the masters of the French school of history, published in the first issue of Le débat magazine, which he had just founded in 1980. The time had come, he said essentially, to put an end to the disorder and terror that was reigning in French criticism and philosophy to the point of interdicting any debate. Posing as the heirs of the literary and artistic avant-gardes, trying to go one better than the incomprehensible poetics of Mallarmé or Artaud, drinking themselves drunk on sibylline prose such as that of Heidegger or Lacan, the Parisian writers and thinkers formed themselves into groups and waged wars of words upon one another without any concern to be heard or understood by one another or by the public. Each sect pursued the unreadable practice of its talent like a schizophrenic. These irresponsible people had torn to shreds the cultural fabric in the same way that clan warfare in ancient times had torn Gaul apart. It was time for some sort of "Roman legion" to put some worthy order into this perverse anarchy and to re-form the order of the mind through debate.

I hope that Pierre Nora will forgive me, but I am too far from home to quote his text exactly. I am relying upon the feeling of stupefaction that struck me upon reading it. We had an enemy, openly setting out to impose a sort of Pax Romana on our internecine strife. It was advancing with "the heavy step of the Roman legions"—I remember that threatening metaphor. The new order was not long in coming—the "new philosophers" in intellectual work, the new subjectivity and transavantgardism in the visual arts, a poetics of procedures and genres, a genetics of texts, a sociology of cultural facts considered to be effects of forces in play within the social field, a history of mindsets [mentalités], which led notably to treating the revolutionary event as a symptom. Everything that is called human science and positive reason advanced with the same "heavy step" in order to impose dialogue and argument on the aggressive and muddled scribblers that we were. This high-minded seriousness had a definite advantage over us—it had no need to make an effort to attract the good favor of popular opinion and the media, which require above all that in matters of thought they should be able to feel that they are on familiar ground. Writings of the Roman party were soon on all the tables in dentists' waiting rooms, as Picabia would say.

My astonishment was as follows: could Montaigne's Essais be the subject of a debate, and could one feel on familiar ground in the course of reading them? Augustine's Confessions? Rimbaud's Une saison en enfer? What about Hegel's Phenomenology, that of Husserl or Merleau-Ponty? And what about Claude Simon's Les Géorgiques, Mann's Dr. Faustus, The Cas-

tle? What was there to debate and to find familiar in *Les demoiselles d'Avignon*, in Delaunay's *Tour Eiffel*, Cage's *Mureau*, or *Répons* by Boulez, in the Thirteenth String Quartet by Beethoven? Was there not in these works of thought, whether their material was language, timbre, or color, a solitude, a holding back, something in excess of every possible discourse, the silence of a terror? And this, not out of capriciousness, fashion, or defiance, but essentially—if it is true, as Apollinaire says—that a work requires the artist to become inhuman. To venture to "signify" something that one does not understand, through means that one does not control, because these means must be freed from those that tradition has controlled—can that happen without terror?

Whether the works were destined for or already had been put into the world Museum and listed in the universal Library, and consequently indexed in the cultural heritage, in memory, in rhetoric, which the system needs to distinguish itself, this did not change by one jot the fact that they never had been "produced" (what a word!) by it, only contextualized—neither with it nor against it—but rather had been born elsewhere, far from any communicational transparency: cultural objects, to be sure, more or less accessible to the community, but irreducible to custom and *mentalités*, thanks to the devastating power that we call their beauty and that withstands the test of time. This resistance and this opacity should have been respected in the course of their reception, even when people strove to comment upon and elucidate them. Commentary is neither a matter of debating nor of finding oneself on familiar ground. It would be far better to give effect to the irreducible remainder and accept losing oneself in it: terror once again.

The works that I have cited as examples were not chosen with the intention of equating our wretched efforts with their greatness, but as a reminder that when it comes to what we call creation, high-minded seriousness cannot be taken seriously, nor are our pretensions of reason reasonable. True scholars and scientists are not unaware that the same is true for scientific inventions: their appearance is no less admirable than in the arts and letters; the state of knowledge in their time doesn't explain why they emerge. Often it resists them.

It does not follow that it is sufficient to render things obscure to attain the excess of which I speak. Nor is it sufficient to respond with a terrible silence to those questions we put to the work in order to make ourselves its defender. Of those whom I have cited, more than one was very civil and ready to enter into discussion. None of this was very important; he didn't possess the secret of the matter any more than anyone else, but he was able to enjoy conversing about it. The distance between the workshop or the writing table, hopelessly solitary, or rather, deserted in favor of an Unknown, and the armchair or roundtable discussions remained too great to cross, and remains so today.

Imagine Flaubert chatting idly about *Madame Bovary* with Bernard Pivot, the television talk-show host. He certainly was capable of it, since he knew how to handle received opinion. But the project of writing, not so much the distress of a *petite bourgeoise*, but the poverty of the model, inherited from Romantic rhetoric, through which Emma Bovary thinks she is expressing and relieving this distress—how would Flaubert be able to make this all too subtle project understood by our dear television viewers? (And how, we should say in passing, would he have made this understandable to reception theorists? As for reception theory, Flaubert engaged in plenty of it in the *Dictionnaire des idées reçues* and in *Bouvard et Pécuchet*).

I cite Flaubert, the Idiot of the family, because like Baudelaire, he was one of the first to confront the stupidity of the system. Baudelaire writes in his notebook: "I have cultivated my hysteria with rapture and terror. Now I still have this vertigo and today, 23 January 1862, I had a strange warning sign, I felt the wind of the wing of imbecility pass over me" (*Oeuvres complètes*, Pléiade, p. 1265). If it is necessary to go as far as imbecility, it is because "the world is going to end." We know this text, this "hors d'oeuvre" as Baudelaire appropriately called it, which describes this outside-of-all-works that the world is becoming before the horrified eyes of the poet. This is the stupid world of total exchangeability, according to the rules of money, the general equivalent of all merchandise, goods, bodies, and souls. Ours (the system) is but the extension to language of this same routine of exchange: interlocution, interactivity, transparency, and debate; words are exchanged with words as use-value with use-value. Poetic hysteria puts an abrupt end to the circuit of superfluous verbal repetition. It confesses to cultivating its retreat with rapture and terror.

What I see as superfluous verbal repetition, Jürgen Habermas and Manfred Frank read as a promise of freedom and equality. Messages are exchanged provided that they are comprehensible, is this not true? And provided that you and I are alternately able to be both the speaker and the addressee? Richard Rorty goes so far as to maintain that this pragmatic condition is sufficient by itself to guarantee democratic solidarity, with no consideration for what is said or for the manner in which it is said. Language can be "white," like that of Camus's *L'Etranger*; it's only necessary to address it to others.

Human languages structurally endow the speaker with the ability to speak to others. But ability does not mean duty. It has never been proved that a deliberate silence is a fault. What *is* a crime is to impose it on others, excluding them from the speaking community, and what's more, we add to this injury another wrong, still more serious because it prohibits speech, and the exiled person does not have the means to appeal his or her banishment. This is the exercise of terror, political, social, or cultural: to deprive another of the power to respond to that deprivation. Whatever one thinks of it, the death penalty, however legal it may be, evokes this crime. But also the child to whom his friends say that they won't play with him, and that the matter is closed, is in truth a victim of a crime against humanity.

It is therefore taken for granted that the human community is based on the capacity for interlocution and on the right to interlocution and that it is up to the Republic to watch over this right and to educate us about this capacity. All this—which is really banal, to tell the truth—must be stated clearly in order to put an end to the accusations of irrationality, obscurantism, terrorism, and sometimes fascism, of which so-called "French thought" has been the target here and there. It would be tiresome to refute in detail each of these points of accusation. The following should suffice: terror and the abjection that goes hand in hand with it should be excluded from the political dispensation of the community to the very extent that it should be undergone and singularly embraced in writing, as the condition of the latter.

This much said, we can allow ourselves to be a bit disturbed about what has founded, and what founds still today, perhaps, the republican community itself. I know that the system is not worried about it and tries to make us forget the revolutionary Terror that occurred in France two centuries ago. Let's say then that the following reflections will be of no importance.

In December 1792, during the trial of the king, held in his presence at the National Convention, Saint-Just turns to the right, where la Gironde is seated: "This man," he declares to them, "must reign or die." The alternative excludes survival. Louis Capet is not able to enter the republican community. As king, his authority came from God. The Republic knows no other law than freedom. When Louis XVI is beheaded in January 1793 at the Place de la Révolution, it is God's word that is being cut off. The Republic, and therefore interlocution, can be based only on deicide—it begins with the nihilistic affirmation that there is no Other. Do we have here the beginnings of an orphaned humanity? This is not how Saint-Just sees it. Nothing is more suspect than an orphan, who incarnates metaphysical melancholy, who keeps the dead father and mother alive through thought. Mourning must come to an end. "Happiness," decides Saint-Just, "is a novel idea in Europe." Happiness, forgetting the murder, is a republican duty. One more effort. . . .

While awaiting this civic paradise, we must be suspicious of gloomy people. This man who must reign or die is not only the king, but any man: reigning as freedom, dying as submission. All motives other than the accomplishment of the law of freedom are subject to suspicion: passions, interests, everything that in the soul of the empirical people lends itself to tyranny. Saint-Just's alternative therefore distinguishes decisively between democracy, which is tyranny, according to Kant, and a holy Republic.

But where should we run the thread of this distinction? Freedom, first of all, is an Idea of Reason, which never is incarnated in practice without equivocation. It is never certain that such and such a decree, pronounced in its name, does not conceal shameful and unspeakable motives. Will we ever be sufficiently free of these, and how will we know? Each one of us, beginning with Robespierre, is suspect to ourselves. Terror is exercised at the most intimate level.

And then, if it is freedom that utters the law, what can the law say except "be free"? Freedom is a pure beginning. It does not know what there was before its action, and also, therefore, the traces left by its previous actions. What can it institute? It can only dread its own works, as well as of all that preceded its present action, all the ancien régime of the soul. Terror, at the intimate level, is exercised without respite.

Was it necessary to recall these well-known matters? It is certainly necessary to remind our adversaries of them. Their interest in consensus is surely not entirely republican, but it is also the interest of the system, as I have said, of its calculations, which Baudelaire called "Prostitution." And even if we give their virtue its due, we should beg them to remember of what crime it is the child. The horizon of universal intelligibility to which they appeal was opened up and cleared with a bloody stroke. A price cannot be put on deicide; reparation cannot be settled by some reasonable exchange, since this very exchange, its freedom, and its right are due to crime.

Terror is not only the historical event that we know it to be. It repeats its gesture of interruption each time that the Republic legislates, each time that a citizen makes a pronouncement. It is freedom that is supposed to pronounce the law for all and for one, but it is never certain that it will not be corrupted through some use to which it is put. The age of suspicion is not about to come to an end. Did Saint-Just know that terror would be the lot of a world devoted to freedom? That each brother would not stop contesting the authority of his brother; that all tribunals would be able to be challenged; that for two centuries, Europe and the world would go to war to decide what shape the law would take and what it would say? Politics became modern tragedy. It is over for now, and we are celebrating in consensus the disappearance of these quarrels of investiture.

It remains the case, however, that the torture continues to exist, for "sensitive souls," of not being what we are, of being an other and not being an other, having to answer to that other and for that other, who, in their turn, do not ask anything clear. Augustine was the first, along with Paul, to reveal this internal division of the ego and the Other, which in the ego is deeper than the ego, deeper to the extent that the ego cannot understand it. Still, Augustine had faith that this Other, the God of love, wanted only good for him.

After the deicide, God did not succumb. Baudelaire writes, "God is the only being who, to reign, need not even exist." So He reigns, but His decrees, even if there are any, are incomprehensible. His law itself is suspect. How do we decide that what the Other inspires in us isn't due to Satan? Evil is not the opposite of good, it is the undecidability of Good and Evil. Just as corruption can pass for virtue, so can Satan pass for God. Bernanos said that faith today is believing in Satan. But it is also to believe that this scandalous act will be forgiven. The law of freedom, without faith permitted, does not have the power to keep this promise. Consensus is not the redemption of crime, it is the forgetting of it. We are asked to help settle the injustices that abound in the world. We do it. But the anguish that I am talking about is of a different caliber than worrying about civics. It resists the Republic and the system; it is more archaic than either; it both protects and flees from the inhuman stranger that is in us, the "rapture and terror," as Baudelaire said.

If works are still possible, if it is not the system by itself that produces them and that addresses them to itself; if, therefore, literature, art, and thought are not dead, it is that they hysterically cultivate this relation with something inside us that has no relation (no regard) to us. Baudelaire speaks of hysteria because this relation must be inscribed—this is what writing means—and it must be traced in the materials of the body, in colors, in sounds, in words as well, which are a superabundant material. Not in order to enter into dialogue with these materials, and for them to "speak"; there is no need of writing for that, but to return them to their silence, to expose oneself to it, and to obtain silence from them.

Jean Paulhan, in *Les fleurs de Tarbes*, subtitled *La terreur dans les lettres*, was amazed that the criticism of his time—(it was during the Occupation, and Paulhan was busy in a network in the Resistance, beautiful expression)—continually deplored that literary writings gave so much space to the material dimension of language. "They're only words," this criticism would repeat, believing like Bergson that language is but a dead scrap left behind by living thought. And this is how Pierre Nora and many others enjoin us to be readable and communicable—in a word, consensual.

But if it is a matter of writing, painting, or composing, what do we immediately encounter? Words, sounds, colors, not raw, to be sure, but already ordered by the rhetorics that we inherit and predisposed by our temperament in what Barthes, following Buffon, called a style: a history, a nature. And writing is the work that aims to silence this learned or spontaneous eloquence. Here terror is at work, imposing silence, both upon what is closest to us, to cut short superfluous repetition, and upon the most familiar expressions. And by the same token, as in the case of the law of freedom, a consistent terror sets in and is suffered from not knowing what is wanted in these mute materials.

The intellectual in former times used to be a happy writer or artist: his works, although obtained in the conditions just described, had the ability in and of themselves to remind civil or political society of the respect it owes to its ideal destination. Intellectuals today have no need to have exposed themselves to the trials of writing. They are called upon by the system to acts of public proclamation by the simple fact that they know a little better than others how to *use* language to repeat the urgent need for consensus. The terror of which I am speaking is the following: if one writes, it is forbidden to use language, it is the Other. We can, we must act as intellectuals before the tribune. But faced with the canvas or the page, consensus is null and void.

TRANSLATED FROM THE FRENCH BY PHILIP R. WOOD AND GRAHAM HARRIS

JEAN-JOSEPH GOUX

Subversion and Consensus: Proletarians, Women, Artists

It often has been emphasized and is more and more recognized: the uniqueness of the West lies in the advent of an economic ideology. Every society has produced, exchanged, and consumed, but it is only in the modern era in the West that the economy has been separated from all religious, political, and moral ends in order to constitute a system ruled by its own laws, which are those of market exchange. In all other civilizations and cultures, the economic phenomenon is not separable from other manifestations of social life; it is interwoven in them, merged with them, indissociable from the tissue of affects and relations that bind human beings together. There is no divided, separable economy, save in Western civilization.[1] The market (the economic) and not the contract (the political), to say nothing of obedience (the religious), becomes the sole regulator of all social life. The logic of market exchange, the synallagmatic or bilateral relation between buyer and seller, a zero-sum game that postulates the quantifiable equivalence between what is given and what is returned, becomes the paradigm of all social relations, the sole principle of every bond, what organizes civil society and governs it.

The effects of this move to autonomization of the economic often have been described, whether with regret or approbation: the old personal bonds of power and dependence, all the complex social ties that attach people to one another by necessarily obscure and affective knots, all these dissolve, leaving, potentially, only the relation required by the exchange of "equivalents," that is to say, the consensus of exchange. Whatever ethical or juridico-political values exist are those that derive formally and necessarily from the structure of the market exchange itself and are at the same time its effect and condition. Thus the individual as the central value and the postulate of equality and liberty. Aristotle, as is well known, distinguished three forms of justice: corrective, distributive, and commutative (or synallagmatic).[2] In the world of the market economy, the third form, the equivalent exchange, not only becomes hegemonic, but also tends to suppress the idea of the other two.

Some, like Proudhon, have seen in this displacement of the mode of justice, in this massive passage from a distributive justice to a commutative justice, the future of humanity, the beginning of a revolution that should be pursued until anarchy: until the suppression of the state, rendered superfluous by the generalized principle of mutualism. But where Proudhon envisioned a mutualist equilibration of exchanges ("service for service, credit for credit, value for value, information for information, property for property")[3] in a pluralist democracy entirely dominated by commutative justice (anticipating the project of modern libertarians like Robert Nozick), Marx discerned, to the contrary, the enigmatic alienation entailed by the necessary recourse to a mediation of exchanges, to what is interposed between the exchanging agents: the general equivalent. Whereas Proudhon retained from the commutative exchange only its equation, its value as balance, equilibration, reciprocity, mutuality, and hence its equity, Marx, following Aristotle, wondered about the medium required to place goods in equivalence: the common measure incarnated by money. There then appeared to him the contradictions and alienations induced by that third object, behind the appearance of dual and mutual exchange. It is the question of this third, this "universal symbolic product" by which individuals alienate their social relations in the form of an object, that preoccupied him.[4] Where Proudhon guilelessly saw only a dual relation (and an undefined multiplicity of dual relations), Marx perceived the problematic institution of a mediator breaking the transparency of the synallagmatic contract and posing the enigma of the intermediary, which, moreover, he compared to language, but as well, through a series of metaphors, to God.[5]

Aristotle has seen that money is not a simple thing, but the common measure, and as such the privileged instrument of commutative justice. This status takes on an exorbitant, exclusive sense in a world that is entirely founded on synallagmatic justice, a world where the authority of persons over persons is excluded to the benefit of the equivalence (or rather the postulated commensurability) of all activities. If social power no longer is expressed directly as the power of persons over persons, it has been crystallized in the general equivalent—a thing that is not a thing, that opens on a virtuality of relations, on the infinity of commutations.

No doubt our questioning of terror and consensus, today more than ever, finds its motive in the enigma of this abstract relation. What is a society (if it is still a society) that is on the verge of completing the process of destruction of all ties, of all forms of subjectivity, of all values that do not enter into the consensus of the synallagmatic relation?

A suspicion still hangs over the nature of this bond. Praised as a guarantee against violence and hierarchic domination, the justice of the market relation appeared very quickly, along with its disappointing and dissolvent counterpart. First of all, the social market relation rests on individual utility, not on the previous existence of a social totality. But further, the ideal of the autonomy of individuals, of their liberty and equality, is accomplished by the market only by depersonalizing the social bond. The personal relations of power and dependence, but also of solidarity, are destroyed, and the relations of individuals are subjected to a neutral and abstract regulatory mechanism. In this sense, the indifference and isolation of individuals with respect to one another can only grow and prevail, along with their universal dependence with respect to the abstract medium of exchange. On the one hand, this medium detaches itself from the exchanging subjects and becomes a foreign intermediary, an autonomous third that alienates them; on the other hand, the exchange destroys the bond produced as it proceeds. The equivalent exchange is without memory and without obligation. It is a relation that cancels and neutralizes itself at the moment of its fulfillment. By its symmetry and instantaneous reciprocity, it is without fidelity or commitment, an abstract relation that exhausts the disaffected mutuality it implies, without leaving any trace.

The suspicion continues to grow: the social bond in the market economy is not a bond (link, knot, attachment) and it is not social, *societas* being an alliance, a union, an association. The market is what, in order to take place, requires the dissolution of all bonds and the destruction of the social.

This modern, postrevolutionary suspicion founded sociology as an attempt by Auguste Comte, and by Marx, to remake otherwise (but how?) what political economy could only demolish. This remaking has not ended. Marcel Mauss, describing the gift in primitive societies as a total social phenomenon, or Georges Bataille meditating on sacrifice, both of them unreservedly opposed to calculable reciprocity, plainly continue the same concern, and each time it is sociology that assumes Penelope's impossible task: to remake, to reweave what political economy (more and more economic, less and less political) destroys and isolates by the cleavage that it introduces and the autonomization that it installs.

Sociology against political economy: those are the stakes of a decisive questioning since John Locke and Adam Smith, Jeremy Bentham and Jean-Baptiste Say, put in place the firm base of modernity, with all its implications of juridical, political, and philosophical correlates for the definition of the individual and its relation to others. How does one think about a sociality that would not be, by its very tendency, reduced to the exchangist operation of the market economy, since this operation creates an antisocial bond? It is to this one question that sociological thought from Comte to Bataille, via Marx and Mauss, has sought to bring a solution.

But it might be that sociology, thus considered, has exhausted its resources: that the reserves of sociality that it has enumerated and promised from its founding by Comte, have been in their turn metabolized in the general logic of pure economic reciprocity. This suspicion deserves consideration. It would at least throw light on a certain image of closure that continues to haunt us under different names, of which "postmodernity" is not the least disturbing and insistent. Has it not been defined, for example, as "the reduction of being to exchange value," or as the dissolution of being "in the undefined transformations of the general equivalent" with no possibility of escaping the play of permutation and commutation by a new restorative aim?[6] This would be from then on the logic of the economy (proliferating, unpredictable), which would conquer every attempt of sociological totalization. This would be the permanent destruction of the bond and of the social by the play of exchange value in a generalized in-convertibility that would vanquish what Auguste Comte pursued as "so-cial reconstruction." Confirmation of this suspicion: not only the visible coincidence between a certain aesthetic postmodernity and neoconser-vatism, but also what, later, I will call "the aesthetization of political econ-omy" as a new, extremely powerful form of legitimation that summarizes this moment of exhaustion of the utopias of modernity by their apparent, and even spectacular integration.

When Comte, strictly a contemporary of Balzac, invented sociology (at the same time that Balzac invented the realist novel), he did so against po-litical economy, principally that of Jean-Baptiste Say. Whereas the econo-mist argues for an absolute right of property and defends the freedom of the market against any usurpation by the state, Comte postulates that "there is society only where a general and combined action is exercised"—if not, there is only an "agglomeration."[7] Comte thus forms the concept of society and of sociology only by rising up vigorously against the "anti-social theory" of economists and jurists "who attribute to property an ab-solute individuality," against all those whose "economic metaphysics" is opposed to "the continuous intervention of human wisdom in the diverse parts of the social movement."[8] The founder of positivism (whose statue, in the Place de la Sorbonne, is periodically cleaned of the graffiti that cover it) did not, however, join the struggle against capitalism. He did not intend to destroy it. He abandoned to it the function of material production. But he argued for a moral authority capable of restoring the social where cap-italism, by its individualistic and mercantile postulates, can only dismantle it. But this philosophical authority for the production of sociability will do its work only if it can find allies. And it is here that Comte seems to have traced out, suddenly, in 1847, the program of postrevolutionary moder-nity: only three groups or agents are called on to make an alliance with the philosophers in order to exercise the moral authority that would make the life of humans together something other than an agglomeration. These are proletarians, women, and artists.

The arguments Comte produced to justify this dogma are, after all, of little importance. That they may at times be disappointing does not weaken the lucidity of the program. Just before the middle of the last century, Comte recognized the possible sources of subversion, which would in fact, most often in a disjointed manner, but sometimes with a will to conjunction, constitute the oppositional resources of modernity. For him the sole, indefinite, inexhaustible reserve, the sole treasury of "social feeling"—which is the highest quality of the human being—can be found only in these three agents. In the antisocial world dominated by political economy (which always manufactures and trades, destroying the social bond), they are, in some way, charged with the free production of sociability.

Proletarians, women, artists: in no class other than the proletarians, according to Comte, is found so powerful a feeling of solidarity, the awareness of the force and support that result from union, self-sacrifice for public need. In its turn, "only the feminine point of view allows positivist philosophy to encompass the true range of human existence, at the same time individual and collective. For this existence can be worthily systematized only by taking as its base the continuous subordination of intelligence to sociality, directly represented by the true nature, personal and social, of women."[9] Finally, it is in art that the unity of human nature finds its most complete representation. Art invites the thinker to quit his abstractions for the study of real life, that is, social life, and it raises practical man to a region of thought where egoism no longer has a place. Better still, it is aesthetic genius that creates utopias, which anticipate the developments of history. And in this sense, poetic idealization finds its place between philosophical conception and political realization. One sees that Marx, Flora Tristan, and Mallarmé, each in a different way, exalts one of those possibilities.

Looking to produce sociability where the industrial and commercial system (the market economy) engenders nothing, in principle, but an unstable agglomeration, Comte thus seeks to assure for his doctrine a triple support, "its popular efficacy, its feminine influence, its aesthetic capacity," without which this reconstructive politics would not be possible.[10] What Comte very clearly praises in those that he lists is the virtue of giving, of sacrifice, of altruism, a relation that is dissymmetrical to the other. It is based on self-forgetfulness, on the primacy of "social feeling" over individual calculation, all of which is contrary to economic rationality, to the pure, calculable reciprocity that is incapable of sustaining sociability, of maintaining society.

The scene in fact opens about 1830. Auguste Comte was preceded in his discovery by the theater. Does not Alfred de Vigny show, with a strange lucidity, those who are excluded by or subjected to mercantile logic? In *Chatterton*, the brutal capitalist, "fair according to the law," condemns the worker, the woman, and the poet to infirmity or death. It is all there as melodrama: the industrial capitalist, a despotic and implacable father who knows nothing but quantifiable value. Opposite him, in revolt, powerless, or desperate, the worker who broke his arm in the machine and who is cruelly fired, the poet who nobly refuses to sell his soul by turning his language into a market commodity and who commits suicide, and the woman who follows him in death, her most intimate feelings overcome by a materialistic and utilitarian society that does not know the imperatives of love. This scene from the Romantic theater will also be the unexceedable frame of a demand and of a utopia.

Isn't it remarkable that the avant-gardes of our century have found themselves grappling with the problem of conjoining in the same irruption the three agents that Comte conceived as the sole resources of sociability in a world governed by market value? It would even be the vocation and the destiny of avant-gardist ambition to rethink, repeatedly and yet always differently, the possibility of such a coalition, the only means of remaking sociability when "economic metaphysics" erects as a norm the formal conditions of its disused and desocializing equilibrations. If there ever have been aesthetic avant-gardes whose programs presented themselves as total and radical, it is in the political and utopian horizon of the possible coalition of the agents that the founder of sociology enumerated. The possibility that these agents might conjoin their power of revolt, in a place to be defined, is what has, in principle, authorized the transitory and fiery constitution of such projects. Isn't that in fact the surrealist hope: to conjoin in the same insurrection what capital, the masculine, and logic dominate and exclude? Such attempts would unite, for Breton, the claims of Marx, the feminism of Fourier and Flora, and the incandescent experiment of Rimbaud in a very unstable precipitate.

Perhaps it is necessary, then, to reinterpret, in order to find it in this broken and fatal genealogy, what was formulated in the post-structuralist commotion. It is necessary because once again, the temptation has arisen to reassemble in the same impulse, but with very different theoretical instruments, the operators of sociability enumerated by Comte.

But at the same time, this ultimate renewal throws a new light on the system that produces this disposition. And it decisively marks its borders, which are those of modernity in its explosion into postmodernity. The enumeration of the agents of sociability would perhaps remain incomprehensible or arbitrary if it were not elaborated within a logic of the third, of the intermediary of mediation, which arrives in this final moment at a new phase of its reign.

The fact that the development of synallagmatic exchange, of which the market economy is the strongest operator, can entail these subordinations would remain unintelligible without taking into account the structural mechanism instituted by the logic of the general equivalent itself. Money, the masculine (paternal and phallic), and language: each of these elements is instituted as a measuring and regulative third, and they necessarily situate, as subordinate counterparts, proletarians, women, and artists, although in different registers—the register of production in the narrow sense, where work and money are exchanged in an always contestable equivalence that takes the form of an equation conforming to commutative justice, but that submits to quantitative mediation, to the postulate of commensurability; the register of sexuation, where the authority of the father situates the law that determines the intersubjective relation and where the phallic simulacrum is the regulative standard of libidinal substitutions; the register of the sign, finally, where the fantasy and its labile energies must submit to the regulative logic of the linguistic signifier and the concept, to the order of discursive reason.[11]

Money, the father, language: these are the centers of equilibration and regulation where exchanges are canceled, are neutralized in an abstract socialization that exhausts antinomies. But above all, they occupy the place of the third that arbitrates, of the Other that governs the balance of contradictory energies, the place of a common measure that effaces differences and resolves discords by the alienation of both sides of the exchange from "a universal symbolic product." This equilibrium, so easily hypostasized as "ideal," "logic," "norm," is surely the quasi-transcendent condition of every relation, but it also determines the point of neutralization of sociability. The tie is maintained only by the unexchangeable, by the constant subversion of the contract, by dissymmetrical mutualities that constantly defy any synallagmatic equation: love, hate, promising, forgetfulness, gratuity, death.

The production of sociability in the modern mechanism, where the general equivalent reigns, could be expected only where these principles of regulation are not incarnated—in opposed and subordinated places, where the work of differences is pursued and where interaction occurs without foreseeable reversal. But this mechanism that Comte, from the start, described so methodically, and that doubtless constitutes the utopia of modernity itself—the utopia by which it desperately sustains its imagination of sociological reconstruction—supposedly has found (in this dramatic form, in any case) in postmodernity its point of breakup and dissolution. Has political economy vanquished sociology? Has Say vanquished Comte? One could perhaps put it thus: unless what has happened no longer even authorizes the designation of the protagonists by those terms, but requires speaking altogether differently, the winner is not political economy as such, but the type of mediatization it has anticipated. It results everywhere in the autonomization of the general equivalent, in the hegemony of the medium of regulation, in opposition to the subjects who participate in exchange, whose full position, whose identity, whose existence, in a sense, it suppresses.

Or further still, what transforms itself in the direction anticipated by economics is the status of the general equivalent, which has become purely symbolic. In another sense, one can say that alienation, in the form that had been feared and criticized, has definitively won everywhere, but that its victory requires changing the concepts that used to designate it.

What has intervened is a historic step in the logic of exchanges. It can be summarized as the autonomization of the medium. Structuralism, in its epochal necessity, will have been but one of the philosophical names of this step (that is to say, after the fact). What had seemed to be the simple, transitory medium of a living relation, provisionally alienating subjects by making their relations something foreign to them, now has become an irreducible symbolic order that constitutes the subjects themselves, instead of altering them, and that constitutes them in their irreducible alienation. The fact that abstract art, Saussurian linguistics, and the capitalism of financial logic should be contemporaries appears in its necessity. They have appeared in a moment of disfiguration of the general equivalent, a moment that brings all the utopias of the reappropriation of the social bond to a halt.

The hierarchizing tension between capitalized money and living work, between masculine rule and the feminine, between conceptual logic and poetic germination is instituted in all its clarity only when the general equivalent takes its full, or figurative, form: at the same time, in a single body, archetype, token, and treasure. Then is put in place a regulative verticality, a dissymmetry between the measurer and the measured, that representative legitimation does not completely succeed in canceling and that it continues to stage.

One can wonder if the claims, at once proletarian, feminist, and poetic, that from 1830 onward have programmed anticapitalist demands are not entirely tributary to the "natural" existence of regulative mediations. It is in their case only (to say it in more brilliant words) that gold, the father, and the spoken word still can be lived as alienating interpositions, as thirds that congeal living relations, but that a greater transparency of exchanges, a deeper personalization of interrelation and communication, could dissolve. As long as money can be thought of as a simple material mediator of market exchanges, that is, as a mere veil, as long as the father remains a person, an interposition with a human face that regulates intersubjective rivalry, as long as language is first speech, a phonic instrument of a live mediation between present interlocutors, then the idea of utopia can be sustained: a more dialogic and interactive world, where the medium of relations would tend toward transparency, where relations among persons would be immediate, instead of alienated in a symbolizing third that becomes exterior to them.

But what is meant by the nearly simultaneous autonomization of art in abstract painting, the accelerated autonomization of the monetary medium in the play of banking signs, and the autonomization of language in the arbitrary and differential play of signifiers is the collapse of that utopia, the hope of which the past century had sustained in different forms. Not *a* utopia, actually: Utopia itself, from Thomas More to Etienne Cabet, as the desirable and possible dissolution of regulative mediations, of the third, of the interposition in which the living and present subjects of interrelation are alienated.[12] But with the collapse of the economic theory that makes money a simple veil, the collapse of the aesthetic theory of figurative representation, or, after the event, the collapse of the psychological concept of the father as a real person and the collapse of the linguistic philosophy of the privilege of the spoken word, the hope of a reappropriation of the social bond loses all meaning, in the face of the acceptance, at first anguished and then playful, of the constitutive agency of structure, of the symbolic order, of writing. The mediation or the medium, that is to say, in a sense, political economy, thus has vanquished sociology. There is only mediation, interposition, medium. Money is not a commodity, that conservable fruit (according to Locke a sort of plum that has the advantage of never rotting), but a sign of operation on values in the banking system. The father is not a face, but a name in a chain of names; language is not a voice, but a trace in the play of traces. Not to speak of the phallus, which is not a penis, but the signifier that designates in their totality the effects of signifiers.

But this disfigurement of the general equivalent marks a moment of the unbraiding of its functions and of the radical hegemony of the exchange function, of substitution, of commutation, over all other functions. Gold, in its naturalist self-evidence, conjoined three distinct functions in one visible body. As the complete general equivalent, it functioned simultaneously as the ideal standard of measure (archetype), as the symbolic instrument of exchange (token) and as the real means of reserve (treasure).[13] The purely exchange function of money, as token (then as inscribed trace), was thus not entirely autonomized. It was also a quasi-transcendent agent of measure and a body. It is thus that all the general equivalents, in their completeness, come on the scene in Vigny, Balzac, and Marx, exciting the anger, fascination, sadness, and helplessness of those who share the same stage on the opposite side of the exchange: proletarians, women, artists.

That this oppositional system is perhaps finding its closure is announced in no other way than by the impossibility (since Beckett for example) of our repeating the scene from Vigny. Not that mutilation, despair, and the desire for suicide have disappeared. But they have taken a form such that the characters of this drama have by now lost even the identity that permitted them to think of those things as support with a human face. In that Romantic scenario, capitalism has not yet entirely done its work. Relations are not yet depersonalized by an abstract mode of social regulation. Being has not yet been entirely consumed by exchange value. Nihilism still struggles against itself. Facing the capitalist (who assumes the face of a despotic father), the proletarian, the woman, and the poet are still, just as he is, part of the dramatis personae. This representative and theatrical possibility authorizes revolt. But when exchange value has continued its work, when neutralization, indifference, and isolation have accrued and been interiorized, when, finally, the absolute primacy of the medium over all live communication has been admitted as an ontological postulate, then modernity will have exhausted its resources of pathos. The autonomy of the media of regulation (money, language, and power), ratified as a constitutive destiny, as an originary alienation that makes all reappropriation, transparency, reconciliation, and self-identity fallacious, will make of this experience a humanist illusion and, forever, a theatrical effect.

The objectivized and autonomized medium of exchange has created its own order. Everywhere there are mediations, substitutes, things substituted, and nothing left to represent to anybody. Everywhere there is communication, but nothing left to communicate and nobody to do the communicating. Money is not what is interposed between living, face-to-face partners of the exchange, as a common circulating measure that permits the interchange of their merchandise and their activities. It is a kind of writing that governs the infinite circulation of debt without any paying off of accounts, or instantaneous discharge of accounting, being thinkable. Monetarism is the doctrine that recognizes the efficacy proper to the monetary medium against the theory of the veil. Similarly for language. There are no face-to-face living speakers who use language to exchange the contents of their thought. Mediation predominates over what it seemed to mediatize. It is thus no longer a question of disalienating oneself from this intermediary in order to attain a greater transparency. Who would disalienate himself or herself, since it is the medium that produces those whom it appears to mediatize?

Whether one thinks of it as the preeminence of the symbolic order or otherwise, the unbraiding of the three functions of the general equivalent and the hegemony of the pure substitute correspond to this moment of disfigurement, when the commutative function acquires (or seems to acquire) an absolute ontologic monopoly. Structuralism and post-structuralism will have been the theoretical, abstract, and fragmented consequences of this critical moment, which we can only begin to historicize.

But what has become of the proletarians, the women, and the artists, protagonists and, above all, antagonists in the representational scene, where gold, the father, and the spoken word display themselves in their glorious capitalist visibility? The question of postmodernism is summed up in this interrogation. In a world that gives an absolute monopoly to mediation (and that recognizes and accepts the cleavage and autonomization of the medium of regulation), one can say that proletarians, women, and artists are more and more difficult to think of as dramatic antagonists. They exist. But the ontological acceptance of the alienation necessary to the symbolic order, to mediation, to the autonomization of the signifier, makes rigorously unlocatable the utopia of reappropriation or of the reserve of sociability that they used to incarnate. No dramaturgy would be able to assign them a place. What the system says (but must one believe it?) is not "there are no more proletarians, women, or artists." Rather, in a way that is at the same time very close and very different, it says "we are all, structurally and ontologically, proletarians, women, and artists," since mediation, the intermediary, the symbolic order, precede and produce what they mediatize. This is our irreducible alienation with respect to the general equivalent, freed now in its pure symbolic function, which produces meaning, desire, surplus value, and play, all of which would be dried up by any attempt at reappropriation or transparency.

The philosophical criticism of the subject obviously coincides with this affirmation. It affirms ontological proletarization, which renders the proletariat unlocatable, but also ontological feminization, which renders the feminine unlocatable, and, finally, generalized ontological aesthetization, which removes from the artist any particular location at the moment that his activity becomes the paradigm of all activity. This domination can be thought of as the dissolution of being in exchange value, that is to say, the domination of the pure symbolic (the inconvertible token) over every archetypal measure and every presentable treasure. The general equivalent always is dominant, more and more dominant, but it no longer is that fixed regulative principle, that ideal standard (which is also real treasure). It is only the element of a structure without a full term, a differential and autonomized token. The stakes no longer are full and complete control by the general equivalent incarnate (gold, father, speech) over what resists the homogenizing common measure (proletarians, women, artists), but rather the process of generalized equivalence itself, taking with it potentially all that is (without any residue) in the movement of synallagmatic economics. The vertical disposition of a still-transcendentalized common measure that rules like a judge (according to Aristotle) has given way to the balance of the exchange, a horizontal structure where the equivalences play themselves out (as in the stock market) without permitting one to assign a determinative site or a substantial value. A mercantile and humanist stage of the general equivalent has given way to its financial, banking, and stock-market regime, where value, which is transitory, neither presupposes nor indicates any regulative law of exchanges. Technically, this change of paradigm occurred starting in 1870 with Léon Walras, when he no longer took as the point of departure of his economic analysis the trading of goods (as Smith and Marx did) but, instead, the market of values in the stock exchange.

It is an understatement to say that the autonomization of the medium constitutes a strong conjuncture. Having arisen first as a cleavage in the economic, this autonomization next extended itself to the aesthetic and the semiotic. But that process could not be beaten back by the utopia of the imaginary reappropriation of transferred contents (as Feuerbach believed) nor that of the transparency of human commerce (as Marx supposed).

A major and perhaps central aporia desperately haunts the long pages that Marx wrote in the interminable drafts for the *Grundrisse*. How can the values of liberty, equality, and individuality, which, he recognizes better than anybody else are strictly corollary to the modern device of the market economy, be maintained and even made to flourish at the same time that the alienating mediatization that has made the market possible up to the present is suppressed? How can commerce take place without the general equivalent? Can one imagine a pure commerce between subjects, which would render the social bond diaphanous? Can one abolish the economic?

Marx never was able to resolve the apparent contradiction between two positions. On the one hand, individuals alienate their social relations in the form of an object. By the formation of a general equivalent, the exchange of activities and products and the mutual relation of individuals are presented to them as a thing. The general equivalent thus becomes a foreign intermediary, an independent third, in opposition to the those participating in the exchange. But on the other hand, as the author of the *Grundrisse* says explicitly, "Exchange value and, even more, the monetary system, in fact constitute the foundation of equality and liberty."[14]

Those two positions perhaps sum up the major vexation of all modernity in its thinking about the social bond. Grappling with the modern process of autonomization of the medium, which at first announced itself historically as a cleavage of the economic, modernity has continued to keep alive the utopia of an abolition of general equivalents. But one could say that postmodernity radically renounces that utopia by making the alienation of the medium itself the condition of meaning and existence.

The theoretical configuration toward which Jacques Lacan reorients Freudian doctrine is significant in that regard. Lacan, starting from language this time, confronts the same problem, that of symbolic mediation. Between subjects, he says, "the symbol introduces a third, the element of mediation." Where Marx designates money as "a universal symbolic product," Lacan says of language that it is "a universal symbolic system." But there is no question of freeing oneself from this symbolic regulative relation: "it is eternal." That relation allows resolution of the imaginary relation of intersubjective rivalry. The dialectic of the self and the other is transcended, placed on a higher plane by this regulative function. Far from being able to escape that mediation, the subject will have to submit to it. And it is the effect in him of that subjection to the symbolic order that becomes his unconscious. The unconscious is, in the subject, "a limitation, an alienation induced by the symbolic system."[15]

Thus, starting from universal mediation, Marx had kept alive the hope of an emancipation, but Lacan sees the eternal fate of a stabilizing subjection to the law and to its irreducible counterpart, the unconscious. When Marx states that man cannot affirm himself practically except by submitting his products and activity to the domination of a foreign entity, a universal symbolic product, he thinks he can relativize that affirmation by a hope of liberation, by the utopia of pure commerce. Such a hope as regards language is unthinkable for Lacan. The subject is divided from itself by the signifier, by language. From the moment one speaks, there is the unconscious. The unconscious is an effect of communication, an effect of the social bond insofar as it is mediatized by the "universal symbolic system" of language.

But also, for all that he makes of the unconscious the effect of the symbolic exchange regulated by the general equivalent, Lacan, without intending it, puts a historical interpretation of the Freudian discovery on track. It had to take place at the moment that the alienation of subjects in relation to the general equivalent took a new form, having been autonomized in a separate order. It had to take place at the same time as Saussurian linguistics, abstract art, and the beginning of financial capitalism.

Just as the importance of financial capital, which had become dominant (to a point unknown by Marx), makes necessary the abandonment of the theory of the monetary veil (for which money was only a neutral instrument without any effect of its own), similarly, the structuralist inspiration since Saussure, whatever might be its variants and philosophical radicalizations, leads to making something other of the symbolic mediation than a transitory means of exchanging or representing whatever could exist without it. Not only does it have its own effects, but it is, some would say, what precedes and produces reality. In consequence, desirable sociability does not lie in the abolition of interpositions, in the impossible suppression of regulative mediations, but, for example, in the play that cuts loose mediation, the symbolic, and writing from all referentiality and measure.

In other words, we are all artists. For we know that it is of the irreducible alienation from the medium, that is, of its play, its fictions, its simulacra, that the resources of meaning are born. If pure communication, pure commerce, can remain an ideal horizon of reconciliation, we know that it will be but a device, among other possible ones, and an aesthetic effect of the technology of the signifier.

Thus, the aesthetic horizon itself is changing its emphasis. Since Kant and Schiller, and up to Adorno and Marcuse, via Comte and Baudelaire, it has remained the fundamental utopia of a society split apart and separated from itself by the economic. But that we are all artists no longer has the idealist and humanist meaning it has for Schiller and Comte. Only aesthetic machinations allow the production of lived experience, and not the reverse. That art has at the same time lost and realized its utopian vocation is the consequence of the process of mediatization whose plaitings we have indicated. In the era of the autonomization of the medium, art is lost and realized. This destiny is inevitably inscribed in what appears more and more as an aesthetization of political economy, which at the same time closes and sets free the whole aesthetic utopia of modernity.

This outcome was in a sense all marked out: proletarians, women, and artists. It is in that chronological order that they have incarnated, since Comte, a sociability seen as an alternative to the cleavage of the economic. Further, aesthetic existence is for Comte the telos of history, its final regime. At the end, says Comte, "social existence, no longer having any compelling practical end, would, like personal existence, take on an essentially aesthetic character."[16] Thus, also, in that chronological order the economic carries along the operators of sociability with it in its commutative logic, dissolves them in the play of exchange value, which leaves, in principle at least, no ontological residue. If the aesthetic dimension has been the unanimous utopia of modernity, the great hope of finally surmounting the cleavage of the economic, this modernity can come to an end only under this still enigmatic sign, whose spectacular insistence and power of legitimation already can be recognized everywhere: the aesthetization of political economy.

Postmodernity is this moment when the telos of modernity is taken up again, assumed, and, so to speak, entirely confiscated by the economic ideology, which offers itself as noncontradictory with the actualization of the aesthetic. It makes this offer before any assignable demand in the spectacle of commodity, mass communication, and the media. What constitutes (not to say usurps) the resources of the social bond is the commercial and aesthetic production of that bond—it is the spectacle of the social bond.

Situations of Current French Thought:
The End of "The French Exception"?

MARC AUGÉ

The French Exception: End or Continuation?

"Consensus," which everybody agrees to regard as a minimal condition for any form of social life (such is, after all, Rousseau's main thesis in *Du contrat social*), is being much talked about in France these days. This could be read as one more indication of the French exception, since neither the word nor the theme seems to be as much debated elsewhere. Most extraordinary, besides, is the fact that the meaning of "consensus" is not unanimously agreed upon. Since French politicians first began to use the word, at a time when the internal disagreements within the Right and the Left never had been as blatant, since historians like François Furet and Marcel Gauchet have attempted to understand its political meaning, other philosophers and social scientists have pointed out the ambiguities of the word and the dangers of the theme. In 1990, an issue of the journal *Le genre humain*[1] was evocatively entitled "Consensus: The New Opium of the People?" More recently, Alain-Gérard Slama's book, *L'angélisme exterminateur*[2] was reviewed in *Le monde* by Josiane Savigneau, and it is quite telling that Savigneau should have entitled her review "The Tyranny of Consensus." In his book, Slama exposes the new moral order as well as the new stereotyped jargon that characterize consensus. He draws up a list of the words and expressions that have become obvious, natural, that everybody now takes for granted, as well as a list of the words and expressions that, on the other hand, are now ostracized and considered obsolete—as if such division was natural, as if the true

57

nature of things suddenly had been revealed to us, setting up an irreversible split between the era of illusion and false debates and the era of
truth and of consensus. Such fear Emmanuel Terray shares when he
writes in the article that opens the issue the journal *Le genre humain* devoted to consensus:

> There is no question that a minimal consensus is the condition for any
> form of social life: the participants should at least agree on the meaning
> of words and the rules of the game. But the game must remain open and
> the future undecided; as soon as consensus applies to the other objects, as
> soon as it pretends to sanction an established order by making it pass as
> "natural," then one should wonder what its cost is. Consensus can be
> maintained only by means of a perverse mixture of blindness and hypoc-
> risy, of lies and tacit acquiescence. To expose such a mixture, to distin-
> guish between what is sound and what is corrupt about consensus, to
> submit any of its forms to the test of criticism, is neither to yield to the
> fascination of nihilism nor to encourage civil war.[3]

It should be clear by now that the debate we are faced with here is quite
specifically political. One can foresee the possibility of an agreement as to
the condition for any kind of democratic political life. But the debate really bears on how broad this agreement can be—and it is a debate whose
originality is dubious, since French Communists or other revolutionaries
for several decades have seemed to put up with a situation they never have
been able to change through radical actions. What I would like to do here,
after I briefly review the themes and the terms of the debate on political
consensus, is to suggest it is ascribable to a wider phenomenon whose signification is literally anthropological and then offer an answer (a cautious
one, of course) to the question my title raises: what future is there for
what has been called the French exception?

The theme of French exceptionality presents itself as explicitly and exclusively political. Its evocation, together with the announcement of its
demise, can be found in the essay by François Furet, Jacques Julliard, and
Pierre Rosanvallon entitled *La république du centre*.[4] From the moment
that the market economy and representative democracy no longer are
questioned, it is the existence of a necessary link between the two that

forms the subject of consensus. Marcel Gauchet has come up with a similar analysis in his contribution to Pierre Nora's *Lieux de mémoire*. If the "Right" and "Left" now appear to him as "memories," it is owing to a number of displacements within time and space. The Right and the Left, Gauchet writes, "testify to the era when French politics was conceived of as universal precisely because the choices it offered were so clear." Thus, 1815 marked the choice between the ancien régime and the Revolution, 1900 signaled the conflict between faith and the Enlightenment, 1935 saw the struggle between socialism and fascism. In those key moments when the reference to 1789 plays a crucial part, the antagonism between the Right and the Left bears on final purposes, on what fundamentally is at stake in political struggle. The universalization of the categories of Left and Right both legitimates and invalidates the ambition that went along with such struggles. As it has been displaced, the opposition between the terms has changed its meaning: it means the necessary coexistence of opposites and no longer the irreducible conflict between principles. France, borne along by the necessary process of the stabilization of democracies, has to renounce the particularity that enabled her to project herself into the universal: "The coming into actual universalization makes it necessary to gauge in retrospect the unique peculiarity of this tradition that claimed to be universal."[5] Such a view understandably invalidates any claim to infer from the French example an interpretation of the history of the world and makes it clear that Marcel Gauchet's semio-political analysis finds its place among the work of historians eager to rethink the history of France through an investigation of her memory.

The main tonality of contemporary history in France thus is attuned to the themes of our time, that is, to the end of "master narratives" and the death of ideologies. If Marcel Gauchet nuances his analysis (he believes indeed in the persistence or in the recurrence of the split between the Right and the Left), it is by changing its subject. Given that the individual is what our society is founded on, Gauchet says, the intellectual and political tension between private powers and public authority will exist. This tension will continue to be called the antagonism between the Right and the Left, but we will have moved from an antagonism in concept, so to speak, to an antagonism in management. It is doubtful that this shift ever will furnish substance for any great intellectual project, and, what is more, it appears, contrary to the illusions of old, as the return in France of a model that has been toned down by the other democracies.

I would now like to make a little aside and consider a few anthropological problems that may first seem somewhat remote from my previous remarks but that eventually will take us back to them. The question of terror and of consensus, as well as that of the role that ideas and interpretative systems play in our understanding and control of the world, cannot, in my opinion, be limited to the political sphere, nor can they disregard the transformations that our world undergoes.

The transformations in our world proceed from changes that are not without effect upon political life and its themes, though they cannot be inferred from them. In relation to political life they come first. The ever-accelerating tempo of history, or, more accurately, the ever-growing amount of information that makes us feel we are immersed in history, makes the task of contemporary historians and of those who reflect upon history more complex: caught up by history, so to speak—a history that therefore no longer is separable from current events—they are tempted, since they do not understand it, to believe it has come to an end. The shortening of distances on the planet, as well as the ever-increasing amount of images, partake of the same media phenomenon: there is hardly any human being today who is not conscious that he or she belongs to the planet earth. Ecology is probably the most sophisticated form this consciousness takes, but the abundance of current or fictitious images introduces in people's relation to space a superabundance, an excess that matches the excess of events that disturbs historical consciousness. This globalization by way of images has its counterpart, in the real world, in the acceleration of means of transportation and of communication. Finally, the individualization of references parallels this excess of events and images. Such individualization corresponds to what might be called the collapse of intermediate cosmologies—by which I mean not only the cosmologies that are traditionally studied by ethnologists (and that colonialism had begun to erode), but also the representations proper to what Durkheim used to call "intermediate bodies," especially political parties and workers' unions. Those representations, indeed, have meant for many a vision of the world according to which everyday life could be regulated and oriented—the same way, say, that religions regulate the daily life of believers. In the religious field itself, individual initiative asserts itself (many Catholics, for example, will practice "their own way"), as if the power religion holds to regulate and direct people's life (its power as an "intermediate cosmology," therefore) was in its turn weakening. In short, it is as if one feature of our modernity has reinvested the individual with the responsibility to create the modes of relation to other people that will make it possible for them to live, to fill up solitarily the symbolic deficit induced by the collapse of intermediate cosmologies and established mediations.

Taken as a whole, those transformations seem to point to a preeminence of the universal, which would seem to go against all intellectual endeavors tending to suggest that it is from the deeper examination of a particular case that a general truth can emerge—a postulate that existentialism, as well as Marxism and structuralism under different forms, held in common in the years following World War II.

The presupposition of the universal is often described today as inducing an "identity crisis." And the historians I quoted earlier always are talking about the crisis of French identity—a theme to which the immigration question is naturally related. I would like to suggest here that the crisis that affects France as well as the rest of the world would be more adequately described and analyzed as a crisis of "otherness." The language of identity is only one of the two languages from which the symbolic threads of social fabric are woven. It applies to what Georges Devereux used to call "class" identities (in the logical sense of the word "class"). The language of identity is the language of ambivalence, in the sense that a reality is ambivalent when it has two characteristics at once: you can be both a private person and a public figure, a father and a husband, a Frenchman and a European. The language of belonging and of class identities also includes the language of politics—a language that gives substantive form to categories and poses questions in terms of inclusion, addition, or exclusion: I am a Scot, therefore British. Is it possible to be a Moslem and a Frenchman? The choice between consensus and terror speaks the language of identity. But the language of otherness, which is the other constituent of the symbolic language of society, places itself under the sign of ambiguity—ambiguity is taken here to refer to a reality that is adequately expressed neither by a quality nor by its opposite, but by a third quality for which there is no other definition than this double negation: neither good nor bad, neither handsome nor ugly. The language of otherness suggests that the truth about people lies not in class identities, but elsewhere. It makes their significance relative and poses its questions in terms of implication, influence, and relations. Whereas the sociopolitical language of identity establishes connections between an individual and the various collective bodies to which he or she belongs or not, the psychophilosophical language of otherness poses the question of relationships between people, or taken more broadly, of the relations between the same and the other. Ritual activity, such as can be observed by ethnologists when they study in various cultural contexts the rites of birth, of death, the rites of passage or of investiture, combines both languages. It metes out to each and every individual his or her place and identity in the society. But it also establishes the individual's most idiosyncratic disposition by determining his or her share of private otherness, his or her hereditary attributes, the ancestral part that returns in the individual. (In all "pagan" systems, the individual is seen as the temporary gathering of elements of various origins.) In those cases, identification is the result of being placed in a series of relationships, rather than the result of being assigned to a substantive category.

The crisis of modernity, from this point of view, could be ascribed to the fact that one of these two languages (that of identity) wins over the other (the language of otherness). In that sense, it would indeed be a crisis of otherness. The phenomena we very quickly described as characteristic of our modernity (excesses of events, of images, as well as individual excesses) affect one of the languages more than the other. Indeed, between the potential homogenization of the whole (the spaces of circulation and of communication associated with the expansion of economic liberalism throughout the world) and the individualization of cosmologies, it is the relation to the other that, even though it is constitutive of individual identity, loses its symbolical framework. Hence an uneasiness that can be felt at several levels, especially in the most advanced, wealthy, and better-protected democracies of our planet, because such uneasiness is individual as much as it is social or, more precisely, because it is, strictly speaking, neither individual nor social, but indeed symbolic, if we take the word "symbol" in its etymological sense, as pointing to a necessary relation between complementary elements. The ever-stronger overlap between such categories as men and women, nationals and immigrants, to say nothing of phenomena that are sometimes improperly described as phenomena of recurrence or of return (the recurrence of nationalisms, the return of religion)—all these testify to the fact that the logic of identity has overcome that of otherness. Because we are unable to think of the other as other (he or she who is neither like me nor unlike me, and who therefore is related to me), we make the other a stranger. An ethnic denomination, a geographical origin, a designation connoting more widely the externality of origin (the "immigrants," for example) indicates a severance of the symbolic bond, as well as a regression of representation to the sole identity factor.

The anthropologist Gérard Althabe has shown very clearly how the "stranger" type has been "invented" or "made up" in the French suburbs since the 1970's. He has shown, in particular, how such invention was induced by the necessity, for workmen and employees threatened by unemployment in those days and eager to identify with the dominant model of prosperity, to distinguish themselves physically from the negative pole where underemployment and ethnic affiliation seemed to go together. Some of them did so by moving from large apartment buildings to small suburban houses that they bought on installment.[6]

The theme of consensus, it seems to me, is in several respects very problematic, and I think we should rejoice over this. It is problematic, first, because it is founded on imprecise assertions: we have no evidence that the model of representative democracy will endure forever in all countries of the world, or that it is necessarily linked with economic liberalism. But it is problematic mainly because it sets the political sphere apart, thus inducing us to question the world in the language of identity. The theme of consensus is therefore not so much a way of interpreting our world as one of the symptoms our world evinces. With regard to such themes as migrations, nationalisms, fundamentalisms, the right of interference or human-itarian action—all of them planetary themes that influence French society and politics and that, I add, are not the subject of any consensus—it is by the French intellectuals' capacity to challenge the recourse to the sole lan-guage of identity that their capacity for innovation and fresh proposals can be judged in the future.

TRANSLATED FROM THE FRENCH BY FABIENNE DURAND-BOGAERT

FRANÇOISE GAILLARD

The Terror of Consensus

Long after we had realized that history could be devious, we still had to learn that it could also be facetious at times. As we rather discreetly celebrated the bicentennial anniversary of the Terror, we were forced to make the following observation: we have left behind what was known as the balance of terror—not only in the geopolitical arena, with the end of the Cold War, but also in the domain of domestic politics, with the disappearance of the notion of the class struggle both as a sociological reality and as an operative concept of social and political intelligibility. The 1980's, at least in France, sounded the dirge for revolutionary eschatology, whose burial, it might be said in passing, is not without implications for the crisis of recognition and of legitimacy that pervades all avant-garde movements, whether artistic, literary, or theoretical. But a detailed discussion of the forms taken by this crisis would stray too far from our present purpose. Let us simply note what cannot be disputed: revolutionary eschatology has collapsed, taking down with it the agonistic representation of society that sustained it. It is indeed clear that the conflictual conception of society has, for some time already, been replaced by a cosmetic vision. This latter goes by the name "consensus."

The first meaning of this term is of course a physiological one, referring to the harmony of several organs in performing a vital function. Any political usage of the term "consensus" thus supposes a belief in the natural and organic order of the aptly named social body. This natural har-

65

mony—which, it must be observed, functions more as a regulatory idea for conservative thought than as a sociological reality—is sometimes seen as the achievement of democracy itself, or (what amounts to the same thing) as evidence of it. In their work *La république du centre*, François Furet, Jacques Julliard, and Pierre Rosanvallon are delighted that an end finally has been put to the particularly French practice of linking the notion of democracy with that of conflict. Registering the profound and recent ideological mutation that we have witnessed, they write that "democracy is no longer a self-contained battlefield for two moral civilizations where two civilizations arising out of a radical conflict fight it out."[1] What Furet and others see in this entente—which, contrary to what he thinks, supposes not so much an adjustment in viewpoints (a rationalization of the political) as a blending of social classes and a homogenization of mentalities, a devitalization of the political—is the very sign of democratic maturity, not to say France's accession, at long last, to democracy. Might he and his friends have forgotten that true democracy cannot exist where a single force prevails, even in a diluted form?

Francis Fukuyama's theses on the end of history appeared just in time to reassure all the apostles of the miracle of consensus that the liberal and democratic state meant no more rending of the social fabric. This amounts to the notion—Furet makes no bones about it—that in a democracy everyone is in basic agreement about the way in which the country should be governed. From another angle, we can say that in a liberal democracy, a protest can be rooted only within democratic and liberal principles and values. Here we see the specter of a logical closure and foreclosure of any alternative to liberalism—hardly cause for worry to all those who are mobilized more by (abstract) human rights than by the (quite concrete) wrongs inflicted upon certain individuals by economic and political liberalism, which seems to be the obligatory escort for our entry into democracy.

The social and political analysis that serves as a basis for the valorization of consensus—which goes so far as to make consensus the categorical imperative of our (not to say all) democratic morality—concludes that we have left division behind us. Henceforth, anything that might resemble the manifestation of a conflict of interest is immediately reduced to the dimension of a simple problem whose natural solution is to be found in, and through, dialogue. Here we recognize the American "let's talk it over" approach, which is expected to resolve all conflicts, familial and other—as if they are all merely misunderstandings. The model for this accord is, clearly, the scientific community, in which agreement ideally rests upon propositions that are accepted by all.

I will not dwell upon the current illusion that consists in seeing the weakening of social movements as an advance along the way to the harmonization of points of view and positions. What I am intent upon showing is that, far from being the regulatory idea of democracy, as it is claimed to be, consensus spells the death of democracy. In order to demonstrate this, it may be necessary to ask ourselves once again from scratch the question of democracy. What, in essence, is democracy? In a very illuminating article, Jacques Rancière reminds all the bad readers of Plato—those blinded by the ideal of *homonia*, which the philosopher seems to contrast with the noise of the agora—that for the Greeks (among whom Plato must be counted), "democracy is neither the compromise of interests nor the formation of a common will." He adds that "its dialogism is that of a divided community."[2] If we read these philosophical texts closely, it becomes apparent that *homonia* is a concept that is pertinent only in connection with the search for truth; as the Greeks knew, politics has to do not with truth, but with injustice, which is quite a different matter. If there is something miraculous about democracies, it is not consensus, but rather the balance of living together on a footing of conflict, which democracies recognize as the very foundation of politics. Indeed, as soon as we understand this term as something other than the sheer exercise of power, doesn't politics consist of managing disagreements without, however, denying them—that is, without "harmonizing" them? If we set this last remark over against the startlingly oxymoronic definition of democracy proposed by Rancière—the dialogism of a "divided community"—it becomes clear that democracy (understood thus—but then, it cannot be understood in any other way) is the most advanced form of politics. This is precisely the conclusion that the philosopher would have us reach. In line with this reasoning, it becomes clear that consensus, which appears by definition as the negation of conflicts in favor of the pursuit of a common sensibility, is one

of the forms—without a doubt the most surreptitious form—of the negation of the democratic exercise of politics; and since previously accepted
definitions merge democracy and politics, consensus is also one of the
forms of the end of politics.

Notwithstanding the current overuse of the term "post," I think Rancière is right to use the term "postdemocracy" for the triumph of consensual ideology. We might also speak of "postpolitics," a diagnosis that would
be confirmed by numerous symptoms, in particular the increasing power
of the juridical in sectors previously occupied by the political. What I
would like to emphasize here are the formidable consequences of denying
the conflicts upon which consensual ideology, which should rather be
termed the ideology of consensus, installs the harmony that it has, per-
versely, made synonymous with democracy. Denying conflicts is a serious
matter, which amounts first of all to denying what characterizes any community, political or other—that is, the agonistic, the dimension of conflict
present in it. And this denial courts grave consequences. Beware, then, the
return of the repressed, for now that conflict has lost its symbolic outlet—
politics—it no longer has a social function. To deny conflicts also means
eliminating from the consensual community all those who are not party
to this consensus, in other words, all those to whom the provisions of the
consensus do irremediable harm: the have-nots, the homeless, the unem-
ployed, immigrants, and so on. Beware, too, the formation at the margins
of the consensual society of pockets of minorities that can be neither integrated nor managed, whose only remaining mode of expression is despair,
or in its more heated form, the explosion of violence not linked to any historical or political goal. Alas, the current situation offers daily examples of
the socially catastrophic effect of this double denial. And let it not be said,
in explanation of the resurgence of hate or of marginalization, with all
their accompanying forms of criminalization, that such phenomena are
only a childhood illness of consensual democracy, destined to be outgrown
in time. "In time": meaning when *Homo democraticus* has understood
that consensus does not represent any thought content, but is a framework ready to absorb all the fallout of unwonted economic mutations and
social upheavals spurred by the advent of a postindustrial age and by advances in knowledge, particularly in the life sciences. The all too familiar

thesis of those who see consensus as a way for mentalities to evolve and for social norms and bonds to be transformed without breaking rests on the idea that consensus is not simply a "thinking in common," but equally, or even more so, a "feeling in common," a common sensibility forged by a cultural background and a common tradition. Because of the conservative force deriving from its flexibility, consensus is thus seen as a sort of moderator of social rhythms and evolution. In other words, consensus is conceived as the only mode for managing public affairs in times of change. In such moments it would offer a legitimate substitute for the more agonistic practice of politics.

It is, I believe, pointless to stress the weakness of such arguments. By touting the virtues of consensus only for periods of change, those who resort to this reasoning are forgetting first of all that perpetual change and the constant challenge of the new are what characterize our modern world; it automatically follows that consensus and its function would become a permanent fixture. They are also forgetting that by founding change upon the elimination of conflicts, they are basing it upon the exclusion of all those whom this change affects adversely. Finally, they are forgetting that, once the process of mutation and innovation thus undertaken is over, it would be impossible ever to reestablish the scene of the political, and that along with its disappearance will vanish any public space in which the intractable—that is, conflict and injustice—can be made manageable. By thus failing to provide for conflict and injustice, consensus is the undoing of public life, provoking a withdrawal from socialization that can unfortunately be observed every day. It is all too easy to list some of the most visible manifestations of this withdrawal: political apathy, social exclusion, and tribal violence. Does this mean that everything our subtle symptomatologists decry as the expression of a postmodern void seeking to fulfill itself through a return to archaic drives is nothing more than the perverse effect of consensus? Such a conclusion is indeed tempting, although the causes and effects need to be charted dialectically. I am certainly aware that to see consensus as a factor in social dissolution, as I am arguing, runs counter to several centuries of enlightened thought, which have seen it as the very expression of the entente and solidarity of the constituent parties of any community. And yet it is difficult today not to remark that wherever consensual ideology takes hold, we observe an infracritical regression in public debate and, as a consequence, a collapse of public life. This state of affairs coincides with (is it even the result of?) a depoliticization of all the questions that trouble civil society and work upon it under the surface.

I would like to return to at least two of the politically worrisome manifestations of the destruction of public life and of ebbing socialization for which I find consensus almost directly responsible: political apathy and social exclusion.[3]

First of all, I will address apathy. Although it is obvious to many, it is perhaps not entirely unwarranted, in the current climate and context, to recall that what divides a society is not so much the problems it faces as the formulation of these same problems in political terms. In other words, the division begins (or comes to light) at the moment when these problems seek a political translation. It could not be clearer, indeed, that it is only when a problem "of society" accedes to a political dimension—when it is "politicized"—that a society, collectively conscious of the problem, but divergent as to its interpretation and its management, can appear to be profoundly divided, and thus that the social equilibrium toward which democracy tends is indeed a balance of conflict. The term "conflict" must be emphasized, for this is the heart of the matter, rather than compromise, which, while purporting to solve a conflict, actually dissolves it instead. With this clarification in mind, it is easy to understand that in order to obtain the harmony to which it lays claim, consensus operates a depoliticization or, if you will, a sort of ablation of the political dimension of the questions that, as the media say, preoccupy the French. This manner of speaking, which is also used by our politicians, is enough to indicate that such discourse is indeed addressed to the consensual community constituted by the French, and not to the political subjects represented by each French individual. It is not difficult to turn a problem into an artificially consensual cause. All that is needed is recourse to an element of pathos, of the emotional, which surrounds the problem with a perceptible halo, instead of undertaking a critical analysis that might reveal its scope and its political ramifications. The best example of this process is to be found in the recent matter of contaminated blood.[4]

The depoliticization machine pulled out all the stops and succeeded in producing the finest, that is the most obvious, of consensual causes. What this example demonstrates in the end is that by deliberately situating itself outside political analysis and reflection, the consensual cause finds only one way to gain adherents, via the risky path of emotion and affectivity. Beware the danger of irrational twists and atavistic regressions. The whiff of vengeance swirling around this affair puts us on guard against the risks run by society when questions of wrong and damage are raised outside the space of the properly political.

That consensus partakes of the deceptive powers of the imaginary and of the affect will surprise only those who, along with the Enlightenment philosophers, wished to see it as a cultural form of reason and an intuition of common sense. It must not be forgotten that what makes consensus true to its prefix, that to which it owes its power to rally and unite, is not so much the idea of clarity and distinction (which, in keeping with its name, discriminates and divides) as it is prejudice. And in this last term, again, the prefix is most telling: prejudice is what is judged before it has even been thought. It is hardly possible, therefore, not to agree with this nostalgic remark by Serge Moscovici and Willem Doise: "in unison even before coming to an agreement, every consensual community inclines, without even realizing it, toward a uniform solution. Thus we may say that its members, rather than forming a consensus, conform."[5] Consensus, as we have seen, makes conflict vanish by eliminating its political arm, but what governs in its place is platitude. Consensus is flat, despite the lust for pathos that chronically gnaws at the consensual society. If it evacuates the agonistic character of social life, consensus also removes its dynamism, leading to the contemporary feeling of a great void of thought and a paucity of debate, despite the ironic inflation that afflicts this last term in the world of thought, as in that of creation.

If intellectuals suffer from the infracritical regression to which consensus leads, then what must be said of those whose social being is affected by the accompanying infrapolitical regression? The ill they suffer has a name: exclusion. And exclusion is another perverse effect of consensus. Have we erected a smokescreen by replacing older representations of society (in terms of class struggle) with a spatializing (and thus postmodern) representation in terms of inside/outside? To understand how consensus comes to generate exclusion in our developed societies, we must detach ourselves from René Girard's apolitical model, according to which community solidarity necessarily implies the rejection of the other. This schema, which belongs to a prepolitical age, in no way accounts for the type of exclusion and relegation now present in our society. Those who are drifting away from us are not, as some would have us believe, to be written off as social and economic mutations; rather, they are victims of the default of the political. Simply stated, this means that they have no natural or symbolic vocation for alterity. Indeed, those excluded de facto by consensus include all those whose interests and whose very existence were, or would have been, taken care of by a conception of politics and of social life based on conflict and division. This can be rephrased as follows: those whom consensus excludes are those whose socialization, and therefore whose maintenance within the social community, depended, or would have depended, on none other than the development of a political awareness of the injustice inflicted upon them. In the place of any political consciousness of social injustice, all that remains is a vaguely bad conscience that forces us, in an excess of cynicism, to consider their cases to be so many problems requiring solutions. It becomes clear, then, that all the underprivileged groups who were connected to society as a whole only because the latter recognized the existence of conflicts within it have become the write-offs of consensual democracy. These are the ones who drift away as if sucked by a force of negative gravity and who are lost in the nameless spaces of the *banlieue*—the place of the banned, of banishment?—where they would be lost from view if it were not for the violent explosions that erupt from time to time, reminding us of their troublesome existence and making us quake at the thought of the barbarians surrounding us. On the horizon of this tide of flotsam and jetsam looms the specter of ghettoization, American style.

But why speak as if this is all in the future? The human devastation that results from this relegation is depicted in Annie Frénaux's recent book *Le journal du dehors*. A notebook of what takes place "outside," in suburban trains and subways, in the megastores of new cities, it is also a journal that bears witness to this world outside, to the universe of those who live outside—who are, in short, excluded. Unable to give political expression to their suffering, the excluded have internalized their exclusion to the point of believing themselves invisible. Thus it is that, in so-called "public" places, such as the metro, they engage in private acts or intimate gestures that generally call for privacy, solitude—"inside." Frénaux observes:

> At the Charles-de-Gaulle-Etoile metro stop, a thirty-year-old man gets in and sits on a folding seat. Suddenly, he bends over and pulls one leg of his trousers up to the knee. You can see his white skin, the hairs on his leg. He grasps his sock with both hands, pulls it up, lowers the leg of his pants. He does the same with the other sock. Later, he stands up, leans against the wall, opens up his vest, and raises his T-shirt. He examines his stomach for quite some time, then pulls his shirt back down. Clearly his acts are not meant to be provocative; they are simply an extreme expression of solitude—the real thing—in the midst of the crowd. Next to him, there is a plastic bag, typical of the homeless. When one is homeless and jobless, the looks of others no longer prevent us from doing things that are natural, but displaced on the outside in our culture.[6]

To be excluded is also to be outside the sphere of visibility. Moreover, other passengers avert their eyes. What they feel is embarrassment, not compassion. This young man is no longer part of the "com" of community, and of its shared suffering. He is beyond the reach of com-passion.

It is no mere coincidence that Annie Frénaux chooses shopping complexes as her sphere of observation. In time it is highly probable that the sense of inclusion will be conferred only by purchasing power—that is, by the possibility of participating in what takes the place of communal ritual in market-economy societies: the consumption of goods. As for the excluded, the wrong done to them will not be not to have been invited to the banquet, but to lack any arena for saying so. Agonistic society was regulated by the idea of integration. Consensual society produces disaggregation and condones the juxtaposition of impermeable communities whose relations are ruled at best by law, at worst by violence. In France, we are witnessing a flood of marginalized populations, and this unbinding of society is without a doubt the most worrisome aspect of the future of our democracies. As Alain Touraine so aptly observes in connection with those who belong to the underprivileged classes: "they used to be exploited; they are turning into strangers."[7] Why then should it surprise us that, in order to recuperate an identity, these "strangers" try to define themselves however they can, in ethnic or cultural terms? Rather, is it not normal—however deplorable besides—that, feeling the press of segregation, they seek modes of aggregation in a communal identity?

TRANSLATED FROM THE FRENCH BY JENNIFER CURTISS GAGE

PHILIP R. WOOD

"Democracy" and "Totalitarianism" in Contemporary French Thought: Neoliberalism, the Heidegger Scandal, and Ethics in Post-Structuralism

Since the early 1980's, in France, Germany, and the United States, "theory"—also known as "left-Heideggerianism" in France or "post-structuralism" in the United States—has been attacked in terms that mobilize one of the more wearisome oppositions upon which the hegemony of capitalism has rested since the French Revolution: terror versus consensus. The opposition is wearisome not just because of the numbing frequency and complacency with which it is invoked, but, above all, because it forecloses the possibilities of the political imagination, seeking to persuade us that we face a choice between only two alternatives: on the one hand, revolutionary terror (whether of the Right or Left) that is necessarily totalitarian; on the other hand, the peaceful and free debates of a civil society (none other than our own) that submits to the democratic rule of majority opinion, if not of consensus. Since the advent of the Cold War, revolution from the Right (fascism) and from the Left (communism) both have been made to serve as what the French call the *caution*, or legitimation, of liberal bourgeois society: "Well, of course, if you don't like us, there's always the gulag." As is well known, contestation of this opposition between terror and consensus has not always gone beyond its mere inversion. Thus, liberal-bourgeois claims for the virtues of consensus within pluralism have been castigated in recent years, in the name of an ideology of "difference," as hollow shams masking an oppressive, even "terroristic" homogenization by the market economy. This criticism is valid, no doubt, in the terms set by the opposition itself—if one chooses, that is, to accept the grounds of the latter.

In a sense, it is surprising that the debate continues to take place in terms of an opposition that is increasingly hoary. Doubtless, in the case of the Heidegger scandal, the context of the 1930's had to be invoked, and Victor Farias's book *Heidegger et le nazisme* appeared before the collapse of the Soviet Union.[1] It is astonishing, nonetheless, how little recognition there has been of the fact that the Heidegger scandal—and the problematization of Heidegger before the scandal broke in 1987, not merely by his philosophical detractors, but by left-Heideggerians—was not so much a settling of accounts with the 1930's and totalitarianism as it was, fundamentally, a further stage in the liquidation of the nation-state—with its rallying cries of race and national destiny—in an age of transnationalism and globalization of the economy.[2] One might, for example, want to give some thought to how the older opposition of terror versus consensus—inextricably bound up with those other oppositions of the Cold War, totalitarian tyranny versus freedom, or homogeneity versus pluralism—has evolved into the more currently topical problematic of the same and difference as a global and "postcolonial" capitalism has swiftly reorganized the terms in which sites and identities had for so long been organized: East/West, North/South, center/periphery, and so on, imposing reassessments as to who "we" and "they" might be.

Be this as it may, there are still persuasive reasons for addressing this controversy on its own terms, however passé they may appear, if only because the oppositions on the basis of which it has raged are still deemed sufficiently virulent to be mobilized for purposes of political advantage: namely, to discredit intellectual and ideological adversaries.

The authors of the attacks on post-structuralism range across a broad front of quite different constituencies: from French neoliberals (Luc Ferry, Alain Renaut, and many others) who maintain that post-structuralism abolishes the humanist subject of modernity, the apparently indispensable basis of liberal democracy, and who have therefore revived the charge of complicity with totalitarian terror that was leveled at the preceding generation of leftists (e.g. Sartre—although this time the totalitarianism in question is Nazi rather than communist because of post-structuralist affiliations with Heidegger); through neo-Marxists (e.g. Bourdieu) and the inheritor of the mantle of critical theory, Habermas, whose theory of communicative action proposes something barely distinguishable from liberal-bourgeois consensus; to a number of American feminists who have suggested that theory's notorious "death of the subject" was an attempt to rob women of subjecthood just when they were busy acquiring it for the first time.[3]

One could be forgiven for imagining that, within such a diversity of response, someone would get it right. And yet discussions of the "death of the subject"—to limit ourselves to this one issue for the moment—have not been satisfactory: on the one hand, defenders of post-structuralism— whether the principal proponents themselves (e.g. Derrida, Deleuze, even the Foucault of the last works and interviews) or their epigoni—have, in their defense, mostly limited themselves to flat declarations of the absurdity of supposing that the death in question ever had entailed an outright abolition, this without condescending to provide the detailed explanations that an often uninformed audience patently requires.[4] On the other hand, no less unsatisfactorily, critics of post-structuralism—even distinguished ones like Jürgen Habermas or Manfred Frank—have failed to understand crucial components of the post-structuralist position, with the consequence that the perfectly legitimate exercise of their right to refuse to make this position their own has not been based upon an informed choice.[5] Finally, there are signs that current negative opinion regarding a number of post-structuralist positions is beginning to congeal into an unshakable *doxa*: it is beginning to be taken for granted in some circles that the debate is closed and the matter settled.

None of this will do.

This state of affairs is all the more unsatisfactory to the extent that there has been little or no effort made to explain the standoff between the neoliberals and post-structuralism in terms that go beyond the technical ones of the debate itself (e.g. competing interpretations of different periods of Heidegger's writings) or the rant of various *mots d'ordre*: "freedom," "the subject," and so on.

I would like to suggest here that the entire debate surrounding the Heidegger scandal, and the reevaluation of Heidegger and his legacy in French post-structuralism, are best understood in relation to what in recent years has been described as the "normalization" of France: that is, the definitive liquidation of the well-known "French exception"—France's revolutionary tradition—a process that arguably began with the absorption and neutralization of the ethos of May '68 as consumer culture (the promotion of "desire," "imagination," and "self-expression") and that was declared to have been completed by well-known commentators in the run-up to the bicentennial of the Revolution in 1989.[6] Put slightly differently, the assault on post-structuralism—and on its challenge to a philosophy of the subject—should be seen as simply one more instance of that complex, ongoing struggle over the progressive alignment of France with the transnational capitalist order of the European Union and the broader global system the latter represents, which has been the principal force shaping French society in recent decades. In this light, therefore, the ongoing Heidegger debates (new grist is added to this mill every year), in their modest way, might be usefully seen in the same context as, say, the debate over immigration from North Africa and the passionate domestic struggle over reducing the budget deficit to bring it in line with prescriptions for France's accession to a European monetary union (a struggle that only recently brought the country to a standstill with massive strikes). Far from being solely an argument over the 1930's, therefore, the Heidegger debates are also, crucially, about the future of France and Europe in the years to come.

While this "context"—it is not something that exhausts or limits the meaning of the text—can be articulated, and must be assumed at the outset, in the broad terms I have outlined above, it is in the interstices of the "technical" arguments swirling around the Heidegger controversy, to which I now turn, that the larger historical stakes—for us today—can be most sharply delineated. This context, in other words, is not something "outside" the texts.

One of the most important reasons for the currently embattled state of post-structuralism has been the failure on the part of its detractors to recognize the origins of crucial components of its positions—especially those regarding the subject—in Heidegger's great *Nietzsche* study. A close examination of this work transforms one's understanding of post-structuralism, especially its positions on the subject. However, even when the centrality of *Nietzsche* has been recognized, the outcome frequently has been incomprehension as a consequence of the text's being read from a pre-Heideggerian point of view. By which I do not mean that one must adopt Heidegger's positions in order to qualify as a valid interlocutor in these debates, but one must, nevertheless, have demonstrated that one has understood his position before one can reject it. At present, I see no evidence of this among his principal critics.

For example, how many of the critics of Heidegger, or of post-structuralism for that matter, know that what these writers mean by the term "subject" is not what we colloquially refer to as "consciousness" but the *sub-iectum*: that is, "what underlies" or is the *ground* of entities?[7] This is the real target of both Heideggerian Being and Derridean *différance*, and is what is castigated by both writers as the basis of "ontotheology." The term "subject," therefore, does not necessarily apply exclusively to the human subject (God, nature, matter, the universe all can be subjects in this sense of *sub-iectum* or ground), although the confusion in this area is not helped by the fact that Heidegger deems the period of modernity (since Descartes) to be characterized by the dominance of humanism: that is, an era in which humanity (whether individually or collectively) for the first time posits itself as the subject—the putative ground of the system of identity and difference of all entities—so that denunciations by Heidegger, or post-structuralists, of the subject, in this period, frequently do indeed coincide with attacks on the human subject. These attacks, however, are directed at humanity as a metaphysical ground, not at the commonly accepted attributes of "subjectivity"—"agency," "freedom," and so on—as naive "constructions" that, from some darkly "nihilistic" or, for some commentators, "authoritarian" motive might be held by Heidegger or post-structuralists not really to exist or perhaps to be simply undesirable. When this is grasped, much of what has passed for significant debate around the "death of the subject" appears strictly beside the point.

For all these reasons, another look at Heidegger is necessary at this time. Such an exercise cannot, however, avoid dealing with the scandal that broke in 1987 upon the publication of Victor Farias's *Heidegger et le nazisme*. The shocking revelation of the full extent of Heidegger's involvement with the Nazis—which, despite the weakness of the book's treatment of more strictly philosophical materials, was recognized as incontestable—supplied the anti-Heideggerians with ample ammunition in their attempts to discredit both Heidegger and his philosophical progeny in France. I believe that the significance of Farias's book has not been fully explored. I propose, therefore, to reexamine the consequences of Heidegger's commitment to Nazism for us via an analysis of the very detailed criticisms of Heidegger in Ferry and Renaut's *Heidegger et les modernes*. This in turn provides a useful vehicle for a reconsideration of the entire issue of the subject and ethics in post-structuralism and current theory, especially in relation to the latter's implications for a democratic politics. (Ferry and Renaut, despite the strangely uninformed quality of their arguments, have the merit of expressing in the bluntest terms the most common and significant of the criticisms leveled against both Heidegger and post-structuralism.) This reconsideration is an attempt to establish, with greater clarity than the principals have managed to do, what exactly is at stake—globally, in the broadest geopolitical terms—in the Heidegger scandal and the recent standoff between post-structuralism and its opponents.

Any defensible discussion of Heidegger since 1987 has had to take Heidegger's Nazism for granted. It has been established beyond doubt that his involvement with the party was not the brief, ill-considered, naive flirtation that it long was represented as having been. Not only would Heidegger seem to have been actively and deeply committed to National Socialism, but his involvement with the party continued long after the notorious *Rektoratsrede*. Furthermore, reasons have been advanced for believing that he was an anti-Semite. And there is his stubborn silence on the question of the death camps.

Not only is it necessary to take Heidegger's Nazism for granted, but it is important to assume it as a point of departure. This is so that we can avoid two equally indefensible forms of evasion. The first would consist in dismissing Heidegger out of hand because he was a Nazi: arguing, in other words, that the political affiliation with the Nazis infects directly the most intimate details of the philosophical works, which are thereby fatally compromised by their complicity with monstrous crimes. The second form of evasion would consist in yielding before the incontrovertible evidence that Heidegger was a Nazi activist while arguing—at least too categorically—that the "man" should not be confused with the "works." While it is doubtless true that to make speeches in support of Hitler is not the same thing as to write *Being and Time*, we need to face what will be for many the unacceptable notion that it is perfectly possible both to be a supporter of Adolf Hitler and a great philosopher, the author of works that—whether one agrees with them or not—remain squarely in the center of our preoccupations today and profoundly topical. Unquestionably, Heidegger was a Nazi. He also wrote *Being and Time*. These two activities are not the same thing. Nor are they entirely separate. They are related. Precisely how, we will attempt to decide presently, but already at this point we must give some thought to the disturbing possibility that Heidegger was a Nazi *because* he was a great philosopher; and that, worse still, he was a great philosopher, in some sense, because he was a Nazi. It is possible to make this assertion, I believe, without entailing or embracing the absurd conclusion that one has to be a Nazi in order to be a great philosopher, or that all great philosophers are Nazis. I will return to this.

Broadly summarized, the most significant positions on the scandal are as follows. For Derrida, the mobilization of the notion of spirit/mind (*Geist*) in the *Rektoratsrede*—a notion that it had been one of the objectives of *Being and Time* to discredit—indicates an attempt on Heidegger's part to demarcate his own position from the biological/racist dimension of Nazi ideology.[8] The recourse to *Geist*, however—like all discourses resisting totalitarianism, racism, naturalism, or biologism in the name of thought, freedom of thought, and so on—entails a complicity with the "subjectity" (*subjectité*) of the modern metaphysical subject. Derrida follows Heidegger in associating the latter with the will to power of a voluntaristic, self-absolutizing project: the domination of the earth that characterizes modernity as a whole and its attendant ideology of humanism. When this theme of *Geist* is combined with the call to authenticity in *Being and Time* as an appeal to the German nation—the latter must assume its authentic destiny in the course of a "great decision," and so on—then the link between metaphysical humanism and Nazi militarism becomes apparent. Hence the paradoxical conclusion reached by Derrida, scoffed at by many, that it is through a surfeit of humanism that Heidegger is at his most Nazi and that Nazism itself is a humanism. This conclusion is articulated still more forcefully by Lacoue-Labarthe.

The left-Heideggerians' critics—most notably Ferry and Renaut—have attacked these arguments as a disingenuous strategy, one that allows for Heidegger's Nazism to be recognized unambiguously while its contamination is nonetheless restricted to the categories of the earlier work and the later, more rigorously and more consistently antihumanistic writings out of which so much of what is essential to post-structuralism itself springs are not discredited. More specifically, they deride the idea that Nazism, an ideology committed to the superiority of the *Volk*, could be described as a version of, or a fortiori the apotheosis of, humanism—which Ferry and Renaut read as a valorization of a universal *humanitas*. Most important and damning of all, in the view of Ferry and Renaut, is a direct relation between totalitarianism and the late philosophy in the latter's antimodern stance, its profound hostility to an autonomous subjectivity and freedom. Ferry and Renaut hold autonomous subjectivity and freedom to be the foundation of democracy and modern egalitarianism, and they argue that in Heidegger they are replaced by an authoritarian *Gelassenheit* (or "serenity") in the face of the history of Being as destiny. This is, of course, the standard apology for the bourgeois subject as the only bulwark between us and totalitarian terror.

We can begin with the issue of democracy. Ferry and Renaut assert that Heidegger's challenge to modernity and the humanism of Descartes and the Enlightenment necessarily leads to a radical repudiation of all the components of the democratic ethos: "mass culture and the world of technology, of course, but also the rights of man and, more generally, the project of resolving by public discussion those questions that the contemporary dynamic of a constant break with tradition ceaselessly presents to us."[9] The fundamental move in this repudiation of the modern democratic ethos is Heidegger's critique of the modern subject:

How can one not grasp . . . that the critique of the contemporary world [by Heidegger] . . . is radically incompatible with the minimum of *subjectivity* required in order that a democratic thought, in whatever sense one understands the term, be possible? Must we not, in order to grant a meaning, albeit, once again, minimal, to the democratic idea, presuppose . . . the possibility for men to be in some way the authors of the choices that they make or should make in common? In short, how can one conceptualize democracy without imputing to man that minimum of will and mastery that Heidegger refuses him because will and mastery, in whatever sense one interprets them, already would contain within them the seed of the world of technology understood as "the will to will."[10]

That Heidegger himself held modern, bourgeois, liberal democracy in scant regard is an indubitable fact. His own political practice is evidence enough for this without our having to have recourse to a detailed exegesis of the writings to confirm or dispute the accusations of totalitarianism and authoritarianism that have been leveled by critics from all quarters, and in any event, his doubts about liberal democracy were quite explicitly expressed in the *Der Spiegel* interview published after his death. What is in question here is whether Heidegger's late "antihumanist" work—the work that comes after the *Kehre*, or turning—is antidemocratic in the sense intended by Ferry and Renaut.

One would have to answer in the affirmative, but only if one accepts the severely limited definitions of democracy and subjectivity supplied by these writers. Let us begin with subjectivity, the minimum of which is required for a democratic thought: "Must we not, in order to grant a meaning, albeit . . . minimal, to the democratic idea, presuppose the possibility for men to be in some way the authors of the choices they make or should make in common?" Doubtless. One could say just as much, however, for every *undemocratic* form of social organization as well, from oligarchies and aristocracies to fascist or communist reigns of terror. No tyrant ever would get very far if his subjects were not sufficiently the authors of their choices to know when to choose to cringe and obey. For, surely, by "subjectivity," Ferry and Renaut cannot mean an absence of constraint or of a limit to the choices available to one (the latter are, after all, notoriously, an integral part of the experience of democracy—that is, liberal capitalism). And if one replies that what is meant here is some fundamental sense of "subjectivity" or "being the authors of the choices one makes" (the two appear to be interchangeable for Ferry and Renaut)—a will to will, for example, a sheer untrammeled expression of subjectivity as pure affirmation of itself as author of itself—then one has difficulty imagining how this might be reconciled with democratic institutions. And, anyway, the general tenor of *Heidegger et les modernes* suggests that this is not what its authors have in mind. What Ferry and Renaut mean by "subjectivity" is what we colloquially mean by "consciousness": the entire panoply of faculties that not only modernity, but other ages have associated with a sentient human being: emotion, perception, the exercise of choice and agency, and so on.[11] And this is what they believe Heidegger has attempted to suppress or eliminate in some manner.

This is, of course, the standard objection made against Derrida, Foucault, and Lacan and the infamous "death of the subject" for which they are held responsible. And if, indeed, this were what Heidegger and his successors had tried to legislate out of existence, then one would have to join forces with Ferry and Renaut and the hordes of other objectors who have howled their indignation at such a patent absurdity. But what has not been understood in all this is that Heidegger is concerned not to *abolish* subjectivity—or being-in-the-world, or the for-itself, or the cogito, or consciousness (or whatever you want to call it, being mindful that all of these terms are inextricably bound up with peculiar historical moments and carry an immense cultural baggage specific to those moments, and that, therefore, these are not merely different names for the "same thing," transhistorically, as it were). Heidegger is concerned to demarcate the historical and cultural limits of a certain kind of "subjectivity," if we must continue to use Ferry and Renaut's term—that of modernity (or humanism, which posits itself as the ground or *sub-iectum* of identity and difference)—and thereby transcend it toward something less malignant and baneful, something that does not, in the celebrated formulation, entail the fateful forgetting of Being, with its attendant "darkening of the world": that is, "the flight of the gods, the destruction of the earth, the standardization of man, the preeminence of the mediocre."[12]

The absurdity of Ferry and Renaut's reading is very easily demonstrated if we consider some of the most important pages of Heidegger's enormous study of Nietzsche.[13] In the course of arguing that Nietzsche's doctrine—"which makes everything that is, and as it is, into the 'property and product of man'"[14]—is merely the ne plus ultra of Descartes's "cogito ergo sum," Heidegger distinguishes modern anthropomorphism very carefully from the apparently equivalent metaphysic of Protagoras contained in his famous "Man is the measure of all things." According to Heidegger, truth in Descartes—and, ultimately, in Nietzsche—is "grounded on the self-certainty of the subject":

> All consciousness of things and of beings as a whole is referred back to the self-consciousness of the human subject as the unshakable ground of all certainty. The reality of the real is defined in later times as objectivity, as something that is conceived *by* and *for* the subject as what is thrown and stands over against it. The reality of the real is representedness *through* and *for* the representing subject. Nietzsche's doctrine . . . merely carries out the final development of Descartes's doctrine, according to which truth is grounded on the self-certainty of the human subject.[15]

Heidegger is quick to add the qualification: "This in no way signifies that the being is a mere 'representation' and that the latter is an occurrence in human 'consciousness,' so that every being evaporates into nebulous shapes of mere thought. Descartes, and after him Kant, never doubted that the being and what is established as a being is in itself and of itself actual."[16]

This is what Heidegger means by "subjectivity," or what Derrida means by "subjectity," *subjectité*, and perhaps, at least in part, what Foucault means by *asujetissement*, or "subjection."[17] It does not preclude other forms of what, for want of a better word (and bearing in mind that it is a term that is problematic for Heidegger), we can call "consciousness." Indeed, it is precisely Heidegger's point that there have been other forms of consciousness. Thus, Protagoras's "Man is the measure of all things" is not simply another instance of the same doctrine as Descartes's or Nietzsche's. It is not even, mutatis mutandis another form of "subjectivism." The distinction between the statement of Protagoras and what Heidegger means by "subjectivity" hinges on the notion of "unconcealment." I will quote an extensive passage in order to reduce to a minimum the appearance that my argument might be based excessively on my own interpretation:

> We today . . . have long forgotten the realm of the concealment of beings, although we continually take it for granted. We actually think that a be-

ing becomes accessible when an "I" as subject represents an object. As if the open region within whose openness something is made accessible *as* object *for* a subject, and accessibility itself, which can be penetrated and experienced, did not already have to reign here as well! . . . By lingering in the realm of the unconcealed, man belongs in a fixed radius of things present to him. His belonging in this radius at the same time assumes a barrier against what is not present. Thus here is where the self of man is defined as the respective "I"; namely, by its *restriction* to the surrounding unconcealed. Such restricted belonging in the radius of the unconcealed co-constitutes the being-one-self of man . . . but not through delimitation of *such* a kind that the self-representing ego vaunts itself as the midpoint and measure of all that is representable. For the Greeks, "I" is the name for *that* man who joins *himself* to this restriction and thus is *he* himself by himself. . . . The way Protagoras defines the relationship of man to the being is merely an emphatic restriction of the unconcealment of beings to the respective radius of man's experience of the world. The restriction *presupposes* that the unconcealment of beings reigns.[18]

To return to Ferry and Renaut, it does not matter very much to us whether Heidegger's account of Descartes, Nietzsche, and Protagoras is correct or convincing. What is important is that, for Heidegger, the Greek was without subjectivity (in Heidegger's very strict sense of the term—as what is characteristic of modernity). And yet it would be patently absurd to suppose that Heidegger means thereby that the Greek was without freedom, or that he was not "the author of his choices."

So much for the absence of the minimum of subjectivity necessary for democracy. But what about democracy itself? On this score, Ferry and Renaut argue that Heidegger's adherence to Nazism was not so much driven by an unreduced residue of voluntarism (i.e., humanism) in the early work (as claimed by Derrida) as it was the product of an attempt to have done with subjectivity (i.e., consciousness) once and for all, an attempt that has not taken the full measure of its own contradictions.[19] Thus, there is a fundamental ambiguity in Heidegger's thought because it is not certain whether the forgetting of Being is solely attributable to Being itself,[20] to the extent that, for example, Being always occludes itself when it unfolds in the particular entity (thus leaving the way open to the temptation of technology and mastery), or whether the forgetting of Being is to be attributed to "man."[21] In the end, it appears that man is responsible for the forgetting of the forgetting. This ambiguity, according to our authors, leaves Heidegger oscillating between two contradictory responses to modernity and the world of technology: either endorsing *Gelassenheit*, serenity, and resignation, the "only a God can save us" of the *Der Spiegel* interview, or attempting to help technology—as the history of Being— achieve its paroxysm by embracing Nazism and thereby, paradoxically, provoking a remembering of the forgetting of Being.[22]

In any event, the essential point for our purposes is that Ferry and Renaut conclude their book with their principal criticism: the later Heidegger subordinates the critical subject of modernity—our only hope for democracy—to the history of Being as a destiny or code, thus repudiating his earlier work, in which the essence of man was said to be his capacity for transcendence of all codes—biological, social, or otherwise. The step from this position to adherence to a German historical mission and destiny with all its disastrous consequences is only a short one:

> In this manner, does not phenomenology, which had, for a while, main-
> tained its distance from Romanticism, risk repudiating its critical heritage
> and striking once more an alliance with the idea that history is our code,
> as indeed the German nationalism that was Heidegger's after having been
> that of the Romantics would seem to indicate? Whether it be by virtue
> of her *Volksgeist* that Germany finds herself invested with a mission of
> salvation, or through the effect of a history of Being in the heart of which
> she would take up once more the extinguished torch of the Greek tradi-
> tion, is not the difference minimal with regard to what would distinguish
> henceforth phenomenology from critical thought?[23]

The objection here, as in the earlier complaints on behalf of subjectivity, and as in most critical responses to Heidegger and to post-structuralism, is to what is perceived as an undermining of the prerogatives of the bourgeois modern subject's autonomy—that linchpin of the capitalist ethos— and sooner or later, the "Western values" of democracy, freedom, and so on. This is, of course, the usual complaint raised in the face of Marxism, which is dismissed as an equally "totalitarian" form of thought and social practice. The problem is that discussion of these issues generally—and certainly in the case of Ferry and Renaut—fails altogether to take the real measure of what Heidegger was trying to do (independently of the question of the success or failure of his enterprise). The question is reduced to a choice between "activity" and "passivity": is it Being that is responsible for the age of technology, or is it perhaps "man"? Who is the agent in all this? Is man simply the passive object of an active and inhuman destiny? Heidegger himself was well aware of these questions[24] and of their naturally—necessarily even—arising within the philosophical space we continue to inhabit. Ferry and Renaut have forgotten that it is precisely this kind of alternative Heidegger was trying to avoid (and more generally, the kind of thinking that generates it and others related to it—the very thought of "subjectivity" in the sense in which we can now understand the term). Heidegger argues that to attribute the forgetting or remaining unthought of Being either to Being or to thinking is to overstate the case, for it lies in both of them to the extent that while thinking and Being can be distinguished, they should not be separated:

> Thinking does not belong with the default of Being as such in the sense that it observes the default, as though Being itself were one thing off by itself somewhere and thinking another that, founded on itself, either troubles itself or not about Being, certainly not in such a way that, as the representational activity of the subject, it would already sustain Being as what is most universally represented by it and in it.[25]

Thinking cannot be said to be separate from Being. How could it be? What would it become if it became "something else," and what would Being separate itself from if not a being participating "in" Being? Even though, of course, "Being persists in a difference with respect to beings."[26] However, in the very fact of what Heidegger calls the "staying away of unconcealment" and the "staying of concealment," in the very default of Being, a locale or "shelter" emerges that is both the advent and locale of Being and the essence of man, for the simple reason that even when man is comporting himself solely to beings he is comporting himself to Being. Being has to be forgotten for beings to emerge. But that does not mean that man is separate from Being. The abode of the default of Being—being here or there—"belongs to Being itself, 'is' Being itself and is therefore called *being-there* [*Dasein*]":[27] "'The Dasein in man' is the essence that belongs to Being itself. Man belongs to that essence in such a way that he has to be such Being. *Dasein* applies to man. As his essence, it is in each case his, what he belongs to, but not what he himself makes and controls as his artifact."[28] None of this is very easy to grasp, and perhaps the clearest evocation of Heidegger's fundamental insight is to be found in the short essay "The Thing," in which a thing—in this instance, a simple jug—is described as being able to be a thing because in it dwells the "mirror-play of the simple onefold of earth and sky, divinities and mortals we call the world."[29]

Which brings us to *différance*. Derrida's notion is only barely distinguishable from Heideggerian Being and owes most of its force to the latter. Summarized brutally, it is what happens to the Hegelian system when the latter loses the Absolute Subject (Derrida himself has pointed, in a couple of places, to "the relations of profound affinity" that *différance* sustains "with Hegelian discourse").[30] In Hegel's *Science of Logic*, difference (with an "e," not an "a") emerges from the unity of the original absolute indifference of pure being, in which and from which nothing can be distinguished.[31] This is expressed as A = A. Being changes into the negative unity that Hegel calls "essence" or "simple identity-with-self" when what he calls the "tedious verbiage" of the law of identity (A = A) becomes apparent, causing nothing (the nullity of what is being stated)—instead of something—to emerge. Identity now turns into difference from itself: "Instead of being the unmoved simple, it is the passage beyond itself into the dissolution of itself."[32] But clearly, all of this is a series of judgments taking place in a *mind* observing its own logical exercises, a mind that must, furthermore, be Absolute Spirit: that is, unconditioned (and especially unconditioned by what it observes). The difficulty that the huge, ever-rising and ever-widening spiral of the Hegelian dialectic tries to contain is that this mind must be a knower whose difference from what is contemplated or posited never can be factored out of the equation (including its difference from itself, so that it can name itself *as* Absolute Spirit). Strictly speaking, this means that ultimately the knower must at some point float free from the multiplicity of conditioned entities in order to be able to contemplate something like pure, undifferentiated being (in the example just cited) in the first place. The latter cannot—within a single unity of being—

coexist with an observer. (Difference and duality immediately would spring into being.) Hegel himself knows this, which is why, contrary to the impression constantly given that the Absolute is a becoming, a hard-won result that emerges only at the end of Hegel's labors, it is in fact always secretly the telos, already at work, that enables each turn of the dialectic to unfold (a circularity that Hegel himself acknowledges, indeed stipulates, at both the beginning and the end of *The Science of Logic*). Which is also why Heidegger described the Hegelian system as the apotheosis of subjectivism and ontotheology, to the extent that the ground of all beings is here construed as an unconditioned subjectivity.[33] In other words, Being is turned into a being, just another being, but one that is miraculously free of the laws of determination, negation, and difference that condition all other entities in the Hegelian system. In short, Absolute Spirit is modeled on the Christian God, *causa sui* (notwithstanding Hegel's claim that "without the world God is not God").[34]

The principal reason for objecting to all of the above—and for the mobilization of Derrida's notion of *différance*—is not so much the nearly universal distaste for God in contemporary academia as it is the following incoherence, which any ground (*sub-iectum*) necessarily generates, and which is common to all ontology in general and to Hegel's system in particular. It will be recalled that for Hegel, the "determinate being" or "quality" of any being is "negatively determined" by means of opposition to an other (the chair is what it is because it is not the table, etc.). The fullest version of this argument can be found in the second chapter of *The Science of Logic*, entitled "Determinate Being," but it already figures prominently in his first major publication, the *Difference Between the Systems of Philosophy of Fichte and Schelling*: "Each entity, on account of its being posited, is counterposed to another, determined and determining."[35] This is the familiar Hegelian critique of what he later calls the "essential illusory show" (*wesentliche Schein*)—the apparent self-subsistence of the entity, but its real incompleteness—which requires that "the mind complete these limits [of the entity] by positing the limits [of a second entity] that are counterposed to the first entity in order to be its determining conditions: but the latter are in need of the same completion, and thus its [the mind's] task is extended endlessly."[36] In sum, the chair is the chair because a subject has determined that it is not everything else in the universe, from the table to the Tarantula Nebula.

Here is the difficulty, however: if a subject determines that the table is what it is on the basis of its not being the chair and, in the final analysis, everything else, then the corollary of this supposition is that the chair, in its turn, needs its difference from the table (and the rest of the universe) in order for the original comparison to function. And so on—"endlessly," as Hegel rightly says. The argument is circular. In terms of space and time—without which, according to Kant, nothing can even appear to a subject—this is impossible, because it defies their constraints: each being would have to exist in its identity "before" it could be the object of a comparison with another being, and "at a distance" from the other, and yet it is this comparison itself that is intended to establish such identity.

In other words, the system or order that gives rise to identity and difference must precede any subject (whatever the latter's identity, human or otherwise). This is what is expressed in Derrida's notion of *différance*. It is also implied by Heideggerian Being, as when Heidegger speaks, in the long passage from *Nietzsche* cited earlier, of the "presupposition of the unconcealment of beings."

In some measure, Hegel implicitly recognized this by stating, at the beginning of *The Science of Logic*, that "the beginning must be an *absolute*, or what is synonymous here, an *abstract* beginning."[37] He understood, in other words, that identity and difference could not be founded in mundane space/time. And yet the same incoherence, outlined above with regard to the example of the table and the chair, dogs Hegel's Absolute and his entire system. As is well known, and stated explicitly by Hegel himself—both in *The Phenomenology of Spirit* and in *The Science of Logic*—the Absolute is both the point of departure and the point of arrival of the system. And yet these two Absolutes are not the same: as Hegel regularly insists, in both works, only the coming to self-consciousness of the Absolute—in sum, its self-exposition in Hegel's works!—makes the Absolute absolute. This faintly ridiculous because redundant expression—the "absolute absolute"—can indeed be found in *The Science of Logic* at page 533 and is meant to distinguish the "end" of the Hegelian system from its "beginning," from the mere Absolute before "the labor of the negative" has brought it to "actuality" in the course of its self-exposition. The latter, however, is a process that must take place in time and space: Hegel himself speaks of it as a "becoming," and his entire system is no more than the unfolding of its "moments." This necessarily entails, however, the circularity and incoherence that we already have elucidated in regard to the example of the chair and the table: the more exalted status of the Absolute and the absolute Absolute does not make their comparison any less problematic. That Hegel himself sensed this difficulty is evinced by the following passage at the conclusion of *The Science of Logic* in which he attempts to assume the circularity, to embrace it as part of his project, to integrate the threat it represents in order to neutralize it:

> It is in this manner that each step of the *advance* in the process of further determination, while getting further away from the indeterminate beginning is *also getting back nearer* to it, and that therefore, what at first sight may appear to be different, the retrogressive grounding of the beginning and the *progressive further determining* of it, coincide and are the same. The method, which thus winds itself into a circle, cannot anticipate in a development in time that the beginning is, as such, already something derived; it is sufficient for the beginning in its immediacy that it is simple universality.[38]

Here Hegel tries both to have his cake and to eat it. It simply won't work, however: if the beginning (the Absolute) is really the same as the end (the absolute Absolute, the outcome of the Absolute's self-exposition) then nothing has happened. There is no difference between the two: and space/time, identity and difference, as well as the subject, are the delusions that the highest forms of Asian philosophy have consistently maintained them to be—maya. If, by contrast, something has indeed happened, then there really is a difference between the two Absolutes and we return to the incoherence evoked earlier in the case of the chair and table: namely, that whoever or whatever attempts to found the difference between any two entities—be they the Absolute and the absolute Absolute—is not in a position to do so because of the circularity entailed in doing so in space/time. This difference precedes any ground or *sub-iectum*.

This is the meaning of the "death of the subject." This is what *dif-*

férance is intended to convey, as an attempt to move beyond a philosophy of the subject as ground or presence—same thing—and not to embrace absence, nothingness, and "nihilism," either. Complaints about threats to freedom, agency, and democracy are strictly beside the point.

Furthermore, we should not be misled by the still surprisingly widespread misreading of Derridean *différance* as a purely "textual" operation (for example by Habermas), in the colloquial or earlier sense of "text," but should understand it to be at work in the "play of the world" as "general text," as indeed what "produces" (in a postmetaphysical sense of that term) or makes possible our opposition between "language" and the "world." Speaking of his work as a displaced reinscription of the notions of being, presence, and so on, without which the relations between ontology and, say, political economy never will be transformed, Derrida specifically states that "it goes without saying that such a reinscription will never be contained in theoretical or philosophical discourse, or generally in any discourse or writing, but only on the scene of what I have called elsewhere the text in general."[39] The reference here is to *Grammatology*, in the early pages of which Derrida addresses the historical reasons for what he calls the contemporary "inflation of language" as the latest theoretical model in the *sciences humaines*. In the early pages of "Structure, Sign, and Play in the Discourse of the Human Sciences" there is a similar explanation for the fact that "everything becomes discourse," a phenomenon Derrida attributes to "the totality of an era, our own."[40] As the passage from "Différance" makes abundantly plain, however, none of this ever was intended to reduce "the world" to the "idealism . . . of the text" that Derrida would go on to denounce in *Positions*.[41] For some time now, we have lived in a world in which "things" have started to look very like "signs," and the latter have taken on many of the properties of "things," a transformation that in much of its socio-economic dimension is very lucidly explained by Jean Baudrillard in *La société de consommation*.[42]

Nobody, to my knowledge, has made the connection between the "death of the subject" (as ground) just explicated and the question of ethics in post-structuralism. We regularly hear the complaint that the latter is incapable of generating an ethics. This is a surprising complaint because it always comes from defenders of the modern (humanist) subject.

What this constituency conveniently has forgotten is that it was the rise of the modern subject and modern humanism that precluded the possibility of an ethics that was anything other than the "decisionism" with which post-structuralism is regularly reproached in this domain. (Heidegger would have called it "voluntarism"—and also, amusingly, given the nature of the criticisms directed at both Heidegger and post-structuralism by conservatives and neoliberals, "nihilism."[43]) In other words, if humanity is the sole source of meaning and value, then the latter never can rest upon any other foundation than choice, a choice that is inherently and willfully unjustifiable in terms of any appeal to a transcendental authority, hypothetical ontology, or "nature of things." Sartre, perhaps better than anybody else, captured this quintessentially modern, humanist conception of values, stating that value can be a value only by virtue of its status as an entirely free, necessarily contingent, and relative choice. This alone distinguishes it from mere "being-in-itself."[44]

In any event, let us see what can be done for those who are in need of religious reassurance (which is what this demand for a self-confident ethics is really about). It is certainly true that post-structuralist writers generally have abstained from ethical pronouncements, although it is no less true that figures like Derrida and Foucault consistently have maintained that their works have significant ethical and political implications and regularly have intervened in the political arena in a manner that leaves little doubt as to at least some of the values they have espoused. Setting aside political activism, however, if one is interested in deriving an ethics from post-structuralism, then the real challenge is to deduce one from what might ostensibly appear to be the most arid, ethically speaking, of its notions: namely, *différance*. If we examine closely the well-known little essay in *Marges de la philosophie* that bears this notion's name as its title, we soon notice a detail that has escaped both those careless enthusiasts of post-structuralism, who have embraced a little too easily and blithely what they take to be its "playful" dimension, and its enemies, who have denounced its "irresponsibility" and "nihilism." To my knowledge, no one has pointed to the importance of the word "order" in these twenty-odd pages, the order (of *différance*) that carries the fundamental oppositions of our language and of our metaphysics. It would be easy to point to the ways in which Derrida, while deconstructing them, has disclosed the *constraints* that the "general system of the economy" of this order of *différance* imposes on us, or how Foucault, far from embracing epistemological nihilism, demonstrated the ineluctability with which we have produced knowledge. More interesting, however, if we are interested in an ethics, is the relation of this notion of *différance* as order to others we already have dealt with: the subject and the totality. If we pursue the line of reflection developed in the pages above, it soon becomes obvious that, far from being the bulwark of freedom and moral responsibility it is represented to us as being by the neoliberals, the subject (*sub-iectum,* ground) is in fact what makes any moral order impossible.

It should be readily apparent from our account of *différance* and the ground, or the *sub-iectum,* that anything that is a ground—that is, anything that does not depend upon what it grounds in order to be what it is (otherwise it cannot be a ground, being grounded by what it grounds in its turn)—cannot be a part of an order. We might be tempted to think that it can constitute the separate and independent foundation of an order (this would be a mistake, however I cannot broach this matter here), but that it cannot be a part of it would seem easy to grasp. What this means, among other things, is that an order (we recall that this is the meaning of the Greek term, *kosmos*) cannot be a totality because, as we have seen in extensive detail in the case of Hegel, the latter can be posited only by a subject that constitutes itself as the totality's ground: that is, as something external to the totality, as something not conditioned in any way or dependent for its existence upon the totality or its parts. In other words, a totality has its conditions of possibility outside of itself; an order does not. This notwithstanding the attempts of the philosophers of totality—from Hegel to Sartre—to avoid precisely this outcome. Thus, according to Hegel, the Absolute is the totality of being. There can be no outside or other to it. We have seen above, however, that this claim does not hold up. Another way of expressing the problem with the Hegelian system is to say that the Absolute is the totality, and yet, logically, if it is to ground the totality, it also must be outside of it.

Because of the incoherences necessarily entailed by the notions of subject and totality (as in the example of the table and the chair), it follows that humanity cannot derive—and would be misguided in trying to de-rive—an ethics from some overview of a putative totality of beings or the "nature of things" as Law: we would have to be implicated in any such to-tality and could not posit it as an object of knowledge. Nor can we, coher-ently, simply shrug our shoulders in the face of this state of affairs and merely assume the necessarily contingent and "relative" nature of our choices in a self-conscious embrace of an unavoidable "decisionism." This, too, posits humanity as *sub-iectum* or ground of value every bit as much as the ultimately authoritarian, "totalitarian" overview of the whole and its Law. Thus, modern humanism generally has asserted (or at least im-plied, without always grasping the nettle of the secret nihilism of its own position) that there is no meaning or value out there independent of what I (or we, as a "culture"), with a greater or lesser degree of understanding of its contingency, posit as a sovereign choice. Many contemporary writers in the area of "cultural studies" subscribe to this position too, without re-alizing the complicity it entails with a liberal capitalism that they believe they otherwise repudiate.

So, according to *différance* and to post-structuralism generally, the law of identity and difference—value—can be neither known nor legislated arbitrarily into existence. And yet there clearly is an order, *kosmos*, if only because without the latter, there could be no identity or difference in the first place, no entities and no minds to ponder them. Even if that order is beyond knowledge ("it is beyond the order of the understanding," says Derrida[45]) we recognize its force. Indeed, we spend much of our time com-plaining about it. Of course, our resistance to the idea of there being an order beyond that of the human subject (whether individual or collective, as "culture" or "society") is in part in direct proportion to the extent to which capitalism has required the premise of the absence of such an order for its full deployment across the planet (the outcome of which has been ecological, to say nothing of political, catastrophe). Once one accepts the notion of order, then the law (of consequences according to the nature of actions) will imply limits to certain actions, an unacceptable boundary to this "freedom" that is the real fear of neoliberalism, concealed behind pi-ous invocations of "democracy."

At a theoretical level, the resistance to any notion of order derives from a fear that this would entail some form of essentialism. On the contrary, it is to the precise extent that the value—identity and difference—of the entity or the sign is "deferred" throughout the general system, and that as a consequence nothing has any inherent identity or meaning, that there can be an order at all. More deeply, however, our resistance derives from the flat refusal to accept that there could be an order (I mean, of course, a trans-human order, a *kosmos*) that permitted genocide, lung cancer, and so on, an order that thereby shows itself to be calmly indifferent to our most cherished notions of justice, our incorrigible, imperious demand that we be happy and that happiness be served to us on our own terms.

Setting these matters aside, however, suffice it to say that if—as we have established—my identity, my difference from you and yours from me, all value and all meaning—come to us, happen, we know not how (after we have put to one side, that is, all those plausible stories we all need to tell, without which we cannot live, about "culture," "late capitalism," the "patriarchy," "modernity," and the like, each of which, like any narrative, inevitably mobilizes a *sub-iectum*), and if, as we have said, we neither can know the law nor legislate it into existence ex nihilo, then, within the perspective of a search for an ethics, at the very least it would seem that extreme prudence is called for as an ethical imperative. Indeed, not just prudence would seem to impose itself as essential, but complete humility. Furthermore, if we take seriously the notion of *différance*, of "the world" as text or *tissage*, a notion that replaces an ontology of substantial, present, beings (however "mediated"), then our intimate and inextricable "intrication" with the henceforth unthinkable "everything else" would also seem to imply, to require—as much as an act of prudence and "self"-interest as anything else—boundless compassion for all "beings" to the extent that the boundaries between self and other with which we customarily operate stand revealed as even more problematic than they proved to be for Hegel, Marxism, feminism, and so on.[46]

With these considerations in mind, it should come as no surprise that the connection between Heidegger and Derrida, on the one hand, and Buddhism, on the other hand, often has been made over the years. Recently, indeed, an entire academic industry has begun to debate the similarities and the differences between the two traditions.[47] It is not hard to see why.

For our purposes here—given our preoccupation with the issues raised by the Heidegger scandal—we might want to reiterate what so many have noticed: that the notion of *différance* bears a striking resemblance to the Buddhist notions of "dependent arising" (or "dependent coorigination") and "emptiness"—as, for example, in the work of the second-century founder of the Madhyamika school, Nagarjuna. He points out that it is only because all entities are "empty"—that is, as we have seen immediately above, cannot exist independently of one another or inherently—that there can be a world of entities in the first place.[48] For an entity to exist independently or inherently, as its own *sub-iectum*, it would not be able to interact with anything else because then it would be conditioned by the latter, and so each entity would have to exist in its own universe, or, more strictly speaking, *as* its own universe. To be in a universe would be to be conditioned by the latter. Indeed, it could not even have parts, because that, too, would make it dependent. It would be pure being, which, as Hegel rightly saw, is the same as pure nothingness.

While Hegel made the conditioned state of all entities a fundamental principle of his system, he nonetheless stipulated an ultimate cutoff point to the endless coorigination—the Absolute Spirit, which is unconditioned. By contrast, Nagarjuna simultaneously can affirm the value of enlightenment, entailing the usual panoply of extraordinary qualities, such as omniscience, while, like Buddhists in general, refraining from positing an absolute *sub-iectum* that ultimately is separate from the relative. This suggests that it is in this area that we might search for the limits to our own culture—especially if we think of the kinds of oppositions that currently dominate the discussions of "the West and the rest," debates over multiculturalism and the scandal of cultural "relativism." In any event, it is not surprising that dependent arising should entail the cardinal Buddhist value: compassion for all beings. It is hard to see how *différance* could entail anything else, either. If, for both systems, every "entity" (as we have seen, these terms are problematic, but unavoidable) cannot be what it is without the simultaneous "existence" of "everything else," anything less than boundless love and compassion for Being and all beings would be a dangerous mistake.

I do not think it can be plausibly argued that compassion necessarily entails democracy. After all, historically, Buddhism has coexisted with and even fostered political forms that Westerners hardly would characterize as democratic. At the very least, however, there is strictly no reason why Buddhism or Heidegger's meditation on Being and its legacy in post-structuralism should of necessity be incompatible with democracy, if one means by the latter the just and equitable co-implication of all members of a society in the political process, a state of affairs that, we should bear in mind, never has obtained in liberal democracy.

"But Heidegger was a Nazi." Indeed. That the entire trajectory of German culture from the Romantics down to Hitler was characterized by a profoundly hostile stance toward modernity is a truism. To add that Nazism represented the acme of this hostility and appeared to millions to represent a viable alternative to the very real ills of modernity and liberal democracy (and especially to the sheer hell of being a modern subject) would be equally unoriginal and equally true. What cannot be evaded is that Heidegger joined the Nazis and engaged in his systematic search for a new form of personhood for the same or similar and historically related reasons as the majority of the millions of others who were the accomplices of National Socialism. It is my personal conviction that, in Heidegger's case, the longing for a form of personhood that transcended the bourgeois liberal subject of modernity entailed a visceral complicity with criminal political forces that went beyond mere "delusion." (One would have to say the same for all of Hitler's supporters.) In Heidegger's case, this visceral complicity was, I believe, the affinity felt by a resentful provincial chauvinist of modest rural origins for all that was worst in Nazism in its hostility to "cosmopolitanism," "rootlessness," and, yes, Jews.

Adorno, in *The Jargon of Authenticity*, is good at picking up the traces of these attitudes, although I would argue that they become something else in Heidegger's philosophical work. Thus, Adorno claims, for example, that Heidegger's condemnation of gratuitous curiosity and trivial magpie intellectualism in the name of the contemplation of Being and the resolute assumption of the enigma of freedom is the same as anti-Semitism.[49] This is too easy. It is reductive of a specifically philosophical context, although it would seem compelling in the historical context of the 1920's and 1930's, and it is no longer the case today that a condemnation of gratuitous curiosity—or, to make the matter more explicit, "rootlessness"—activates the same anti-Semitic resonances it once did (i.e., anti-Semitism, no less than anything else, has a history).[50] That Heidegger's work can be read today as hostile to liberal democracy is certainly true. But the work does not necessarily entail Nazi totalitarianism, either in the sense that a reader unfamiliar with the context of the 1930's would, after reading *Being and Time*, be more inclined than previously to support authoritarian or fascist forms of social organization, or in the sense that a totalitarian social order can be deduced from it.[51] (I should add that the same can be said for the *Nietzsche* study, which I believe I have demonstrated at some length.) Although it remains the case—and this is the force of the criticisms leveled by Adorno—that the work emerges from, and necessarily bears the traces of, not merely the entire world of Weimar Germany hurtling toward National Socialism, but a real, visceral complicity with those criminal forces that would reach their paroxysm in the Holocaust. In other words, when one reads *Being and Time* in the context of the 1920's and 1930's, or perhaps simply as a German, one necessarily is struck by the historical and linguistic resonances that de facto link the work to atrocities. (But, as I have tried to make plain, we are not just talking about "context": in other words, *pace* Derrida and Lacoue-Labarthe, I hold Heidegger's complicity with crimes to be evident as early as *Being and Time*, notwithstanding the work's publication prior to Hitler's accession to power.) This explains the outright and unqualified repudiation of Heidegger by both Adorno and Habermas, just as it also goes some way toward explaining the more receptive attitude of the French, from Sartre to Levinas, Deleuze, and Derrida.[52]

We are, however, treading on very dangerous ground. Are we not perhaps suggesting, with our argument about different contexts, that we can forget the context of the 1930's and, ultimately, the Holocaust itself? There is a sense, in other words, in which to suggest that we read Heidegger "differently," and differently "today," is to abandon the victims of unspeakable crimes, to repudiate their memory, to make oneself the partner in crime of the revisionists—like Robert Faurisson and Jean Beaufret—who would have us believe that the Holocaust never happened in the first place, or that its horrors have been much exaggerated.

I would argue, however, that we can both read and use Heidegger "differently," and "today," yet sustain the memory of the sinister origins of this work. After all, nothing short of outright repudiation can avoid contamination altogether. But then, one might well find oneself having to extend the repudiation nearly to the entirety of the German philosophical tradition as far back as Hegel. Levinas, for example, has pointed to the complicities between the Hegelian system and anti-Semitism. And it is always possible, I suppose, to imagine philosophers (they would have to be from Oxford, somehow) stating their willingness, their eagerness even, to do without "Continental" philosophy altogether, but it is hard to contemplate this alternative with any seriousness. Indeed, can we plausibly imagine getting "outside" of the text of German philosophy at all? Even if one wanted to have nothing to do with the latter, one would still be haunted by it without realizing it, so much is it a part of our cultural programming.

We are, in other words, brought up against the limits of our own thought. Any use of Heidegger is an affront to the victims of the Holocaust and their families. But we cannot do without Heidegger.

It is at this point that the exemplary importance of the *affaire Heidegger* becomes apparent. The conundrum just articulated above is one we face—or should be facing—with all thought. This is the meaning of Walter Benjamin's celebrated seventh Thesis on the Philosophy of History: that every cultural product—at least, for Marxists, since the Neolithic revolution, when social classes and economic exploitation first appeared—is "a document of barbarism," drenched in shit and blood, rendered possible only by the exercise of massive, criminal, socially organized and institutionalized millennial violence.[53]

Even supposing that we accept Benjamin's thesis as a general proposition—something the academy in the United States can be counted upon to resist strenuously, so stubborn is the need here to be able to give oneself *bonne conscience*, to believe that one can find some clean space to occupy and from which to speak—it may be argued that Heidegger's case is an especially stark and unattractive instance of the complicity of "culture" with crime. In other words, we can distinguish degrees of criminality and general ugliness. We also can attribute degrees of responsibility. But while the special ugliness of Heidegger's case is not in question, in this particular instance we need to temper this otherwise impeccable line of reasoning with the following considerations. Totalitarianism, whether Nazi or communist, and its attendant crimes, have served for too long as the legitimation of the Western democracies. It is especially important in the present atmosphere of self-congratulation over the collapse of the tyrannical regimes in the East and the Iraq War to reiterate what has been stated often enough before, but rarely faced head-on: not only do we not have to consider Western democracy the only alternative to totalitarianism, as the opposition of "terror" and "consensus" would have us believe, and as the critics of post-structuralism would have it, but as it has been historically constituted, the crimes and atrocities of the modern West rival anything Nazi or communist totalitarianism ever perpetrated (the most significant difference being that the Western democracies have not practiced genocide on "white" people within the borders of our own nation-states). The catalogue of crimes, after all, is not unimpressive, if familiar, and I mention them here only because they are consistently downplayed. If indeed we are to invoke complicities with evil forces in the case of Heidegger, we would do well to recall that the bulk of the capital it took to launch the Industrial Revolution and the "democratic" institutions of which we are so strangely proud, which capitalism requires for its efficient functioning (the only reason we have them), was amassed in the course of the pillaging of India and in the slave trade. Shameful episodes of this kind and others—the murderous colonization of the Americas, Africa, Australasia, and huge tracts of Asia, the Vietnam War, the destruction of the biosphere, the fact that we do not have genuinely democratic institutions, and a neocolonialism as destructive as the colonialism it replaced—are not aberrations in the history of the modern West, as Ferry and Renaut, or Habermas, would have us believe, but integral to it, and integral to the kind of subject Heidegger and Derrida decry. A being that sees itself faced by objects that are either representations of its own will to power or, alternately, something not merely distinct from, but something separate from itself, a being that posits itself, in the final analysis, as *sub-iectum* (whether as God, Absolute Spirit, or the modern subject of humanism) can exercise only violence. Thus, the minimal democratic rights enjoyed by the "individual" in the

West, and his or her standard of living, the individual's very constitution as a particular version of personhood, in all its juridical and economic features, all are inseparable from, and functionally integral to, conditions in the "Third World." The integration of France into the European Union and the Heidegger debates, which are topical to the extent that they problematize notions of national identity, culture, and race, are simply episodes in a novel deployment of a global capitalist system that now finds racism, national identity, and national culture obstacles to its implementation. Finally, it should be emphasized that, for Heidegger and Derrida, both Nazi and communist totalitarianism were merely variations of a larger cultural space that constituted the West as a whole in a continuity with the Greeks and the Christian tradition. The full consequences of this position have barely begun to be explored in all their ramifications.[54]

In conclusion, it should be emphasized that it should go without saying, but still does not, that to reiterate these familiar arguments is in no way to suggest that the universal complicity with criminality somehow exculpates Heidegger's collusion with Nazism as one engages in a kind of metaphysical shrugging of the shoulders in the face of universal and ineluctable horror. On the contrary. It is true, however, that we do need to face the possibility that it is the vile Nazi, Heidegger, an anti-Semite, who was the first thinker of the West to articulate forms of thought that might eventually lead us in the direction of something beyond the loathsome barbarism of so much for which we currently stand. If this seems extreme language, then we might want to bear in mind the fact that, from the point of view of the diversity of cultures and the diversity of fauna and flora, Western modernity (under which one would have to include communist regimes[55]) and its subjectivity, which is its basis, are the worst catastrophe to have hit the biosphere since the giant asteroid that, we are told, destroyed the dinosaurs and countless other species in the last known major extermination some sixty-five million years ago.

In short, we have not yet done with Heidegger.

M A R K   P O S T E R

Postmodernity and the Politics of Multiculturalism: The Lyotard-Habermas Debate over Social Theory

Remarkable changes are taking place in the European social and political order concerning Eastern European socialism, the demise of the Soviet Union, the political, economic, and cultural unification in Western Europe, the emergence of ecology as a political question, the transformation of "private sphere" issues into public concerns, the question of postmodern culture, the impact of advanced technologies on everyday life and the secular trend toward a general globalization of the economy and cosmopolitanization of identities. In this context, social theory is faced with a staggering task of reconceptualization, of treating themes that challenge and stretch the viability of traditional orientations, those of Locke, Mill, Marx, Weber, and Durkheim. Within the framework of an emerging new politics, the stunning controversy between Jürgen Habermas and the French post-structuralists has dominated the arena of social theory since the late 1970's.

Despite the acrimony that has characterized the controversy, one fundamental issue unites the protagonists: all agree that social theory must give new priority to language. In *The Postmodern Condition*, Jean-François Lyotard spoke of language as basic to the social bond, in part as a consequence of the dissemination of computer technologies.[1] Similarly, Habermas in *The Philosophical Discourse of Modernity* urged a turn to language in social theory.[2] Earlier orientations toward society as an arena of actions and a structure of institutions are replaced by a focus on the symbolic level. Lyotard defines the current "postmodern" age as "incredulity toward metanarratives," by which he means the inability of our intellectual heritage to make sense of our present circumstances. In a similar vein, Habermas declares "The paradigm of the philosophy of consciousness is exhausted" and urges a shift to "the paradigm of mutual understanding."[3]

Despite this convergence of tendencies, the differences between the positions far outweigh the similarities. The issues that divide Habermas and French post-structuralists may be gauged by looking at the degree of viability each is willing to accord to past theoretical frameworks in the present conjuncture and the concomitant need each position senses for new theoretical departures. In general, French theorists regard the Western intellectual tradition as an obstacle to understanding the present, or more accurately, as a discursive structure of domination, rather than a basis for a new critical standpoint, while Habermas views their point of departure as a fall into irrationalism. Habermas attempts a reconstruction of historical materialism and aspires to the completion of the Enlightenment project of emancipation. Lyotard, Foucault, Derrida and other related French theorists signal "incredulity toward the metanarratives of emancipation," predict the demise of humanism, and call for the deconstruction of the Western philosophical tradition. In the one case there is an effort to revise and conserve; in the other, an urge to break out in new directions.

This divergence of views has in many cases been acrimonious: Habermas regards Derrida, Lyotard, Foucault, and the rest as "Young Conservatives," and Manfred Frank, more disparagingly, characterizes Lyotard as a "neo-fascist."[4] Lyotard for his part has been equally forthcoming: the perspective of Habermas's communicative rationality is "terrorist."[5] Advocates of Habermas's position, such as Seyla Benhabib, dismiss Lyotard as a "liberal pluralist" or "quietist."[6] While from outside these camps, especially in the United States, it may appear that Habermas and the post-structuralists have much in common and together constitute the main hopes for a renewal of critical social theory, the participants are not at all as sanguine, viewing each other rather as a chief enemy than as a potential ally. The single hiatus within the general enmity is Habermas's short memorial essay on Foucault's death, where a somewhat promising picture of Foucault's work is given.[7]

Habermas diagnoses the present conjuncture as a mixture of serious dangers with some hope. The dangers come from the intrusion of "the system" into "the lifeworld."[8] Habermas accepts the Weberian, Lukaçsian critique of modern social institutions as characterized by increasing differentiation of functions, but also by generalized instrumentality. While the system of modern society becomes ever more complex as an articulation of specialization, its mode of practice, instrumental rationality, is homogeneous. In the corporation, the state, the military, and the schools, the process of reification, of treating human beings as things to be used efficiently for one's own ends, steadily extends the domain of its sway. Outside this system stands the lifeworld, the domain of the everyday, where symbolic exchange operates according to a noninstrumental principle. In the lifeworld, communicative action is based on a different principle of rationality.[9] Symbols are exchanged without the imperatives of the system for profit, control, and efficiency. Hence, the opportunity for a critical use of reason in communication is possible.

The lifeworld, for Habermas, is the seedbed for the growth of emancipatory language use and action. All language, he thinks, contains the potential for a free society, since it embodies, as a "universal pragmatic," the validity claims of truth, justice, and beauty. Communicative action contains a kind of rationality in that one may presuppose that speakers intend the truth, mean to express themselves, and are motivated by norms of justice. Even if these conditions are never met in practice, Habermas posits an "ideal speech situation" in which they may occur, a situation in which the force of the better argument, not social position or coercion in any form, alone may prevail. When these conditions are fulfilled, social interactions are governed by the autonomous, critical use of freedom by each participant.

But Habermas goes further. The ideal speech situation contains the telos of consensus. The fundamental rule of communicative rationality is that the parties attempt to reach agreement; their differences are erased in an attempt to attain unity of mind and purpose. Habermas posits the sign of consensus as a universal, necessary principle of all speech. The true conditions of emancipated society are fulfilled when the universal pragmatics of speech are instituted formally as a public sphere that aims at consensus. With the notions of consensus and the public sphere Habermas puts forth a vision of the completion of Enlightenment rationality, setting this in opposition to the system rationality of liberals like Niklas Luhmann, who content themselves with functionalist operationality or instrumental reason as the basis of a free society.

Habermas traces the emergence of the public sphere and the actualization of communicative rationality back to bourgeois efforts to resist aristocratic hegemony. In his earliest work, *The Structural Transformation of the Public Sphere,* he traced the rise of a public sphere in coffeehouses, salons, and lodges, relating it to the spread of print culture in newspapers. In these social spaces a type of public speech was instituted that was characterized by a disregard for status, a putting into question of new areas of common concern, and a principle of inclusivity, that is, that anyone who chose to could participate. Habermas sets as the basic condition for this public sphere the culture of the bourgeois household. In the newly constituted "privacy" of the family, a new subject emerged that was transferred to the "public sphere" of the coffeehouse. The bourgeois who felt himself comfortable, at ease, human, and morally affirmed at home also felt autonomous, critical, and free in the setting of the coffeehouse. "The communication of the public that debated critically about culture remained dependent on reading pursued in the closed-off privacy of the home."[10] In sum, Habermas thinks that the culture of the white, male bourgeoisie instituted a form of communicative practice that if reinstituted in the late twentieth century provides the basis for universal freedom.

Habermas makes this argument despite the fact that the emancipatory politics of the 1970's and 1980's have concerned in good part an analysis of the limitations of bourgeois models and a critique of the position of the white, male subject and its pretensions to universality. Feminist, antiracist, and anticolonial discourses in many ways have put into question the generalizability of the rational subject. They have shown how this universalization has worked against minority cultures, how it has served the interests of the established subject positions, how it makes Other all groups, races, and, sexes that do not conform to its image of autonomous individuality. Arjun Appadurai speaks directly to Habermas's attempt to universalize the bourgeois public sphere when he writes: "The master-narrative of the Enlightenment (and its many variants in England, France and the United States) was constructed with a certain internal logic and presupposed a certain relationship between reading, representation and the public sphere."[11] What Habermas sees as the completion of the Enlightenment project of emancipation Appadurai sees as an extension of Western domination.

Appadurai argues that a new global culture is being set into place by dint of telecommunications technology and a general increase in worldwide intercourse. The incipient synergy of computers, telephones, and televisions produces a cosmopolitan culture in which ethnic difference is evoked and registered. An enormous constellation of images, narratives, and ideas is shared across the globe, but indigenized by ethnicity and culture in very different ways. The key term "democracy" translates differently in different ideological and cultural landscapes. Neither universality nor homogeneity adequately expresses the emerging global culture. Rather, a form of cosmopolitanism better captures the mixture of shared experience and difference without denying the enormous disparity of economic well-being that exists. Habermas, on the contrary, perceives in the new communications technologies only a corruption of communicative rationality:

> In comparison with printed communications the programs sent by the new media curtail the reactions of their recipients in a peculiar way. They draw the eyes and ears of the public under their spell but at the same time, by taking away its distance, place it under "tutelage," which is to say they deprive it of the opportunity to say something and to disagree. . . . The sounding board of an educated stratum tutored in the public use of reason has been shattered: the public is split apart into minorities of specialists who put their reason to use nonpublicly and the great mass of consumers whose receptiveness is public but uncritical. . . . The consensus developed in rational-critical public debate has yielded to compromise fought out or simply imposed nonpublicly. . . . Today conversation itself is administered.[12]

Going to the movies, listening to the radio, watching TV, messaging by computer or fax machine, using the telephone, are all for Habermas only degradations of communicative rationality, examples of the colonization of the lifeworld by the system. One of the serious limitations of the theory of communicative rationality is that it cannot articulate language differences in electronically mediated communication, perceiving only the lack of what it calls "rationality."

But another interpretation is possible, one that derives from the French post-structuralists, Habermas's opposition. As I have done in *The Mode of Information*,[13] one can study the way subjects are constituted in these new, electronically mediated language situations, looking for precisely those configurations that call into question the privilege of the autonomous, rational individual, not to go behind it to some "rationalist" position, but to test the possibility of emancipation in new subject positions, as Appadurai suggests. At this point, aspects of the theoretical strategies employed by Lyotard, Baudrillard, Foucault, Derrida, and Deleuze are most appropriate because they have initiated the project of examining the role of language in the constitution of subjectivity and they have done so with an effort to move outside the parameters and constraints of the Cartesian/Enlightenment position. From Habermas's vantage point within those parameters, it appears that post-structuralists advocate irrationality; but from the vantage point of post-structuralists, the position of rationality, with its particular relation to representation, reading, and privacy (the ideal speech situation of the coffeehouse), is itself a stumbling block to the discovery of contemporary cultural processes that promote and reproduce domination.

The issue dividing Habermas and French post-structuralists is the relation of language to the subject in the era of electronically mediated communication. Habermas's position has the advantage of arguing for continuity with the Enlightenment liberal tradition, asking only for an extension of democracy to institute a public sphere for the enactment of communicative rationality, for a critique of incursions of the system into the lifeworld. French post-structuralists contend that Habermas's theory of communicative action based on a "universal pragmatics" of validity claims substitutes for the autonomous individual an interaction or practice of communicating subjects. Habermas, in their view, fails to reconceptualize the subject in relation to language, to articulate the way language constitutes the subject in different patterns. Habermas, in their view, reduces cultural or symbolic interaction to communicative action and further reduces this to the "rationality" of validity claims. Habermas' critique of instrumental rationality in favor of communicative rationality does not get to the root of the problem of modernity, of the project of Enlightenment.

The subject for Habermas remains pregiven, prelinguistic, and the movement of emancipation consists in removing structures of domination that have been placed on top of it.[14] Emancipation consists in a lifting of burdens, a releasing of potentials for freedom already contained by the subject. As constituted by transcendent, universal attributes of speech, communicative rationality requires no cultural change, no reconfiguration of the subject, no restructuring of language. The Habermasian critique of post-structuralist positions on the ground that they do not distinguish between rationality and manipulation, between the legitimate influence of the better argument and sheer illocutionary force, does not convince.[15] The problem raised by Lyotard and others is not to find a defense of rationality, but to enable cultural difference, what the Enlightenment theorized as "Other," to emerge against the performativity or rationality of the system. From the post-structuralist perspective, the telos of consensus that Habermas evokes is itself a form of domination, since the authority of the better argument to which all participants must submit necessarily erases the difference of subject positions and stabilizes or essentializes one subject position in particular. And it is thus a form of coercion.

The effort of post-structuralists has been to articulate the mechanisms through which language is more than constative, representational, univocal, the ways in which word and thing do not gel into an eternal stability. This critique has uncovered the figure of the subject that stood behind such stability and the dualist metaphysic of subject as agent/object as passive material that provided its foundation. The theory of writing in Derrida, of the imaginary in Lacan, of discourse/practice in Foucault, of the differend in Lyotard, of the hyperreal in Baudrillard, are all aimed at subverting the paradigm of the subject and its relation to language that has dominated Western culture at least since Descartes and the Enlightenment. Whatever epistemological force one may accord to the work of the post-structuralists, one must acknowledge the fruitfulness of their pozsition in relation to the politics of feminism and anticolonial discourse, as well as to the emergence of the mode of information. In both cases, a convergence exists between the post-structuralist effort to reconstruct the figure of the rational subject with the inscription of noninstrumental, destabilized subjects in electronically mediated communication, on the one hand, and critique of white, male culture from positions outside of it on the other hand.[16]

Thus far, however, it must be acknowledged that the French critique of the subject has not led to a new politics. Habermasian critics, not surprised by this deficiency, complain that post-structuralists have no political agenda, maintain no clear norms to guide practice, have no general perspective on social development and no vision of a better future.[17] While these complaints must largely be sustained, post-structuralists reply that these are precisely the issues that must be expunged from the discourse of intellectuals. The "normal" expectations of such discourse from the Enlightenment to the 1960's were that it should provide a coherent sense of the social world, distinguish salient historical trends, specify groups suffering structural domination and therefore having potentials to mobilize for change, and finally depict utopian possibilities.[18] Habermas's theory of communicative rationality accomplishes all of these tasks, whereas the French post-structuralists achieve probably none of them.

The French thinkers, in particular Foucault, Derrida, and Lyotard, strive to rid their discourse of concepts that present a closed or sutured understanding of society, by which they refer to theories that totalize from one level, reduce multiplicity into unity, or organize discourse toward an end or telos that is usually utopian. Any concepts that fix identities, stabilize meanings, or resolve the nature of society are improper and politically dangerous, contend the post-structuralists.[19] Because of these self-imposed restrictions, French post-structuralist theory fails to satisfy certain assumptions about completion. The reader often is bothered by missing elements or gaps in post-structuralist discourse that Habermasian writing, by contrast, furnishes or fills. Some readers go so far as to complain that French post-structuralism can say nothing "positive" about "reality," that it is "narcissistic," or, worse, "nihilist." The French writers reply that they do not want to reproduce at the level of theory the pattern of reason as control that is found both in society and in the tradition of critical social theory. Critical theory in the past, they argue, was able to define the radical moment of society and ground progressive politics only by constituting a suspect theoretical subject. This subject was a stable point of knowledge set against a passive world of objects that it was to establish a position to control through its discourse. In this sense, criticism must avoid the metaphysical gesture of grounding itself in the absolute, even at the cost of failing to satisfy "logical" demands for coherence and closure.[20]

Lyotard exemplifies the post-structuralist reluctance to closure. In *The Postmodern Condition*, he warns that the trend toward computerization implies the reduction of language to the level of "performativity" or efficiency. The theoretical concept in this case represents the real as a closed system governed by instrumentality. Society is seen as a unified system of information flows in which the goal of theory is to insure the maximum ratio of sense over noise. For Lyotard, theory here becomes a "terrorist" denial of difference. In response, he urges critical theory to move to a notion of the unrepresentable, to what cannot be captured by concept, what resists the logic of performativity, and what therefore can serve as a basis for an idea of justice based on the acceptance of an agon of multiple discourses or differends. Theory retreats to locate the minimal conditions for justice, withdraws to the defense of the little narrative against all positions that assert grand gestures or metanarratives, all projects of Enlightenment that solve "the riddle history" or dialectically realize the Absolute Spirit. The sense one gets from reading Lyotard is that, to quote Dick Hebdige quoting The Talking Heads, we are on the road to nowhere, not on the grand boulevard of progress.[21]

Post-structuralism's apparent retreat to a minimalist position might be interpreted as the pessimism characteristic of white, male theory in an age of decolonization (the decentering of Europe) and feminism. The easy assumption of the voice of the universal that has been a hallmark of white, male, Western theorizing no longer rings true. Attention now must be paid to the gender and ethnicity of the thinker, not because of some simple, unilinear determinism of these factors, but because the positionality of the theorizing subject inevitably bears traces of sex and race. In addition, we learn from the history of the comfortable appropriation of the universal by white, Western males that any such appropriation gives cause for concern. When one accepts as an inevitable condition that theoretical subjects are fully genderized and ethnically specific, a new form of dialogue might begin in a context of what I would call "differentiated cosmopolitanism," as opposed to the flat homogeneity of earlier claims to universality as exemplified by Habermas.

Differentiated cosmopolitanism is furthered by the thickening and intensification of communication across boundaries of locality, a process enabled, but not completely shaped by electronic forms of communication. Previously subjugated voices are more readily brought to one's attention and previously private speech and practice of elites are available for all to see. President Bush's regurgitation at a Japanese state dinner illustrates the latter and the well-known photograph of the Vietnamese girl running on a road with her body contorted by pain illustrates the former. Elite control over information slips from its grasp as infobites from dominated groups bleep through communication channels. While the global communication village is not at all a democracy, enough local knowledges do make their appearance to shatter the uncontested hegemony of white, male, Western culture. I believe this structural feature of the present warrants the periodization "postmodernity."

And yet such postmodern cosmopolitanism urges the post-structuralist further toward a minimal theoretical posture. Another bastion of modernist social theory is the assumption that a community of face-to-face individuals is definable, however different its form may take in the varieties of Enlightenment traditions. Postmodernist minimalism then might equally be interpreted as a response to the collapse of any hope for a free community in an age of electronically mediated communication. One may argue that critical social theory, from its beginning through the recent work of Habermas, has assumed as the goal or history, or at least as a possibility, a democratic social order in which face-to-face relations between individuals transpire with a minimum mediation of structures of domination, hierarchy, or asymmetry. But the dramatic spread of electronic communication systems, which undoubtedly will rise even more precipitously once the computer, the telephone, and the television are systematically integrated, toll the end of community in any shape it hitherto has been imagined. The mode of information betokens a restructuring of language so drastic that the figure of the subject that it will constitute cannot readily be discerned. Relations of mind to body, person to person, and humanity to nature are undergoing such profound reconfiguration that images of community are presented, if at all, only in science-fiction books and films. Post-structuralist theory, I contend, reflects these changes by redefining critical discourse to bypass reliance on either the autonomous, rational individual or the democratic, face-to-face community.

French post-structuralism has the advantage over Habermasian critical theory in facing squarely the question of the postmodern, of the prospects of critique in an age that no longer enjoys the supports, metaphysical and social, of the modern, Enlightenment era. The issue of the postmodern evokes a consistently negative response from Habermas in *The Philosophical Discourse of Modernity*, where he attacks Derrida and Foucault as postmodern irrationalists. Among the French theorists, only Lyotard consistently has employed the category of the postmodern, and even then only ambivalently. Nonetheless, French post-structuralists, I argue, defend the modern/postmodern distinction in the sense that their critique begins by putting into question the validity of modern positions. Because they confront squarely the dilemma of the subject in the postmodern age, they are surer guides to a reconstruction of critical social theory than Habermas. In the present-day context of German unification, Eastern European and Russian social and political reorganization, and general European centralization, French post-structuralists may appear deficient for speaking very little on urgent affairs. Yet as these issues become sorted out, Europe surely will face the problem of the postmodern, and the work of the post-structuralists likely will become an important resort in the discussions.

The issue of the postmodern addresses political topics at a very general level. Recent post-structuralist works like Lyotard's *The Inhuman*[22] and Donna Haraway's *Simians, Cyborgs, and Women*[23] register the depths of postmodern culture in a recognition of an emerging "inhuman" or transhuman social order. The referential anchor of the individual recedes in social prominence as global communication networks (Lyotard) and human/machine combinations (Haraway) replace older figures of man versus nature and individual versus society. If we are witnessing a general reconfiguration of the most fundamental features of the sociocultural, some care must be taken in connecting the theme of the postmodern to particular or local political issues. When focusing on the politics of postmodernity, there is a danger that the general processes at stake will become confused with or reduced to the politics of modernity. For example, the controversy over multiculturalism, which is often identified as a postmodern issue, easily slides into the terms and references of liberal politics, of pluralism, and even of the American consensus politics of "the melting pot." I will discuss the relation of multiculturalism to postmodern politics bearing in mind the above considerations.

The term "multiculturalism" generally refers to curricular reform at institutions of higher learning. As more and more minorities attend these institutions, the easy assumption of the universality of Western culture, the Eurocentrism of many basic courses in the humanities and social sciences, increasingly appears incongruous. In campus after campus, controversial curricular reforms have been initiated by faculty and more often by administrators to include non-Western or minority components in courses on literature and history. For conservatives such as Lynn Chaney, multiculturalist reforms signal a deep threat to the quality of higher education since it happens that, for her, "excellent" and "white" are indissociable adjectives. Some liberals attempt to assimilate multiculturalism to consensus politics: here, racial and ethnic minorities in the present context are equated with European immigrants of earlier decades and are to be treated similarly. Curricular reform for this group means devoting study to African-Americans, for example, along with Italian, Jewish, and Irish immigrants. In both cases, liberals retain the notion of pluralist consensus by which all communities are welcome to melt down their identities in the crucible of modern democracy, capitalism, and urbanism.

A third position associates multiculturalism with postmodernism, and it is to this position that I want to address my remarks, because it opens the question of politics in relation to postmodernism. The argument in this case is that the inclusion of non-European cultures in the curriculum introduces a multiplicity of viewpoints that corresponds to the postmodernist celebration of difference. An essay by Tom Bridges, for example, argues that "anyone wishing to pursue the reform of the curriculum along multiculturalist lines simply cannot avoid confronting and dealing with the issues raised by postmodernism."[24] Postmodernism and multiculturalism share a rejection of the universalist claims of the Enlightenment, he contends, making them interdependent and politically similar. Lyotard's appeal for the small story over the grand narrative and Foucault's call for an "insurrection of subjugated knowledges" fit into this profile. In such a spirit, Foucault wants "to entertain the claims to attention of local, discontinuous, disqualified, illegitimate knowledges against the claims of a unitary body of theory which would filter, hierarchise and order them in the name of some true knowledge and some arbitrary idea of what constitutes a science and its objects."[25] The suspicion of the Enlightenment posture of universal rationality appears to emerge with equal, parallel ferocity among postmodernists and multiculturalists.

But this alliance is a troubled one, and it is troubled in ways that reveal the limitations of both positions in the effort to extract themselves from Enlightenment positions and politics. In the case of the postmodernists, the difficulty concerns their repetition in denial of the Enlightenment posture of critique, their replication of Enlightenment forms of critique (the writing of discourses), and their address of universalist themes (society at large for Lyotard consists of differends) while at the same time denying universalist claims. In its rules of formation the discourse of postmodernism retains these crucial Enlightenment characteristics. While postmodernists attempt to avoid foundationalism, the systematic elaboration of theory out of an ontologically secure subject position, they have not completely altered the discursive form of modernity or its institutional apparatuses.

In the case of the multiculturalists, the difficulty concerns a reliance on subject positions that reproduce Enlightenment notions of agency. Minority discourse may function critically as an other to Enlightenment subject positions, but the assertion of validity for minority positions often reproduces the fullness of identity that is a major problem in the Enlightenment position itself. In a recent collection of essays representing a broad array of many of the best writers on the question of cultural difference, the issue of identity, agency, and subject position appears over and over again as the bane of critical thinking.[26] The colossal problem is one of asserting the emancipatory potential of multiculturalist subject positions while avoiding the essentialism or self-identity that is associated with Enlightenment forms of resistance. Over and over, writers on this topic reiterate the warning that the position of the other is neither a guarantee of ethico-political superiority nor a fixed, coherent wholeness. The critical potential of the "other" position must be carefully extracted from the structure of its domination.

With postmodern discourses such as those of Lyotard and Foucault, it is often noted that non-Western minorities function as an empty alterity, providing a standpoint of critique of Western logocentrism, but one vacant of specificity.[27] Yet when that position of alterity is "filled in" or "completed" by multiculturalists, the resulting subject position often becomes a self-identical one, and its culture is uncritically affirmed. For example, when some Asian-American students are asked in class to present a critique of the writer under discussion, they refuse and justify that refusal by referring to their local culture's or family's prohibition of criticism. It does not matter to them that the writer in question might be a racist or antimulticulturalist. The fact that the writer is read in the context of an institution of higher learning is enough to forestall criticism. In this case, the resort to the legitimacy of the minority culture prevents the critique of positions that would refuse that culture's presence in the curriculum. This example is by no means unique, and the same problem is found in any number of "other" positions. In other words, the postmodernist validation of minority discourse as a consequence of the critique of Enlightenment universalism, when set into the academic multiculturalist arena, may allow no doubts to be raised about the specificity of ethnic and racial discourse, even when the text in question denies the critical function of education in favor of instrumental ones. If a multiculturalist curriculum would decenter learning from Enlightenment universalism and include the experience of non-Western groups, postmodernist configurations of critique may well be incapable of providing an adequate framework for that study.

This political limitation of postmodernist thought, however, ought not to surprise anyone. In my view, postmodernism is a fledgling position, one registering changes in society (the demise of colonialism, the spread of electronically mediated communication, etc.) that have only just begun to revolutionize the structures of modernity. Postmodernism anticipates a future in which these tendencies will no longer be emergent, but dominant. In the meantime, the major modern political tendencies, shorn, to be sure, of their legitimating metanarratives, continue to plod along, blanketing the play of forces with discursive regimes that hold back or disguise postmodern developments as much as they can. In this complex, ambiguous situation, multiculturalists must choose between a Habermasian universalism that denies their enunciative position altogether and a postmodernist differentialism that affirms that position, but cannot fully defend that affirmation.

FRANÇOISE LIONNET

Performative Universalism and Cultural Diversity: French Thought and American Contexts

Ideas about national specificity are closely tied to certain idiosyncratic notions of culture in France, and as Pierre Bourdieu has eloquently shown, "culture" for the French is both French and universal: it is the *culture générale* that informs every educated person's background; it is synonymous with "high" culture and with the ability to engage in speculative thinking about the nature of such concepts as "thought" and "culture" and about their vexed relationship.[1] To be French is to have learned to think beyond mere particularisms, regionalisms, or ethnicities. It is to transcend difference. The French school system socializes its pupils into believing that the goal of education is to accomplish the Enlightenment ideal of helping individuals rise above mere regionalisms and tribalisms in order to adopt such republican values as can be beneficial to all peoples at all times. As one commentator puts it, "To be French is to be the member of both a particular nation and a representative of a universal ideal, to be other is (at minimum) to be only particular, a condition that may be escaped only by becoming French."[2] Hence the politics of cultural assimilation, which continues to be implemented—ostensibly "for their own good"—as regards immigrants from Africa or citizens from the *départements d'Outre-Mer* who come to live in France.[3] Public discourse about "Frenchness" generally implies this universalist ethical dimension: France is a *terre d'asile*, a land of asylum, for those fleeing from political persecution, religious fanaticism, or economic hardship and already won over to the universal ideals symbolized by the Revolution.

These ideals are frequently opposed to what is perceived as the "American nightmare" of identity politics and infinitely fragmented social realities, where cultural relativism leads to the breakdown of the social contract. As a headline from a 1991 issue of *L'Evénement du jeudi* proclaims: "Puritanism, Ultrafeminism, the Assault Against Privacy, Moral Rigidity: America, or The Dictatorship of Minorities."[4] In the same issue of this popular magazine, an interview with Tom Bishop is entitled "The Minorities Risk Becoming a Small Dictatorship," and the icon of the Statue of Liberty with a gag on her face adorns each page. This series of articles on American contemporary culture stresses the gagging of the democratic ideal of free speech. It attributes this situation to the shadowy double of American democracy, a spreading puritanical obscurantism. Such extremism, it is argued, undermines the search for truth and justice, even within those institutions of higher learning whose mission it is to enlighten and educate: censorship and self-censorship have replaced the free and open discussion of ideas.

The contrast between these representations of the ideals of a "universal" culture, on the one hand, and the barbarisms of minorities, on the other, offers a productive way to think through issues of terror and consensus in a cross-cultural and transatlantic context. French responses to and misconceptions about the alleged breakdown of democratic consensus in the United States have been filtered through the American Right's misleading reflections on public discourse in the universities and beyond. French perceptions also are influenced by the fact that democratic consensus seems to be playing an ever more important role in the French public sphere.[5] Rather than examine the broad questions of political philosophy that arise from these issues, I want to look at the cultural underpinnings of the situation as I have just described it. I want to underscore both the provincialism of French claims to universality and the genuine influence that French thinkers since the Enlightenment have had on the global production of knowledge. Contemporary French philosophers are both credited with and blamed for having forced a reexamination of the ideological basis of this production of knowledge, of the ground upon which claims of universality and enlightened modernity can indeed be made.

It is true that ideals of democratic universalism are part of a legacy of the French Enlightenment that has been appropriated by many different cultures. Each has nevertheless put its own stamp on these ideals. As Arjun Appadurai explains: "Democracy has clearly become a master-term with powerful echoes from Haiti and Poland to the Soviet Union and China . . . [but] this is complicated . . . by the growing diasporas (both voluntary and involuntary) of intellectuals who continuously inject new meaning-streams into the discourses of democracy in different parts of the world."[6] There is no transcultural consensus on the meaning of democracy, and the unstable or culturally coded nature of the concept can help explain why notions of "terror" or "consensus" have become rather limited ways of thinking about politics and intellectual debate at the end of this second millennium. The process of decolonization in the 1950's and 1960's has also shaped a debate which has increasingly been demonized under the term *la pensée '68*. The colonial experience is the underlying concern of thinkers of porosity, discontinuity, and the refusal of *arche*, an-archy such as Foucault (who lived for a while in Tunisia) and Derrida (an Algerian Jew). It is from this political context that they draw the urgency of their thought, an urgency that inhabitants of other cultures sometimes have difficulty appreciating.

The dissemination of this *pensée '68* has had a very profound influence within the field of American cultural studies, and selective aspects of this *pensée* have been imported and have migrated through the American system of higher education. I propose to look here at the phenomenon of cultural diversity both in France and in the United States, seeing French thought as one element in this diversity, one singular element that has had a particularly strong effect on the dynamics within this diversity. In this view, "French thought" might be seen as a commodity, appropriated and transformed by its transatlantic passage.

What has been particularly interesting in the 1980's and 1990's is that the appropriation of, say, post-structuralist methodologies within American cultural studies often goes together with the expropriation of the original purveyors of such theories. Rampant Francophobia has often coexisted with the enthusiastic rejection of all master discourses, the French "master thinkers" being relegated to a sphere of noninfluence, much in the spirit of their own denunciation of either the alliance of power and knowledge (Foucault) or the "grand narratives" that have legitimated thought and action since the Enlightenment (Lyotard). Some American scholars have learned the lesson well, rejecting the French masters in favor of the creative use of theories that they adapt for their own purposes, sometimes linking the hegemony of "theory" to a legacy of terror imposed by their philosophically minded colleagues in departments of French and comparative literature. In such a context, "Frenchness" becomes a code for a set of approaches and practices that are said to obfuscate, colonize, and unsettle local ("native") attempts to make sense of the diversity of American culture. French singularity becomes associated with intellectual terrorism when it is not simply discounted as elitist and "politically incorrect."

Ironies

I am interested in asking whether we can begin to rephrase questions of singularity and identity in ways that are more productive, less constraining, less nationalistic. I do not think that it is possible to talk about an exclusive identity of French thought, of any thought for that matter, at a time when massive transversals of one realm of culture into another have become a universal phenomenon, when the university itself is a truly transnational body that brings together scholars from around the world, and when electronic communication allows researchers to communicate with each other instantly. At a time when disciplinary boundaries are crumbling, we are as likely to find "French thought" taught in departments of English and history (e.g. Lacan, Derrida, Foucault), anthropology and performance studies (e.g. de Certeau's influence on the study of "the practices of everyday life"). Is this the result of the success of what is called "French theory" in this country? Is it also due to the general interest in the rest of the Francophone world and its diverse cultures in what can be termed (after Deleuze and Guattari) "minor literature"? To what extent is the perceived "dictatorship of minorities" an amplification of the lessons drawn from contemporary French philosophy, and if it is, what can we say about the (seemingly universal?) impact of the critique of instrumental reason on contemporary cultures and disciplines in the United States?

The current tensions or *crispations* within French intellectual culture that have led back to the ideology of consensus in France actually appear as a series of attempts to come to terms with the very real political challenges posed by the end of the colonial era. The intellectual metaphysics of French culture has been threatened, like the political order, from above as well as from below: from the new Europe, as well as from immigrants from the "South." Indeed, French intellectual culture has been porous from above for quite a long time. Sartre himself openly proclaimed that the purpose of *L'être et le néant* was to effect a certain rapprochement of Hegel and Heidegger—two thinkers not notably French, but from the far southwest of Germany. Similarly, Husserl was the inspiration for a great deal of Merleau-Ponty's work. Foucault explicitly takes off from Nietzsche, and inexplicitly from Heidegger, as does Jacques Derrida.

In general, French philosophy since the war can be viewed as a series of very acute commentaries on German philosophy. Paris has thus played a mediating role in the cultures of the world: it has taken German categories and rethought them in connection with the very real challenges to Aristotelian metaphysics posed by the end of colonialism and the rethinking of questions of hybridity in theory, culture, and race. True, this mediating role is something of a demotion: French thinkers are not, in general, nearly as original as they are taken to be. But the mediating role is important. How might we conceptualize it?

Thinkers in Germany or the United States certainly have not been able to play this role. Germany never had the kind of colonial empire that France and Britain had, and thus never needed to conceptualize the identities of its foreign subjects the way the French did. Nowadays, such insiders from outside have shown up with a vengeance: East Germany is something akin to a colony of the West, to which it is having to conform. The streets of Western towns are full of non-Germans who, in spite of their ignorance of German culture and even the German language, fully meet the criteria for "Germanhood" propounded by the German state: German ancestry. Similarly, this mediating role cannot be played by America, which is almost entirely composed of insiders from outside, but which remains pragmatically resistant to the need for theory. Both countries, in their efforts to articulate the situation in which they find themselves, may make increasing use of the categories and gestures of French thought, which in that way acquires a kind of universality: not the dominant (terroristic) universality of the single model to which all others must conform, but a de facto and impermanent universality grounded in the pragmatic usefulness of a paradigm that provides conceptual tools to help us understand the complex relationship between insiders and outsiders, "same" and "other."

The figure of Hélène Cixous, as an example of these paradoxes and as one who provides such a paradigm, kept haunting me as I was pondering these issues. In "Sorties," Cixous writes: "The paradox of otherness is that, of course, at no moment in History is it tolerated or possible as such. The other is there only to be reappropriated, recaptured, and destroyed as other. Even the exclusion is not an exclusion. Algeria was not France, but it was 'French.'"[7] Concepts introduced into the academy by way of foreign-language departments have been assimilated into the discursive practices of scholars intent on challenging the epistemological premises of their disciplines. These concepts have represented a certain kind of otherness to the hegemony of Anglo-Saxon positivism, and otherness, as Cixous perceptively writes, is a category that always is in danger of being coopted and assimilated. Academic institutional practices in this country have been radically transformed by the successful assimilation of approaches and analytical procedures initially associated with "French" intellectual life. But just as Algeria was not France, yet was considered "French," we might draw a similar analogy about "theory" or speculative discourse that is more German than French. But "theory" has now been thoroughly Americanized, domesticated, cut loose from its "origins" in the pedagogical practices of French departments, and widely disseminated by specialists in other fields, who, like Deleuze and Guattari's nomads, have thoroughly deterritorialized it, multiplying its ramifications and rhizomic structures across a curriculum that now bears its imprints.

In other words, the boundary between inside and outside, domestic approaches and foreign practices, has disappeared. At the very moment when scholars are making widespread use of "French thought," it is no longer useful for them to acknowledge or even recognize their debt to it, since this displacement of thought, its cultural exile and distanciation from an "originary" place, enacts a radical separation between signifier and signified, between so-called "French theory" and "Frenchness," thus performing the "becoming minor" of theory, the dismantling of forms and categories that ostensibly could determine or fix "Frenchness" within American academic circles. The transgression of current disciplinary divisions, and within disciplines, of divisions between theory and practice, is what characterizes "cultural studies" as the field that best reflects the changes both encouraged by the vitality of American academic institutions and opposed by the conservative Right.

Multiculturalism may have acquired a particular kind of urgency in this country—despite conservative campaigns against it—in the wake of the Clarence Thomas–Anita Hill fiasco of 1991 and the Los Angeles riots of 1992, an urgency that many French intellectuals seem to have great difficulty appreciating, if one is to judge by the distorted coverage given to the issue of "political correctness" in the French media. France has had its own share of riots and scandals, especially in its *départments d'Outre-Mer*, but the political response to these has been rather subdued and ineffectual, marked by a gradual veering toward the Right.[8]

The influence of "French thought" on the American academy has been contested on several grounds. If it is true, as Naomi Schor has said, that "Franco-American intellectual relations are at a (cyclical?) all-time low,"[9] it seems to me that this situation is the result of mutual misunderstandings and of the interesting paradox identified by Cixous: French thought cannot be tolerated "as such," at the very moment when it is being appropriated and destroyed as "other." Here, exclusion is not exclusion, it is the extreme form of the assimilation and absorption of concepts that never were "purely French," always have been hybrid, or *métis*, and continue to be transformed by the arrival of diverse social agents on the intellectual scene, agents with the capacity to create new cultural realities and to act in terms of them. These are, for example, specialists in Francophone and (post)colonial literatures, writers and critics, who, like Cixous herself, have been questioning the very definition of "*francité*," or French singularity, and what it includes, occludes, or excludes.

As is often the case in transcultural processes, the proliferation of nonliterary, noncanonical objects of study across a curriculum increasingly influenced by the thinkers of discontinuity and disjuncture has forced, in turn, a reexamination of the practices of foreign-language departments, opening up French studies to the examination of cultural practices, to visual media and oral and written materials from a variety of Francophone contexts, to what some might still consider marginal, peripheral, and ephemeral practices, but what most of us who have been working in minority discourse for the last two decades consider a long-overdue recognition of the fundamental diversity of the Francophone world within and outside the hexagon, and of the need to understand and reconceptualize modernity in relation to the phenomenon of colonial expansion since the Renaissance.[10]

If there is one singular convergence among French-speaking intellectuals who are read here and who have been influential in this country—from Albert Camus to Jacques Derrida, from Edmond Jabès to Nathalie Sarraute, from Emmanuel Levinas to Marguerite Duras, from Julia Kristeva to Tzvetan Todorov, from Aimé Césaire to Maryse Condé, from Edouard Glissant to Abdelkebir Khatibi and Assia Djebar—it is their common experience of multiculturalism, of exile and displacement from either *la France coloniale* or Central Europe, and the fact that they are bilingual or multilingual, although they choose to write in French and their intellectual achievements are very much part of a certain cosmopolitan "Parisian" scene. But more often than not their otherness has been "reappropriated, recaptured, and destroyed," as Cixous puts it, both in France and in America, in a move that antedates the current fate of French theory in this country with respect to the nationalist myth of a monolithic and universalizing French culture.

As Cixous goes on to add, in a more personal and private register: "Me too. The routine 'our ancestors the Gauls' was pulled on me. But I was born in Algeria, and my ancestors lived in Spain, Morocco, Austria, Hungary, Czechoslovakia, Germany; my brothers by birth are Arab. So where are we in history? . . . Who am I? . . . What is my name? . . . Who is this 'I'? Where is my place . . . which language is mine? French? German? Arabic?"[11] Known in this country as a "new French feminist," to borrow the title of a famous anthology published in 1980, Cixous is positioned at the intersection of several cultural currents and shares the fate of millions of displaced people, émigrés or immigrants, intellectuals or manual laborers, who contribute to our understanding of the hexagon as the always already hybrid space that it is.[12] The writer Leïla Sebbar stages the existence of those who inhabit just such a space in her novels *Shérazade* and *Les carnets de Shérazade* about a young Beur woman and other second-generation immigrant youths who survive on the periphery of mainstream French culture, acting out their marginalized or clandestine existence in squats and flea markets, in the *quartiers* of Barbès, Belleville, or Crimée.[13] The "Paris" of Leïla Sebbar's characters has a topography quite unlike the one that, say, American tourists would easily recognize. It is also not the *Rive Gauche* of cosmopolitan intellectuals. But by the same token, the "independent, unassimilated, unscrupulous, often intelligent, sometimes violent . . . rootless, alienated youth" that populate her novels are the Parisian analogues of the young people of New York or Los Angeles, cultural nomads all.[14] Sebbar's novels represent an intervention in the field of French literary culture that produces a change in the way this field is perceived. Her work emerges as a performative utterance that changes the relational dynamics of all objects in this heterogeneous field. Thus, to look at French culture from the place where Sebbar writes across its borders is to discover a different sense of "Frenchness."

The "we" that constitutes "French identity" today manifests more diversity ethnically, regionally, and culturally than many other European countries. Abdelkebir Khatibi has attempted to conceptualize a "thinking otherwise," a "thinking the 'we'" inspired by Heideggerian, Deleuzian, and Derridian philosophy that undermines the intellectual imperialism of institutional discourses and disrupts traditional fields of knowledge. He defines it as a "historical chain in which being is woven and that is woven by being on the margins of metaphysics."[15] He echoes what Edouard Glissant has called "the poetics of relationality," an aesthetics of interdependence and deterritorialization, an "aesthetics of reversal and intrusion . . . of rupture and suture . . . of the variable and continuous, of the invariable and discontinuous."[16] Glissant's narrative critique of all totalizing discourses is a project aimed at articulating the specificities of the Antilles in relation to the diversity of a global context, the "tout-monde."[17] His project consists in forcing hegemony to rethink itself together with what it

represses or renders unspeakable, taking into account the mutually determined histories of the metropolis and its satellites.

Using concepts that originate in Greek and German philosophy, Khatibi
and Glissant give us the tools to conceptualize this hybridization, this
weaving or *métissage* of cultural forms that has been the lived reality of a
majority of the world's peoples from the beginning of the Roman Empire
through the Conquest of 1492 to the current "modern world system" of
Immanuel Wallerstein. In this system, the historical position of France has
been a place of contact and transculturation since the Middle Ages. As a
métis nation, it incorporates influences from the North and the South,
Christian, Jewish, and Islamic. It eventually was forced into a kind of artificial unity by linguistic policies (put in place after the French Revolution)
that periodically need to be reaffirmed precisely because they are imposed
in an arbitrary way and are in constant danger of losing ground.

Languages and Identities

In such a context, I propose that the Terror dates back not to 1793, but
more accurately to the fifteenth century, when Claude de Seyssel, advisor
to Louis XII, urged him to follow the example of the Roman emperor and
to impose his language on the whole nation. The primacy of the French
language as a fundamental element of the national ideology subsequently
has been reaffirmed at each important juncture of French history: in 1539,
with the *Ordonnance de Villers-Cotterêts*; in the eighteenth century, by
the intervention of the Abbé Grégoire; in 1975, by a new law governing
the use of French and meant to protect its purity; and most recently, on
June 22, 1992, with the decision of the *Congrès* to enshrine French, along
with the national anthem and the flag, as a fundamental symbol of the Republic and an essential principle of its constitution.

The linguist Henri Giordan has stated that with this decision, France
became "the only country among the Twelve [the countries of the European Economic Community] whose constitution guarantees the privileged
position of an official language without reference to the other regional languages."[18] This continued attempt to impose an artificial homogeneity on a
very diverse nation represents an interesting departure from the apparent

defense of cultural pluralism voiced by François Mitterand in a statement
he made on March 14, 1981: "The time has come for a statute on the languages and cultures of France. . . . France must not be the last European
country to refuse to its citizens the elementary cultural rights recognized
by the international conventions that were signed by us."[19]

By contrast, the ruling of June 1992 indicates that the old nationalist
reflexes remained (as was confirmed in the 1993 spring legislative elections that brought the conservatives back into power). The radical cosmopolitanism of French intellectual life during the past two decades is now
in danger of being subsumed under a new rhetoric of "lost or hidden authenticity that, once uncovered, yields a single, immutable national identity."[20] The early-twentieth-century conservative ideology of "True
France" seems to be back in style in the late 1980's and early 1990's. As
Herman Lebovics writes in his study of French cultural identity:

> The idea of France [that this ideology] consecrates is profoundly static
> and ahistorical, indeed antihistorical, for despite all vicissitudes of
> history—monarchy, republic, empire—a vital core persists to infuse
> everything and everyone with the undying if seriously threatened
> national character.
>
>   This conceit is idealistic in metaphysics. Its epistemology is dualistic:
> revealed truths dominate the spiritual realm, but it is strongly empiricist
> in the human sciences.[21]

Viewed from this perspective, the ideology of "True France"—as developed during the first half of the century by conservative Franco-French[22]
and as critiqued by Lebovics—has much more in common with the pragmatic and commonsense approach associated with Anglo-Saxon empiri-
cism than with the image of "French" speculative discourse familiar to
American academics. The wars over cultural identity may simply be a
symptom of the fundamental instability or discontinuity of concepts and
formulas, which yield their most interesting and performative results
when they are free to travel across cultural boundaries, working over and
transforming traditional notions of identity and culture, as is in fact happening across the globe today.

For Gérard Noiriel, the historical study of migrations is an indispensable prerequisite to the study of contemporary patterns of cultural contact, and "the deconstruction of the Nation as a collective entity in favor of an approach that looks at individuals first" is the only approach susceptible of yielding an accurate representation of "French" identity.[23] Contemporary French political life has been deeply marked by "l'immigration de masse," and he argues that it is time to "break away from the beautiful narratives that underscore quiet, restful, even reassuring views of history, these narratives of consensus appropriate to the study of rural *longues durées* and with which we have become familiar thanks to the best specialists of rural French history."[24] These always have been linked to a long history of xenophobia with a dramatic effect on French political life. During the Dreyfus affair, for example, Emile Zola's strong motivation for supporting Dreyfus may have been rooted in his personal exposure in the 1880's to the increasing prejudice against foreigners that severely affected his own father, an Italian immigrant.

A century later, in the 1980's, xenophobia again became a major issue in France. It is currently being fed by the same myth of a unified France grounded in the ideology of universal values. The pressure to homogenize continues to increase within the confines of the hexagon.[25] In the United States, by contrast, we seem to have reached a different sort of intellectual, cultural, and political consensus, one that recognizes both the need for ethnic pluralism and multicultural education and the usefulness of conflict as a way of airing out differences.[26] This need is currently being translated into concrete reforms at different levels of the educational system, from elementary schools to postgraduate humanistic studies. These are by no means entirely satisfactory, and their effectiveness will have to be tested. But the system is attempting to be responsive.

Noiriel makes an interesting comparison between French and American traditional views on the question of assimilation, suggesting that (contrary to appearances) American sociological views on the importance of "ethnicity" have much in common with Sartrean views on "authenticity," since both underscore the need to act in terms of one's freely chosen ethnicity and essential nature, to perform one's identity, to become what one is—that is, to acknowledge either the constructed nature of one's identity or to choose to select only one element of one's background.[27] The difficulty is that the freedom to choose this authenticity also can make one the target of racism and xenophobia. The passion for the universal stems from the desire to fight off those particularist ideologies that confine immigrants to playing the role of the other to mainstream culture, hence to the uncomfortable position of being an exotic commodity to be feared, envied, or hated. Noiriel suggests that it became urgent for the French to develop a "parler autrement," a way of speaking otherwise about the issue of immigration so as to avoid falling into the trap of the "cloisonnements identitaires," walled-in identities, which he, too, sees as the hallmark of American pluralism.[28]

This "parler autrement" is what the deterritorializing of French theory in this country is in fact all about. The symbolic demand for cultural difference on American campuses, for example, often is mediated by a set of practices that are an act of emergence from the "unsaid" and the "unthought" of hegemonic and homogeneous discourses. Cultural theorists in this country increasingly are pointing to the performative value of these interventions. These can generate new forms of solidarity among the fractalized group identities of "minorities" who distance themselves from the ideal of homogeneous nationhood, yet reconstitute themselves as smaller groups whose discourses often are incommensurable with one another, but who value solidarity nonetheless. Such an approach can help disenfranchised and disempowered groups fight for rights without falling back into conventional ideas of territory and nation.

The work conducted in 1991–92 by the research group on minority discourse in residence at the University of California Humanities Research Institute at Irvine is instructive in this regard. Influenced by Deleuze and Guattari's concept of "minor literature," Abdul JanMohamed and David Lloyd have stated that "the task of minority discourse, in the singular [is] to describe and define common denominators that link various minority cultures. Cultures designated as minorities have certain shared experiences by virtue of their similar antagonistic relationship to the dominant culture which seeks to marginalize them all. Thus bringing together these disparate voices in a common forum is not merely a polemical act,"[29] but a constructive attempt to develop strategies of empowerment. As Lloyd explains:

What is perhaps most immediately striking about the historical experience of minorities in general . . . is its determination by processes of dislocation rather than enracination. That continuing dislocation has taken many forms, materially and culturally, including the internal colonization of an already hybrid Chicano/a population and its continuing patterns of labor migration and acculturation; the enslavement and Diaspora of African-Americans and their continuing economic dispersion; the genocide and displacement of Native Americans in an effort precisely to loosen their claims to "local" land rights; the immigration and exploitation of Chinese and Filipino workers, and so forth.[30]

The goal, then, is to imagine points of commonality, to search for common denominators. Although this appears to mirror the current French preoccupation with a politics of consensus, it is nonetheless very different from the kind of stability that consensus implies. Rather, it points to a common logic and to another sort of universality: not the universality of a set of static principles (democracy, freedom, and human rights), but the dynamic universality of the paradigm, of a particularly clear instance of something that has other instances elsewhere.

So construed, French theory becomes, not a statically portable entity, but a dynamic one, a set, not of principles, but of practices that are embodied in one place, but can be approximated elsewhere as needed. As a set of publicly observable paradigmatic practices, French theory is, in short, a performance: a "performative universal." It is what allows us best to understand culture, not just as "performance," but as a "performative" in the Austinian sense.[31] So construed, then, French theory is recognized to be, like Hélène Cixous herself, woven together out of other things. In particular, these other origins include certain categories derived from recent German thought, which itself derives rather immediately from the ancient Greeks. And as it pursues its own trajectory, French theory weaves itself into the social and political realities of a decolonized *Francophonie* and a multicultural academy. Seen in this performative perspective, French theory is not a transportable commodity, but an activity of interweaving thought and reality, a universal activity of hybridization and *métissage* recognized as a transnational phenomenon that erodes claims of singularity and showcases the creative and appropriative gestures of cultural agents as they fluidly negotiate the "variety of ideoscapes" and "the disjunctures . . . central to the politics of global culture."[32]

Mission and Limits of the Enlightenment

JEAN-MARIE APOSTOLIDÈS

Theater and Terror: *Le jugement dernier des rois*

Used as a proper noun, the word "Terror" defines two periods in the French Revolution. The first Terror, flaring up between August 10 and September 20, 1792, was a direct result of the Prussian invasion. It would lead to the king's arrest and to the September Massacres. The second Terror raged between September 5, 1793 and July 28, 1794. This involved the slaughter of the Girondins and the arraignment before the Revolutionary Tribunal of many suspects, many of whom were subsequently guillotined. The conflagration reached its peak between April and July 1794, when Robespierre, at that time Master of the Convention, imposed absolute rule. It is to the second Terror that we will refer, with particular emphasis on the history of theater. More precisely, we will attempt to understand how theatrical performances staged in Paris at that time may or may not have afforded endorsement of the new government by reenacting onstage what was taking place in the street. In other words, we will examine the connections between the political Terror and its spectacle[1] by focusing on their common source, the moment when one strove for perfect reenaction of the other.

Theatrical Life in Paris During the Terror

Throughout the period of the Revolution, Paris had two active theaters, the Théâtre de la Nation and the Théâtre de la République on the rue de

Richelieu. Besides the national repertoire, each of these theaters advertised new plays that would serve as extensions of ongoing public discussions. Thus, the same topics were bandied about onstage and in the street; in both cases, they aroused tumultuous debate. Thus, on January 3, 1793, the Théâtre de la Nation staged a new play by Citizen Laya, entitled *L'Ami des lois*, a spectacle that sought to ridicule the leading figures in the revolutionary government by presenting them as bloodthirsty cutthroats. The public easily could recognize that Nomophage represented Robespierre, while Duricrane had all the characteristics of Marat. The play was a great success among the moderates before being banned eleven days after its premiere.[2] Vying with its rival, the Théâtre de la République chose the very day of Louis XVI's execution, January 23, 1793, to stage a play by Olympe de Gouge, *Le Général Dumouriez à Bruxelles*, which so aroused public ire that it was closed down after a mere two performances. If one is to believe eyewitness accounts, the play was judged to be insufficiently radical by the audience, which displayed its disdain by climbing onstage and dancing the Carmagnole around a Liberty Tree in the scenery.[3] At the end of August, following *L'Ami des lois*, the Théâtre de la Nation staged an adaptation of Richardson's novel *Pamela*. This again provoked the disapprobation of the critics due to the supposedly counterrevolutionary nature of some verses. Not only was the play banned after a dozen performances, but on the night of September 3, its author, François de Neufchâteau, was arrested, together with the actors of the Théâtre de la Nation.[4] Although they seemed doomed to the Revolutionary Tribunal, that is to say, to the scaffold, by some miracle they appear to have escaped it. In any case, their arrest left the field open to their rivals. In the months following, only the comedians from the Théâtre de la République, who were regarded as being more radical, were permitted to stage performances. Onstage, they became, to a certain extent, the official voice of the Reign of Terror. Three plays characterize this period: *Le jugement dernier des rois* by Sylvain Maréchal; work by the comedian Dugazon entitled *Le modéré*; and *Les contre-révolutionnaires jugés par eux-mêmes*, a comedy by a "canonnier révolutionnaire," or a revolutionary gunner, named Dorveau.

Thus, the life of the theater during the Terror had extremely strong parallels to political life, which was attuned to the rivalry between the

Girondins and the Montagnards. Correspondingly, the actors of the Théâtre de la Nation were antagonistic to their more radical colleagues from the Théâtre de la République. The latter did, in fact, succeed in eliminating their competitors, at the same time as the Paris Commune got rid of the Girondins. They did so by transforming their theater into an echo chamber that would amplify questions raised in the political space. We can observe the mechanisms of this artistic terror in the best-known of the plays staged during this period, Sylvain Maréchal's *Jugement dernier des rois*.

'Jugement dernier des rois'

Since the government patronized the performances of this comedy, it can be considered as one of its ideological expressions during the Terror. During the sessions of November 14, 1793, the Committee of Public Safety sponsored the purchase of three thousand copies of the work. Its example was followed by the War Ministry, which ordered a further six thousand to be sent to the troops. The play was being staged not only in Paris, but also in the provinces, in Rouen, Lille, Grenoble, Metz, Le Mans, Beauvais, and Compiègne. A second edition of the text was published in Vienne, in Isère. Soon, the play would spawn many freer adaptations, closer to street theater. For example, in Boulogne-sur-mer, at the time of the capture of Toulon, the mob participated in a sort of revival of scene 5 of *Le jugement dernier des rois*; the monarchs of Europe appeared in a procession. They were dragged to the Place de la Fédération and thrown to their knees in front of the Liberty Tree.[5]

What does this comedy tell us? At first it appears in the guise of a "prophecy," or dream. According to the author, as in the example set by the French, the sansculottes of all nations have put an end to the monarchies of Europe. The dethroned kings are condemned to spend the rest of their lives on a desert island. The sansculottes who accompany them there discover that the island not only is inhabited by an exiled ancient, but that furthermore, it is volcanic. They decide to abandon their cargo of kings. Once there, the monarchs constantly quarrel and show themselves to be incapable of organizing their existence. The volcano puts an end to their bickering by drowning them in lava.

The depiction of the sansculottes' disembarkation on the island with their prisoners can be seen as an imaginary representation of republican France; it is the re-presentation of a founding action that already had taken place a few months previously in Paris: the judgment and execution of Louis XVI. After the entry of the crowned tyrants, a sort of public trial takes place, which brings to mind those of the *tribunaux d'exception*. Thus, in his play, Maréchal rediscovers the primary meaning of the theater, that is, as judgment, and a popular judgment indeed. Each tyrant is brought before the masses in chains and in the grasp of a sansculotte who announces the charges against the accused, and the accused makes his defense heard. The audience's verdict is clear from its laughter. Therefore, to begin with, the title of the play can be understood as referring to the Revolutionary Tribunal. Established on March 10, 1793 by the Convention, this had seen an increase in both its staff and its powers, which now extended well into the provinces. It is also known that the tribunal's sentences were carried out within 24 hours with no chance for appeal or revocation. Onstage, the sansculotte doubles for Fouquier-Tinville, the Public Prosecutor. This is his indictment speech: "It is in the service of this handful of craven cutpurses, and for the pleasures of these nefarious rascals that the blood of a million, nay, two million men, the worst among whom was more worth than all of these together, has been spilled on close to all the points of the continent and beyond the seas."[6] What the theatrical tribunal publicly reveals is the underpinning of the politics that the revolutionaries were fighting. The prosecutor exposes the sexual relations between Catherine II and Stanislas, the future king of Poland; he reveals the collusion between the émigrés and the European powers; the pope's negative role is heavily underscored; and so on. Contemporary history is thus duplicated and reproduced in fictive space. State secrets, once a privilege of the monarchy, are now disclosed to the public.

The play offers not only a lesson in history, but above all a lesson in civics. It aims at testing the reactions of the spectators, at educating their politics. The lesson does not stop at the immediate spectators. In order that it may bear fruit later, it addresses itself to future generations by underscoring the exemplary nature of the events taking place in France: "Generations to come, can you believe it? Here are those who held, in the palm of their hands, in balance, the destinies of Europe" (p. 1321). In order for the spectators to understand the meaning of what they are actually experiencing and to develop a consensus, they must be able to project themselves forward in their imagination to a future when they can see their own accomplishments through the eyes of succeeding generations. It is only in this light that the public executions, the sentencing of the king and queen, the punishment of the aristocrats and federalists, can pass for just and necessary acts, indispensable to the founding of a new order of society. In this way, the theater allows an economy of experience. Overcoming, as it does, the limits of time and space, it places present events in a universal light. Thus, the spectacle constitutes a double for episodes that, deprived of this reenactment, could not be transformed into exemplary actions.

The Volcano, the Mountain, the Guillotine

The final eruption of the volcano constitutes the apogee of the performance. So that the drama of the last scene might be suitably emphasized, the play's producers received twenty pounds of saltpeter and another twenty pounds of powder from the government, a sumptuous gift at a time when, due to the war, these products were a rarity. In order to comprehend the tremendous power of terror associated with this last scene, we must be able to decode the various images that are included in it. In the volcano itself, I see a direct allusion to the catastrophes that unfolded less than fifteen years previously. Ever since the eruption of Vesuvius in 1779, the image of the volcano had haunted eighteenth-century consciousness. The Marquis de Sade, in his prison cell, was no more able to escape the specter of this event than any other member of the public; his letters dated September 7, 23, and 29, 1779 and addressed to Carteron, his valet, are entirely consecrated to the subject. In the *Histoire de Juliette*, which he wrote later, Sade reaffirms his interest in the region of Naples: "In no other part of Europe," he writes, "is Nature as beautiful, as imposing as in the environs of this city. . . . Here, she is all aflame; the disorders, the volcanoes of this Nature, always evil, plunge the soul into a turmoil that renders it capable of great actions and tumultuous passions."[7] In *La nouvelle Justine*, the monk Jérôme makes the following confession: "One day, observing Etna, whose bosom spewed forth flames, I wanted to be this famous volcano."[8] For Sade, as for his contemporary Maréchal, the volcano was an instrument of natural punishment. Like an earthquake, this catastrophe would permit the emergence of a new order. The imaginary of catastrophe was not new in 1793; it was part of an underground current that rose up during the whole of the Enlightenment, the functioning of which Annie Le Brun has attempted to retrace.[9] However, the Revolution brought this current to light. In some ways, it succeeded in realizing it within its social and political space. Sylvain Maréchal's play renders it visible by baring its foundations. The play is prophetic only inasmuch as it announces a revolution still to come, one that will be universal.

The mountain has yet another significance. It is the visible incarnation of the "the Mountain," the radical movement that dominated the Legislative Assembly, whose orders resembled the flow of lava altering the country's flesh indelibly. As did "the Mountain," the mountain frightens the moderates; it threatens, engulfs its enemies. A speech by Chaumette, the *procurer-syndic* of the Paris Commune, illustrates this eloquently: "And you, Mountain, forever illustrious in the pages of history, be the Sinai of the French! In thunderbolts, lance the decrees of Justice and the will of the people! O sainted mountain, become a volcano whose lava may devour our enemies! No more quarter, no more mercy for traitors! Let us cast the barriers of eternity between ourselves and them!"[10]

Finally, there is a third image that is revealed during the mise-en-scene of the volcano, that of the guillotine. The kings have been unloaded onto the island because it appears appropriate to their punishment (p. 1311). From the very beginning, the volcano is interpreted as being an instrument of torment for the kings, and this is repeated several times during the play. Its presence in the background dominates the scenery. Its tall outline speaks to us of the guillotine. In its fiery red sparks, we can see the jets of blood spouting forth at each decapitation.

The volcano serves as a metaphor for the guillotine because it executes naturally. The sansculottes do not wish to be executioners: "Crowned monsters! You should have died a thousand deaths on the scaffold; but where could such executioners have been found, that would willingly soil their hands with your vile and corrupt blood?" (p. 1321). Thus, an appropriate method of punishing these tyrants must be found, obviating the need of sullied hands: "The hand of Nature will hasten to ratify, to sanction the sentence handed down by the sansculottes against the kings, these rascals so long privileged and unpunished" (p. 1321). In this way, the volcano plays the same role on the island as the guillotine does on the Place de la Révolution. It executes without causing suffering. Because it is a machine that delivers death in a "mild" manner, the instrument for beheadings is associated with nature. It renders the revolutionaries innocent of the death warrants they pronounce. It is a just instrument, egalitarian and neutral, the true incarnation of the republican spirit. It also guarantees the revolutionaries' loyalty to their ideals, which is why it is called "the sainted guillotine."[11]

Maréchal's play, then, celebrates the founding instrument of the Republic, this guillotine that not only has freed the people of the tyrant's yoke, but has raised them up in the monarch's place. The guillotine serves as a sort of instrument for republican baptism, a scarlet baptism that is accomplished by blood, rather than water. In Maréchal's play, the sansculottes make a solemn profession of faith at the feet of the volcano, or scaffold: they swear to remain united and to preserve the same ideals: "For myself, I vow instantly to obliterate from the book of free men whosoever might, in my presence, sully the air with such remark as might favor a king or other such monstrosity. Comrades, let us swear it one and all" (p. 1322).

Because it embodies a triple significance, and is simultaneously Vesuvius, "the Mountain," and the guillotine, the volcano of the theater plays an essential role in the mise-en-scene of the Terror. Its final eruption presents a living tableau of all catastrophes possible at the time. It duplicates the intensity while showing the ineluctable character of a revolution in which nature combines with political power to found a new order.

The First Manifesto

The *Jugement dernier des rois* must be understood as the first manifesto of the literary history of France, a manifesto presaging those of the avant-garde movements such as Dada or surrealism. In the artistic domain, it prepared the way for the *Manifeste des égaux*, which Sylvain Maréchal was to write a few months later. It is, above all, a literary manifesto, in the sense that it breaks with the aesthetics of the previous generation. The author actually introduces a reversal by means of his text, not only of themes, but of the literary forms of the ancien régime. He accounts for this in his discourse entitled "Aux spectateurs de la premiére représentation": "Citizens, you remember how, in times past, in every theater, the most respectable classes of the sovereign people were vilified, degraded, and ridiculed in humiliating fashion in order that kings and their court lackeys might laugh? I thought it high time to repay them in kind, and in our turn be amused" (p. 1307–8). The main inversion engineered by Maréchal consists of presenting royalty not in tragedy, but in farce, the most despised literary genre. What was at the top is now at the bottom. Thus, the author rediscovers the origins of the feast, the saturnalia mentioned in an early version of the text.[12]

For Maréchal, it was a question of breaking with the theater of the "court lackeys," in other words, all of eighteenth-century theater. In fact, the Age of Enlightenment was also that of private theater, performed at court and for the aristocrats. The forms imitated classical theater, but the imagination of the preceding century was gone. Authors of comedies copied Moliére, those writing tragedies aped Racine and Corneille. It was the time of autonomized literary forms within the sphere of the aesthetic. They seemed hackneyed, relating not at all to the actual preoccupations of the majority of the public. Consequently, Maréchal sought to break with this tradition. Rejecting the principles laid down by Diderot in *Le paradoxe sur le comédien*, he furthermore demands that the actors feel what they are saying, that they be totally involved in the performance. The emotions onstage must parallel those in the street, and the spectacle must harmonize with the concerns of the public. One can see that, to him, fictive space must almost exactly reproduce social space. It is by the sharing of emotions that a consensus may be achieved: the will of the people. The community of ideas must be reproduced in a community of feelings in order to be consecrated, in order to occupy the imaginary position of the king. This is the reason for his insistence on natural and sentimental language, expressed by gesture, which the savages in the play share with the sansculottes.

Maréchal's comedy is also a manifesto in that it dares to shatter the limits of art in order to change it into action. It does not deal with a directly political action, but with a symbolic one that unfolds in a space doubling for public space. Thus, *Le jugement dernier des rois* constitutes a first draft of the theater of cruelty as advocated by Antonin Artaud around 1933.[13] The play returns to the beginnings of literature, to a time when genres were subject to neither division nor hierarchy. In it, the tragic and the comic are linked: gravity merges with buffoonery; the republican eloquence of the sansculottes is in stark contrast to the vulgarity of the monarchs, who themselves behave like flunkies. It constitutes the first model for a true revolutionary literature. Breaching the narrow confines of the *scène à l'italienne*, it addresses itself to the spectators by presenting to them topics drawn from their everyday existence. By prolonging the great revolutionary celebrations,[14] it also breaks with psychological theater and the study of social mores that characterized the French stage of the eighteenth century. Finally, by capturing the imagination, as much by word and image as by sound or animated tableau, it creates a total spectacle that returns, by means of horror and derision, to the origins of religious theater.

Thus, Maréchal's play strives to exceed mere performance. It introduces a rupture between a "before" and an "after." If it is spectacle, it is an unbearable spectacle, constituting what is almost a literary guillotine.[15] It was, in fact, presented in each city, just as each city boasted an actual guillotine. However, once the revolutionary period was over, it was not performed again. It was discarded, together with the instrument for beheadings. It inspires horror, as testified by the commentaries of Etienne and Martainville, the first historians of the theater of the Revolution.[16] The historians who come after them do not display any greater fondness for this play. If it is mentioned at all, it comes under the heading of bad taste. Like the guillotine, it fascinates and repels at the same time. It attracts insofar as it is despicable, its charm relying upon its ignominy. It arouses the powers of horror and abjection. To Maréchal, as later to Antonin Artaud, the stage is a privileged space of the act itself, physical, cruel, overwhelming, the repercussions of which must extend even into social space.

Terror and Consensus

What conclusions may be drawn from this brief overview of Maréchal's text? We may say that terror can engender a consensus only by moving from social space to symbolic space. It must be deployed as a symbol, it must reproduce itself in a spectacle in order to attain a power of authority without which it cannot survive. In other words, for terror to provoke a consensus, it must be used symbolically. It must become a threat, a show of force, rather than force itself, as a means, as in 1793, in the spectacles of Maréchal or the revolutionary festivities, each in its own way enacting political themes in social space. The deployment of these images is favorable to the emergence of a consensus because the constraints no longer are experienced directly and because the images establish so many mediations between power and its subjects. Of course, in the long term, the spectacle risks producing an inverse effect, of engendering an inflation that will cause it to lose all symbolic efficacy. However, 1793 was still the time of foundation. The society of the spectacle, as would be denounced by the Situationists, was not yet come.

PIERRE SAINT-AMAND

Hostile Enlightenment

The concept of wrong is the original and positive, and the concept of right, which is opposed to it, is the derivative and negative. . . . The concept of right contains merely the negation of wrong.

—Schopenhauer

In the view of Ernst Cassirer, Enlightenment thought was inhabited, even obsessed, by a paradox: the question of the origins of humanity. Haunted by its origins, the Enlightenment was condemned to a process of continual regression with respect to itself. Fundamentally, the question of origins, the problem of establishing law, runs counter to the central project of the Enlightenment, that is, the development of rationalism with a view to progress. More precisely, Cassirer writes, "A fundamental feature of the philosophy of the Enlightenment appears in the fact that, despite its passionate desire for progress, despite its endeavors to break the old tables of the law and to arrive at a new outlook on life, it nevertheless returns again and again to the original problems of humanity."[1] The specter of origins is the skeleton in the closet of Enlightenment political philosophy, the evil spirit that haunts it, the ever-present threat of incompletion. I propose to probe the recesses of the Enlightenment, to expose it to a veritable crisis of law. Indeed, by stripping away its soothing illusions, we can bring this self-proclaimed Age of Reason closer to us, and perhaps its humanism will speak to our anxieties at last. The political thought of the Enlightenment belongs rather under the (Machiavellian) sign of pathology and suspicion, of original immorality, of an accursed share, an element of evil that pervades communication among men. We must do violence to the Enlightenment in order to correct its transfiguration of the human, to redress the illusory emancipation it claims to confer upon mankind.

Following the lead of Michel Foucault (although not focusing as he does on the institutionalization of domination), I would like to dismiss the Enlightenment ideology of "universal reciprocity," of progress from warfare and its replacement by the rule of law.[2] The priority accorded to hostility over universal benevolence follows the same process Marshall Sahlins analyzed with regard to Hobbes's "warre." Benevolence is designed to repress the violence, "to overlay it and deny it as an insupportable menace." It is the desired "transfiguration" of its true opposite.[3]

In *L'Ere du vide*, Gilles Lipovetsky made the following remark: "Violence has failed, or nearly failed, to attract the attention of historians."[4] It is this often-overlooked problem that I wish to bring to bear upon my consideration of right in the eighteenth century. This is the problem that, gnawing unseen at the bowels of the social body, insidiously vitiates both the major theoretical advances of the social pact and all forms of political or national organization. For the political thinkers of the period, it was as if the time of violence was gone forever, as if Enlightened man had embarked upon an irreversible process of civilization, a future for which the stage had to be cleared. From this point forward, violence could be conceived only as what lies beyond the realm of theory. Constance, a character in Diderot's *Le fils naturel*, exclaims with cheerful optimism and a candid naïveté: "The time of barbarism is past. The century has become enlightened. Reason has grown refined, and the nation's books are filled with its precepts. The books that inspire benevolence in men are practically the only ones read."[5]

And yet: what if it could be shown that the development of the conception of right in the eighteenth century sprang from an archaic source that, rather than being far removed, was still close at hand? One might, for example, examine the phenomenon of war, which was for the eighteenth century the most extraordinary social catastrophe. In fact, for thinkers from Montesquieu to Kant, not to mention the Abbé de Saint-Pierre, war remained the distant, unquiet front at the outer limits of the philosophes' political reflections. But I would like to start with less ambitious, more elementary concerns.

To begin with, let us consider the article on "Society" in the *Encyclopédie* of Diderot and d'Alembert.[6] This article defines society in its ideal form. The closely related concept "sociability" depicts human reciprocity as leaning naturally toward the good: sociability "is the disposition that leads us to bring to other men all of the good that can be asked of us, to reconcile our happiness with that of others, and always to subordinate our particular advantage in favor of the common and general advantage."[7] According to the article, a sort of natural proclivity leads us to seek out the company of others and to share our happiness with them. It might safely be said that the anthropology of the Enlightenment philosophes is exclusively characterized by exchange or sociability. In *Emile*, Rousseau writes: "No society can exist without exchange."[8] But let us return to the *Encyclopédie*. It instances two reasons for the social development of man: first, the faculty of speech with which he is endowed, and second, his ability to imitate. Affective imitation is what makes social exchange possible; the first social behaviors are the result of mimetic affect, such as sympathy and pity or the desire to congregate. Nicolas Boulanger conceived of reciprocity only in its benevolent dimension.

What if reciprocity is to be conceived as a dissociative force, a convergence of heterogeneities? Marcel Mauss illustrated this ambivalence in the instance of the gift. Indeed, reciprocity for Mauss cannot be limited to the sense of economic rationalism. On the contrary, as illustrated by the example of potlatch, the gift system studied among Native Americans of the northwest coast, reciprocity is fundamentally agonistic. In Mauss's theory, the gift always implies a countergift; it is governed by an antieconomical principle. Reciprocity for Mauss is founded on dispute before it is founded on exchange. The obligation to "return the gift" must be understood with the full force of ambiguity inherent in the phrase: not only positively, to match or reciprocate the gift in a similar presentation, but also negatively, in a subtractive gesture exacting further sacrifice from the original giver. This obligation to reciprocate results in contests of prestige, confrontations that end up eclipsing the original exchange. Rivalry becomes the rule of reciprocity because there is never full equivalence in the mirroring gestures: each gift incites the receiver to outdo the previous giver in generosity. As Bataille insisted, the gift is always a gift of retaliation. In other words, the gift can only contradict itself: "it leads to suddenly aggravated strife, even when its intention was to eliminate discord."[9] This system of escalation is aptly described by Mary Douglas, who writes: "conspicuous consumption is succeeded by conspicuous destruction."[10]

One might well apply to Enlightenment thought the same reproach with which Pierre Clastres taxed Lévi-Strauss—and indeed, this parallel between Lévi-Strauss's approach and the ideology of the philosophes, with their emphasis on sociability, goes a long way toward explaining Lévi-Strauss's naive admiration for the Enlightenment, and for Rousseau in particular. The point of Clastres's objection is that "to misjudge violence is to misjudge society."[11]

Indeed Clastres observes that Lévi-Strauss pays minimal attention to the phenomenon of war in primitive society, almost to the point of suppressing violence. According to Clastres, Lévi-Strauss asserts the ontological priority of exchange over war. It is exchange that is original and positive; war is considered only negatively. Lévi-Strauss's anthropology appears as the exact obverse of that of Hobbes. Primitive society is articulated on the basis of reciprocal exchange, rather than reciprocal conflict. In other words, Lévi-Strauss substitutes friendship for hostility.

There are more precise examples of the return to origins in political texts, examples with a focus on a specific type of reciprocity: vengeance. I will deliberately avoid invoking sociological evidence to confirm the persistence of vengeance in eighteenth-century society and the war waged by the philosophes against this archaic ritual. Rather, my aim here is to demonstrate that the philosophical texts of the period, their abstraction notwithstanding, do not diverge widely from the old models of reciprocity. My intent is not to show that the eighteenth century was not really embarked upon the process of civilization as described by Norbert Elias, or the "politics of decency" defended by Peter Gay;[12] nor do I wish to refute Susan Jacoby's view of the "containment of revenge" during the Enlightenment.[13] My interest lies instead in the fundamental ambivalence of reciprocity and in the varying notions of justice as defined by different philosophes. Certainly, the eighteenth century saw considerable advances in the field of legal justice (advances that were associated with Beccaria and Voltaire, among others). This progress is proof of the modernity of the Enlightenment. But it is also clear that during the same period, considerable effort was expended in idealizing human relations and distancing philosophical thought from certain types of violence relegated by it to the distant past as part of some remote, immemorial era. For these reasons, the wholesale return to violence and its legitimation by the apparatus of the state during the French Revolution were all the more shocking, brutally putting an end to the peaceful interlude enjoyed in the course of the eighteenth century.[14] The assassination of the king could in fact be seen as the most spectacular instance, the immeasurable culmination, of revenge—as a "sovereign vengeance," as one diehard defender of the Revolution insists to this day.[15]

In the *Encyclopédie*, vengeance is defined simply as the opposite of sociability. It is not a part of the social economy. And since sociability is considered natural, vengeance is not. "Stifling the very principle of goodwill, [vengeance] replaces it with a feeling of hatred or animosity, malicious in itself, opposed to the public good, and categorically condemned by natural law."[16]

Vengeance represents a model of reciprocity that the Enlightenment refused to consider. As a form of response to the other, retaliation falls, curiously, within the treacherous logic of the gift. As an antagonistic form of the gift, vengeance is a relation of hateful obligation, a dangerous debt. In vengeance, the desire for recognition, the symbolic foundation of the gift, is exaggerated to the point of delirium. Vengeance institutes a relation of malevolent reversibility, of spiteful reciprocity, between individuals. *Lex talionis*, the law of the talion, is the diametric opposite of the contract: it goes to the extreme of singling out the partners in exchange, rather than universalizing them. In this, the talion is the obverse of the contract, which transcendentalizes and exteriorizes ad infinitum the object of exchange. Before expanding upon this point, however, let us consider Montesquieu's views on reciprocity.

For Montesquieu, reciprocity cannot be antagonistic from the start. Man is originally, fundamentally weak. Restricted by his vulnerability, he lacks the physical means to be violent. On the contrary, if there is reciprocity at this stage, it is in mutual fear. Men are brought together by a mimesis of fear: "the marks of this fear being reciprocal, would soon engage them to associate."[17] While all forms of unsociability are later banished from the pure form of government as conceived by Montesquieu, nevertheless they return to undermine the equilibrium of governments. Antisocial elements constitute both the defining boundaries and the internal vice of government. In a monarchy, rivalry is sublimated into courtesy. Thus tempered, this competition among noble individuals miraculously produces a sort of social harmony. Democracy sublimates rivalry into a desire for equality. The government that most explicitly embraces vengeance is the despotic government. This government is the antithesis of the others: the despotic government could be said to have absorbed the violence of the two other types of government. It embodies their monstrous potential.

Despotism can be the result of the democratic crisis. In this case, it appears when relations of reciprocity have disintegrated fully. It is the outcome of a generalized, violent struggle for power. Democracy is corrupted when equality is carried to an extreme, when each individual covets the position held by the other, when identical desires obliterate existing hierarchies and blur the differential order of society into a dizzying homogeneity.

While monarchy is, for Montesquieu, one of the most stable forms of government, it contains a practice feared by him: the duel. According to Montesquieu, the duel is a throwback to primitive social structures. By virtue of this violent practice, monarchy escapes the logic of the modern world. The duel is a type of primitive social behavior belonging to the socialization pattern that anthropologists term "blood society." Dueling is essentially wasted energy and fatally wasted blood. L'Esprit des lois sets forth honor as the monarchic principle par excellence, as a very particular system of moderating passions. Of all the elemental structures of primitive societies, honor is the one retained by Montesquieu—but without the element of vengeance. Honor itself is tempered, stripped of any possible recourse to force, detached of its frenetic hubris, of its formidable expenditure. It becomes a struggle for prestige, a type of socialization requiring respectful recognition of the other. Honor has become reciprocal adulation; it has been aestheticized into courtesy and flattery. As Louis Althusser so perceptively pointed out, honor has been taught its manners: it has been "educated."[18]

It is possible, however, for honor to return to its origins, as in the duel—a flagrant example of untempered honor, with a full complement of bellicosity. The duel particularizes to excess the desire for the same (prestige). It is nothing but a heinous duplication. The violence called forth by the duel tends to escape containment. It spills out of the private sphere to unleash the contagion of violence throughout the community. Montesquieu's critique of the duel focuses on the contagious aspect of the spectacle of conflict: the epidemic potential of the duel seems to come from the individual's ability to identify with the representation of violence. The duel enacts its name ad infinitum in a perpetual series of conflictive pairings. It sets the stage for a veritable theater of cruelty.

Unlike Montesquieu, Rousseau declared his opposition to laws prohibiting duels because, for him, it was futile to pit law against honor. For Rousseau, the drop in the frequency of duels was due not to respect for laws banning them, but to decaying social mores: specifically, to the effeminization of warlike values and to diminishing aggressiveness among men.[19] The *Lettre à M. d'Alembert sur les spectacles* includes a long digression on the practice of dueling in which Rousseau proposes instituting a tribunal of marshals, which he dubs a "Court of Honor," for the purpose of redressing offenses. This court, which Rousseau conceives as free of violence, relies above all on a hypervaluation of honor to prevail. Still, it must be said that this tribunal also admits bloody violence, however legitimized by its restriction to warriors and their military personnel. In this court, the inefficacy of law is replaced by the omnipotence of opinion. What Rousseau seeks to preserve (but through a logic that is totally unlike Montesquieu's) is the system of honor, but without physical force or cruelty. In *La nouvelle Héloïse*, the argument against dueling is made even stronger. The recourse to this infamous practice is based on a kind of reasoning worthy only of wolves.[20] The defense of honor by force is a corruption of true virtue. The use of force to uphold honor is a useless *supplement* to probity.[21]

I am inclined to say that the philosophe who, in a direct response to Montesquieu, as we will see, gave the most depth to the concept of vengeance is Sade, in whose work vengeance makes a most ostentatious comeback. Given Sade's definitive rejection of Enlightenment idealism and his thorough corruption of the rationalism of the period, it is not surprising that vengeance appears in his work, running the whole gamut of the unthinkable. In Sade's view, evil is synonymous with human relations; violent reciprocity is ineluctable.

Sade's work turns on its head the principle of goodwill, the ideal form of reciprocity put forth by the philosophes. The well-being of the other never is the aim of the Sadean subject. On the contrary, he is animated by an unmitigated devotion to the propagation of evil—crimes, murders, vengeance. Sade's work might be said to eroticize vengeance, which is propagated by means of the orgy itself: in every combination and permutation, the orgy relentlessly perpetuates the circulation of vengeance. It gives vengeance a framework, a context where it is sublimated or recast as pleasure. By pluralizing vengeance, the orgy strips vengeance of any origin.

Marcel Hénaff speaks of a contract of revenge in Sade's work: "This exchange is a sort of challenge, he writes, a glorious and sacrificial dissipation. . . . Thus, the formula 'Do to me what I did to you,' so often repeated during orgies, issues out of this competitive response, out of this wasteful excess that casts the partners into a delirious expenditure of energy and erotic figures."[22] For Roland Barthes, as well, revenge is the essential characteristic of the Sadean relation and is indispensable to the erotic combinatorial process: "it ensures the immorality of human relationships."[23]

Sade is the anti-Montesquieu of the Enlightenment. Indeed, he mentions Montesquieu in *Juliette* only to denigrate him as a second-rate philosopher. Sade exposes, and opposes, the idealistic dimension of Montesquieu's political science. Montesquieu's ideal of justice is unacceptable in Sadean politics. It must be replaced by an implacable judicial relativism, by private passions and interests—precisely what Montesquieu was at pains to repress in order to demonstrate the possibility of peaceful cohabitation. Sade seizes upon the weakest point of the *Lettres persanes*, where Montesquieu envisions the possibility of a human society without justice and doomed to reciprocal violence (a vision Montesquieu quickly repudiates in the name of man's natural sociability):

> We are surrounded by men who are stronger than ourselves. They can do us harm in a thousand different ways, and three-quarters of the time they can do it with impunity. What peace of mind it is for us to know that all these men have an inner principle which is on our side, and protects us

from any action that they might undertake against us! But for that, we should be perpetually afraid. We should walk about among men as if they were wild lions, and we should never be sure for a moment of our possessions, our happiness, or our lives.[24]

Sade is well aware of a deceptive blind spot in Montesquieu's vision. In describing a justice without a divine point of reference, Montesquieu writes that it would be "a horrible truth that we should have to hide from ourselves."[25] Justice must be guaranteed by an external principle, some kind of transcendence, such as God or a model; or rather, justice should inspire in men a reciprocal imitative benevolence that in turn serves to guarantee justice: "even if there were no God, we should nonetheless still love justice, that is to say, make an effort to resemble this being of whom we have so exalted a conception, and who if he existed would be just necessarily. Even if we were to be free of the constraints of religion, we ought not to be free of those imposed by equity."[26]

The judicial bond would thus be a product of reciprocal identification with an idea, a phantasm of benevolence.[27] But left to their own devices, human beings are incapable of justice. They become wolves and lions, preying on each other. What lies hidden behind these metaphors of bestiality is man's effort to project his own violence outside himself and to deny his own inhumanity, or rather, to deny the savage, dog-eat-dog element of his humanity. Montesquieu no sooner mentions a natural instinct for justice than it becomes a pretext for rivalry within the group: whoever is able to be more just than the other, whoever is better able to display this sentiment by transforming it into flattering narcissism, into an impression of domination, will end up placed above the others: "When a man takes stock of himself, how satisfying it is for him to conclude that he has justice in his heart!—it may be an austere pleasure, but it is bound to cause him delight, as he realizes that his state is as far above those without justice as he is above tigers and bears."[28] Clearly, justice—or the benevolent mirroring that seems to produce it—now has been metamorphosed into an obscene competition, turning each person into an imperfect mirror of the other. Justice becomes a spectacular duel. This simulation of goodness is revealed in all its falsity: it masks the worst of intentions.

Sade appropriates this competition into the mechanisms of justice. He immediately relativizes, personalizes, narcissizes the idea of justice. He makes it into a human structure riddled with egotistical and contradictory impulses, into a sublimation of our passions:

> Let us have the courage to tell men that justice is a myth, and that each individual never actually heeds any but his own version of it; let us say so fearlessly. Declaring it to them, and giving them thus to appreciate all the dangers of human existence, our warning enables them to ready a defense and in their turn to forge themselves the weapon of injustice, since only by becoming as unjust, as vicious as everybody else can they hope to elude the traps set by others.[29]

According to the Sadean ethos, everyone should have access to the privilege of administering justice. Private access to justice is a guarantee of social peace: the dissuasive effect of direct violence is greater and more compelling than that of law. Sade pursues his argument in part through absurdity: "My neighbor's passions are infinitely less to be dreaded than the law's injustice, for the passions of that neighbor are held at bay by mine." Here is the example that he gives: "Never will Tom be unjust toward Dick when he knows Dick can retaliate instantly." In a note in *Juliette*, Sade proclaims that "vengeance ought to be tasted in private and by him alone whom the deed has outraged."[30] In principle, law is iniquitous for Sade because it is possible for it to be wrong. The law is a poor executor of justice and a feeble substitute for private vengeance. But above all, the law usurps the rights and passions of the individual. Its rationalism spirits away the spectacle of one's own egotism. According to Sade, therefore, all forms of natural justice ought to be restored. Similarly, when Sade objects to judicial reparation as subtracting from or devaluing the intensity of the original offense—in contrast to the full equivalence of immediate vengeance— he is refusing to consider the sacrifice involved in judicial retribution.

Justice does indeed defer. And because of this, it moderates, preventing further outbreak of direct confrontation, obviating the infinite renewal of the cycle. Nietzsche denounces the law for the same reasons in *On the Genealogy of Morals*. Like Sade, he expresses a nostalgia for those heroic times when tribal vengeance reigned as the only form of justice. Law, for its part, manifests itself as pure violence, as a castration of individuals' passions: "Submission to *law*: how the consciences of noble tribes all over the earth resisted the abandonment of vendetta and were loath to bow before the power of the law! 'Law' was for a long time a *vetitum*, an outrage, an innovation; it was characterized by violence—it *was* violence to which one submitted, feeling ashamed of oneself."[31]

Like Nietzsche, Sade subjects justice to a public flogging, denouncing the violence that is at the very root of law, the original violence concealed beneath the concept of right. Right is a form of countervengeance, an ultimate, omnipotent revenge that prohibits any further propagation of the desire for vengeance. Sade restores cruelty to its role as the dynamic impetus behind social relations. Cruelty for Sade is the sheer and unabashed display of human inequality, of the natural antagonism that is the inevitable result of every confrontation between human individuals. It contributes to the disintegration of human bonds, the disbanding of the human herd. It is, literally, *inconsequential*: their primitive roots notwithstanding, the rituals of cruelty staged by Sade do not lead to the accomplishment of any end, nor are they redeemed by any form of transcendence. Their function is one of loss, of waste for its own sake. They continually repeat the desire to escape the social order, to liberate the actors from all social taboos. Sadean atrocities—torture, cannibalism, murder—are performed in an absolute vacuum of significance, without the backing of any mystical transcendence. Perhaps Blanchot has put it more aptly than any other commentator on Sade: Sadean cruelty is apathetic, it is "the ultimate . . . incandescent lack of sensitivity."[32]

In tracing a path from Montesquieu to Sade, I have tried to locate the blind spots in Enlightenment attempts—through the idealization and excessive rationalization of social practices—at a massive foreclosure of violence. We see, however, that in the writings of the philosophes, dissension and differences surface.

It could be said that the philosophers of the Enlightenment confused politics with morals, subordinating the former to the latter. The *Homo politicus* of the Enlightenment is first of all the man of civic duty and virtue. (This is the credo that would be taken up by the revolutionaries in 1789.) The philosophes did not see that any rationalization of political activity had to take into account antagonism between men. Blinded by universalism, they refused to see the political as profoundly agonistic in nature. Some philosophers, however, seem from the outset to stand apart from this general chorus of pacifist consensus, this blind idolatry of benevolence and optimistic reciprocity. They do not leave to us the task of uncovering the labor of negation.

One of the most eloquent is Simon-Nicolas-Henri Linguet, who in 1767 wrote *Théorie des lois civiles*, in which he refuted Montesquieu. Linguet writes:

> Other writers, more comfortable with calm, cannot imagine that battle cries or the clash of weapons could have marred the birth of the world. They endeavor to banish such an inhuman roar from the cradle of society. They desire this institution to be the result of free and unanimous consent: but it repulses them to see it being born amidst commotion and delivered by soldiers: it pleases them to suppose that it is the product of the mild-mannered relationships of agriculture and trade. They would prefer that ploughshares, rather than swords, be the basis for first governments, and they would have laws fashioned by the callused hands of laborers, rather than the bloody hands of heroes.[33]

Linguet denounced Montesquieu's project as an enterprise of idealization, an exercise in flattery that gilds over origins, deceptively substituting one history for another. For Linguet, on the contrary, society is born of blood, in the submission of farmers to gangs of soldiers. At the origin is no contract of goodwill and of mutual help, no shared needs, but rather violence and force.

We could also name the Scotsman Adam Ferguson, who writes in his *Essay on the History of Civil Society*: "Mankind not only find in their condition the sources of variance and dissension; they appear to have in their minds the seeds of animosity, and to embrace the occasions of mutual opposition, with alacrity and pleasure." He takes it as axiomatic that "in treating of human affairs, we would draw every consequence from a principle of union, or a principle of dissension."[34]

Certainly Kant is the most "critical" when he propounds the thesis of the unsociable sociability of humankind. In Kant's view, the social institution and the foundation of law are free from any form of angelism, any unrealistic optimism. Here reason sets itself against nature. Reason, the will to repair evil, confronts violent behavior. It thus opens the way to an ethics of responsibility. Armed with reason, Kant writes, even a "people comprised of devils" can succeed in living according to law, "if only they possess understanding."[35]

What in Kant's view can bring peace among nations can also do so among individuals. As Claude Lefort writes of Kant's plan for perpetual peace, "peace can . . . be founded only upon the idea that relations among men are relations among equals [*semblables*]."[36] Indeed, Kant reforces us to rethink humanism. He ushers in a lucid form of humanism that is wise to the inhumanity of man. Likewise, his cosmopolitan universalism can help us conceive of a "pluriversalism," or, if you will, a pluralism enriched by the diversity it embraces, welcoming the multiplicity of individual desires and interests. Another name for this openness to converting what is foreign, external, and potentially antagonistic is "hospitality," which neutralizes generalized hostility.

It is perhaps time to reread the political thought of the Enlightenment through the lens provided by the political philosopher Carl Schmitt, who focuses on hostility as the very foundation of all political activity. Without endorsing his authoritarianism, we can recognize that his anthropological pessimism—to say nothing of the fascist context in which he wrote— inspired his exploration of the relationship between violence and the formation of the state, impregnating his work with a "dark history."[37] It is along these lines that he criticizes Enlightenment humanism as a sort of extravagant exoticism of thought:

A relativistic bourgeoisie in a confused Europe searched all sorts of exotic cultures for the purpose of making them an object of its aesthetic consumption. The aristocratic society in France before the Revolution of 1789 sentimentalized "man who is by nature good" and the virtue of the masses. Tocqueville recounts this situation in words whose shuddering tension arises in him from a specific political pathos: nobody scented the Revolution; it is incredible to see the security and unsuspiciousness with which these privileged spoke of the goodness, mildness, and innocence of the people when 1793 was already upon them—*spectacle ridicule et terrible.*[38]

By positing a co-implication of violence and law, of law and discord, the philosophers of dissensus provide us with a more complex approach to the social phenomenon. In any case, they make it possible to assess what is incomplete and ideologically stunted about their optimistic counterparts. A lucid political ethics must see that the threat of unsociability, of violence, will not be obliterated from philosophies whose intention is to tell mankind its history. Reminding people of hostility, the nemesis of their great pacific projects, places them face-to-face with their responsibilities and thus keeps them from lapsing back into barbarism.

TRANSLATED FROM THE FRENCH BY JENNIFER CURTISS GAGE

SUSAN RUBIN SULEIMAN

The Intellectual Sublime: Zola as Archetype of a Cultural Myth

Reflecting in 1947 on the situation of the French bourgeois writer—which was also, of course, his own—Sartre sardonically remarked on the power of certain preexisting models: "we have known, since we were adolescents, the memorable and edifying features of great lives . . . it's not bad to start one's life like Rimbaud, to begin a Goethean return to order in one's thirties, to throw oneself at fifty, like Zola, into a public debate. After that, you can choose the death of Nerval, Byron, or Shelley."[1] We recognize here the caustic, self-ironic voice of the author of *Les mots*, parodying everything he once held sacred. But as far as Zola is concerned, at least, Sartre exercised a very different voice as well in speaking about him during those years. In the highly earnest "présentation des *Temps modernes*," written in 1946, he evokes Zola at a crucial moment in his argument; this time not as a parodic cultural stereotype, but as an exemplar of the engagé writer: "I hold Flaubert and the Goncourts responsible for the repression that followed the Commune because they didn't write a line to prevent it. Some will object that this wasn't their business. But was the Calas trial Voltaire's business? Was Dreyfus's sentence Zola's business? Was the administration of the Congo Gide's business? Each of those authors, at a particular time in his life, took stock of his responsibility as a writer."[2]

Voltaire, Zola, Gide—the next name in the series would obviously be that of Sartre himself. Interestingly, the three precursors are evoked in exactly the same role: each intervened by one or more acts of writing in the

159

public sphere in order to protest against an injustice affecting a third party. Each one was impelled by a specific circumstance to "take stock of his responsibility as a writer" and to conclude that he had to consider another's misfortune as his own business. What was at stake in each case, Sartre's argument implies, was a general principle affecting the whole community: the responsible writer acted as a spokesman not for a single person or group, but for values of universal significance and scope.

This figure of the responsible writer drawn by Sartre corresponds to what Michel Foucault would later call the "universal intellectual": "he who bears the values of all, opposes the unjust sovereign or his ministers and makes his cry resound even beyond the grave."[3] Foucault's grand phraseology here is surely somewhat ironic, for he was convinced that the universal intellectual—traditionally embodied in the person of the "great writer"—was fast disappearing; and Foucault did not mourn his passing. In his view, the universal intellectual who had been modeled on the jurist or the defender of universal law (he mentions Voltaire as the prototype) was being replaced by a new type, the "specific intellectual," whose model was not the jurist, but the expert, the scientist. Foucault's prototype for the specific intellectual was Robert J. Oppenheimer.

Although writing at a distance of thirty years and coming to quite different conclusions, Sartre and Foucault both were struggling with the question of what it means to be an intellectual coming "after"—after the 1930's, after World War II, after the bomb, after the great precursors—in short, "post." This question is still with us today—I would say, more than ever with us today. What is the role of intellectuals in the age of e-mail and ethnic cleansing, a.k.a. "the postmodern age"? *Are* there any intellectuals in the postmodern age? And if so, how do we recognize them?

Elements of the Myth

Setting our own problems aside for a while, I want to look somewhat closely at the cultural model of the "universal" intellectual as it was constructed around the person of Emile Zola. I prefer to call this cultural type the "sublime" intellectual, a terminological shift whose rationale will appear as I proceed. What is involved, of course, is not the actual man, but an idealized figure who acts as both vehicle and protagonist of a powerful cultural myth. The main outline of this myth (consisting of the archetypal figure and his story) was put into place around Zola during and immediately following the Dreyfus affair (roughly, from 1898 to 1906—Zola died in 1902). It is a measure of the myth's power that it was repeated, with no modification of its chief elements, throughout the interwar period, and that it received its most detailed elaboration as late as 1978, in the eight-hour television film whose title reflects both the chief theme and the power of the myth: *Zola ou la conscience humaine.*

What exactly does the myth of sublime engagement comprise? Consider the following excerpt from one of its best-known versions (which provided, incidentally, the subtitle for Stellio Lorenzi's 1978 film):

> Zola had attained glory. Famous and at peace with himself, he was enjoying the fruit of his labor when suddenly he put an end to his rest, to the work he loved, to the peaceful joys of his existence.
>
> But you know, gentlemen, that one can find peace only in justice, rest only in truth. Is it possible to keep silent about those who seek the ruin of an innocent man? Silent about those who, knowing they will be lost if he is saved, go after him with the desperate bravado of fear?
>
> . . . Justice, honor, thought, everything seemed lost: everything was saved! Zola had not only revealed the miscarriage of justice, he had denounced the conspiracy of all the forces of violence and oppression that had come together in order to kill social justice, the republican ideal, and free thought in France. His courageous words had awakened France.
>
> . . . Let us envy him: he honored his country and the world by his immense literary oeuvre and by a great deed. Let us envy him, for his destiny and heart endowed him with the greatest fate: he was a moment in the human conscience.[4]

These ringing words, pronounced by Anatole France at Zola's funeral on October 5, 1902, have been quoted often since then. I chose this text precisely because of its grand eloquence, its reaching for the sublime.

In more down-to-earth terms, what does the story told by Anatole France entail? First, it entails a heroic choice: the great writer, having attained the summit of his glory and rejoicing in the fruit of his labors, tears himself away from rest, from the work he loves, and from the peaceful joys of his personal life—for what? In order to defend an innocent man unjustly accused and at the same time to defend the universal principles of justice, honor, and free thought. This choice is, in my terms, sublime for at least two reasons. It is made not for any personal interest or gain, but for the general good, and it involves personal sacrifice and risk, requiring not only an abstract kind of courage, but physical fearlessness as well. Anatole France could be sure that all who heard him remembered the mobs outside the courthouse screaming "Death to Zola!" as the writer left his trial every day in February 1898; they remembered, too, that Zola had been burned in effigy in cities and towns all over France after the publication of his broadside *J'Accuse* on January 13, 1898 in the daily *L'Aurore*.

The sublime, (or, if you will, heroic choice) leads to an act that manifests disinterested conviction and personal courage. In addition, the act has two characteristics worth noting: first, it is a piece of writing launched into the public sphere—it thus differs less in kind than in genre from the writer's usual activity. Second, it is effective: the pen acts here literally like a sword. As we know, *J'Accuse* had an immediate, dramatic effect: the libel trial against Zola (which he had intentionally provoked) indirectly reopened the Dreyfus case. Admittedly, it was not until the summer of 1899 that Dreyfus himself was retried and his captivity ended, but Zola's *J'Accuse* had given a whole new turn to the Dreyfusard struggle.[5]

So far, we have four major plot elements and four major character traits for a story of sublime engagement: in the plot, an initial situation of fame, comfort, and solitary labor is followed by a heroic choice, which produces action in the mode of writing and leads to struggle or renewed struggle. The corresponding character traits are: authority, disinterestedness, courage, and effectiveness. Each of these plot elements and character traits can be expanded and variously embroidered or emphasized in a given representation. Furthermore, the material outcome of the struggle is less important than the heroic choice and subsequent action. In the best circumstances, the struggle provoked by this choice and act will result in triumph for the hero and his cause, but even if there is no material triumph, there is a moral triumph, and that is what finally matters. At the time of Zola's death, Dreyfus had not yet been fully rehabilitated or officially recognized as innocent (that happened in 1906); in addition, Zola had been condemned in his own trials for libel, and that judgment never was officially annulled. Yet Anatole France could speak of Zola's action, quite correctly, as having produced a victory for truth and human conscience.

The fifth and final trait of sublime engagement is only implied in Anatole France's speech, but one finds it explicitly stated in other works. In terms of character, I call it "modesty." Its corresponding plot element is a return, if not to the initial state of happiness and comfort (sometimes the peace is ruined forever), at least to the writer's main activity: solitary creation. France mentions, in describing Zola's heroic choice, that he "tore himself away from the work he loved." After his trial, even during his year of forced exile in England (his lawyers had advised him to leave in order to avoid imprisonment), Zola resumed writing novels. His last cycle of visionary novels (*Fécondité, Travail, Vérité*) were all written and published after 1898; *Fécondité* was written in England.

This last trait is important in distinguishing sublime engagement from what might be called "professional" or routinized engagement—that of the official party writer, for example. Modesty, or the return to one's primary work, corresponds to what Maurice Blanchot has called the "intermittent" status of the intellectual. In a famous 1984 essay (inspired, interestingly, by a new narrative history of the Dreyfus affair), Blanchot wrote: "When the intellectual—the writer—makes his decision and takes sides, he . . . takes himself away from the only task that matters to him."[6] This suspension of the writer's activity is dangerous (true writing, Blanchot believes, has nothing to do with the "public" writing of a *J'Accuse* or of any other polemic), for the writer risks losing "la parole inattendue," the unexpected word that constitutes his true calling. Yet, Blanchot concludes, the risk must sometimes be taken—and independently of any further action, the writer's temporary renunciation of his solitary activity requires great moral strength and courage. Blanchot's point, however, is that the renunciation must be temporary: "Ever since they have borne that name, intellectuals have done nothing else than cease momentarily being what they were (writer, scientist, artist) in order to respond to ethical demands, at once obscure and imperious, since they were demands for justice and freedom."[7]

Blanchot's theory of writing is totally different from Sartre's, yet his view of the intellectual is astonishingly close, here, to Sartre's heroic view in 1946 of a Voltaire or a Zola. Indeed, despite one or two significant differences, Blanchot's vision of the intellectual corresponds to the sublime paradigm.

Representations of Zola as "Sublime" Intellectual

There is an extraordinary range of genres and modes of representation, both in his own time and later, in which Zola appears as the exemplar of the cultural myth of sublime engagement: biographies, personal testimonies by family and friends, eyewitness accounts of the trials following *J'Accuse*, films, plays, novels, as well as the annual homages by writers, known as the *discours de Médan*—not to mention the thousands of visual representations in the form of cartoons, photographs, and postcards, which could be the subject of a separate study.[8] I cannot claim to have read and looked at more than a sampling of the various narrative genres, but I have read or seen at least one of each—and even that adds up to a considerable number.[9] I will discuss a few works I find especially significant or interesting. Underlying the discussion are two questions: What makes Zola particularly attractive as the vehicle for such mythologizing? How useful is the sublime paradigm in thinking about the role of intellectuals in contemporary French (but also European and American) society?

Some of the most interesting narratives published in Zola's own lifetime belong to the genre of *impressions d'audience*, eyewitness reports on the Zola trials of 1898 and also, in some cases, on Dreyfus's retrial in Rennes (1899). Usually published as daily newspaper articles, some *Impressions* were subsequently reissued in book form. Among the latter, one of the best-known and most pleasurable to read is by the libertarian feminist writer Séverine, *Vers la lumière*.[10]

Séverine's vivid, evocative prose succeeds in capturing the atmosphere as well as the daily drama of those highly publicized trials. In an opening chapter, she describes a visit she made to Zola shortly before his first trial—and it's quite fascinating to see how firmly in place the elements of the sublime paradigm already were in this brief report. Zola, surrounded by the tasteful, even luxurious surroundings of his apartment (signaling the initial state of fame and comfort), receives his visitor with calm self-confidence: "He has accomplished his duty . . . He therefore possesses what always accompanies such certainty, the peace of his conscience." At the same time, he burns with "the interior flame of his conviction," a conviction founded on disinterested examination of the facts in the case: "based on proofs, on evidence, his conviction grows, irreducible, invincible."[11]

Later, Séverine quotes Zola's famous riposte to General de Pellieux, an army witness at his trial who had made a deprecating remark about him: "Each man serves the country in his own way, by the sword or by the pen. M. de Pellieux has doubtless won some great victories; I have won mine. By my works, French thought has been carried to the four corners of the world. Between the name of de Pellieux and that of Emile Zola, posterity will make its choice." Later still, Séverine quotes Zola's closing speech to the jury, which presents a particularly eloquent version of the sublime paradigm. (It didn't prevent the jury from condemning him, however.) Thus authority, disinterestedness, and modesty all figure in this short passage: "I have behind me neither political ambition nor the passion of a sectarian. I am a free writer, who has devoted his life to work, who will go back into the ranks tomorrow and take up his interrupted task."[12] The other character traits and plot elements of the myth are equally present in the speech, which Séverine quotes in its entirety.

The fact that we find Zola himself repeating the cultural myth on his own behalf suggests that it was already in place, and no doubt in his mind, at the time he wrote *J'Accuse*. Stellio Lorenzi's 1978 film *Zola ou la conscience humaine* suggests this by having Zola read Voltaire's *Traité sur la tolérance* (with a voice-over actually quoting Voltaire's text, written at the time of "l'affaire Calas") just before he himself sits down to write *J'Accuse*. This scene is pure conjecture on the filmmaker's part, of course, but a believable one. It indicates the existence and the power of this cultural myth for Zola himself, hearkening back to Voltaire, even though it was by and about Zola that the myth became fully elaborated in the twentieth century.

Zola's case provides not only a full, but a hyperbolic version of the myth, for several reasons. The Dreyfus affair itself was hyperbolic, attain-

ing a national and international notoriety that no other judicial case before it had attained. And Zola was not only a well-known writer before he
wrote *J'Accuse*, he was one of the most celebrated writers in the world, a
media star before there were media stars, and someone who elicited un-
usual degrees of public hatred as well as admiration for his work.[13] In pub-
lishing *J'Accuse*, he not only was unusually effective, since by a piece of
prose he succeeded in provoking a swift and violent reaction from the government; he also was unusually courageous, facing down crowds screaming for his death and accepting exile for close to a year, separated for long
stretches from his family and friends. And he was unusually modest, returning to his craft and completing a lengthy novel during his forced residence abroad. It was a true story of sublime engagement, almost too sublime to be true.

Admittedly, this was only one version of "Zola's story." For every sublime representation of him, one can find one or more abject representations, especially in the visual field, where the best-known caricaturists
(Forain, Willette, Caran d'Ache) were convinced anti-Dreyfusards.[14] But
here is the interesting fact: Zola's enemies, numerous and often vicious in
their criticism (some never had forgiven him for his attacks on the army
and the church in novels published in the 1890's) did not contest the
power of the cultural myth of sublime engagement—they only contested
its correspondence to Zola's story. According to the abject version of the
story, Zola was not a great writer before writing *J'Accuse* but a *cochon*, a
pig, a disgrace to French letters. Besides, he wasn't even really French,
since his father was Venetian. ("Those with insight have always felt that
there was something foreign, something anti-French even, in Zola's talent," wrote the militantly anti-Dreyfusard novelist Maurice Barrès in
1898.)[15] Furthermore, his motives were not disinterested—he was simply
seeking publicity, and in any case he had been "bought" by the Jewish
"syndicate," nor was he courageous in going into exile, but was a coward
unwilling to face prison.[16] Note that this version of the story does not reject the sublime paradigm as such, it merely denies Zola's right to it. His
enemies did not contest the power of a great writer's authority, disinterestedness, and courage. It was *Zola's* authority, disinterestedness, and
courage that they denied.

Nevertheless, one may wonder whether the myth of sublime engage-ment (independently of Zola) is not characteristically a myth of the Left. Historically, all of the great figures who have been associated with it, from Voltaire to Sartre and including Hugo and Zola, were linked to positions characteristic of the Left, ranging from anticlericalism to anti-authoritari-anisms of various kinds. At the time of the affair itself, anti-Dreyfusard intellectuals like Ferdinand Brunetière and Maurice Barrès strongly criti-cized an idea that is essential to the myth of sublime engagement: that "intellectuals" (as the term was starting to be used) had the right, the obligation even, to intervene in social and political debates in the name of universal values. This criticism was soon abandoned because, as Christophe Charle has noted, the anti-Dreyfusards quickly understood that "in order to reinforce their own cause, they had to gather some well-known names and thus recognize what they had at first denied—the legitimacy of polit-ical interventions by 'intellectuals.'"[17] Nevertheless, one has the impres-sion (which should be tested) that the elements of the myth are more of-ten found in the discourse of the French Left, which has generally evoked universal values, than in that of the Right, which has been more oriented toward particularisms.[18]

As far as Zola is concerned, two other facts about him helped to rein-force the cultural myth: first, the public debate of 1908 concerning the transfer of Zola's remains to the Panthéon (the question was debated even in the National Assembly) had the effect of bringing the Dreyfus affair, and specifically Zola's role in it, once again into the limelight—and to the front page of newspapers. In that case as well, some people glorified Zola while others heaped abuse on him, but the notion of sublime engagement itself was not questioned. Second, during the interwar years and right on up to the 1960's, Zola continued to function for the Left as a heroic figure (despite his ambiguous relationship to Marxists and socialists during his lifetime). A number of highly laudatory biographies were published about him during those years, emphasizing his role in the Dreyfus affair and praising his selflessness, his courage in acting on his conviction, and his lifelong friendship for the downtrodden and the workers. The 1952 biog-raphy by the Communist journalist Jean Fréville, *Zola semeur d'orages*, is not untypical in its fulsome praise: "Zola fought the battle that, from generation to generation, opposes those who want to maintain hierarchies . . . and those who want to see them disappear." And further on: "His immortal *J'accuse* . . . condemns forever the enemies of the people, who have changed only in name; it inspires the combatants for democracy in their constantly renewed struggle against the partisans of fascism and Hitlerism."[19] As this last sentence suggests (alluding to the Communist line during the Cold War), Zola continued to function as an archetype of the cultural myth because the myth lent itself to being constantly readapted according to the needs of the moment. Even while firmly situated as a historical actor involved in a specific role, Zola could be seen as the permanent, atemporal embodiment of a fighter for truth and justice.

This is precisely the figure of Zola that appears in two popular films made at a distance of forty years. Despite some significant differences between them, both of these films realize, almost to the letter, the mythical scenario of sublime engagement as I have outlined it. *The Life of Emile Zola* (1937), directed by the German émigré filmmaker William Dieterle, who had left Germany after Hitler came to power, won three Oscars that year: for best film, best director, and best actor (Paul Muni in the title role). About this film, one can say with only the barest exaggeration that all of its details are false historically but true mythically: it shows us the writer's well-earned fame and peaceful life before the storm, his heroic choice, his dramatic act of writing, and the struggles that ensued, and it shows us the man himself, not only a great writer, but one who was disinterested, courageous, effective, and modest. Dieterle falsifies the facts for the sake of heightened dramatic effect, which also has the effect of reinforcing the elements of the myth. Thus, he makes no mention of Zola's articles before *J'Accuse*, as if Zola had no involvement in the affair before January 1898. (In fact, Zola began campaigning on the Dreyfusard side in the fall of 1897, and all his articles were published a few years later under the title *La vérité en marche*). This reinforces the moment of heroic choice, making Zola's decision to write *J'Accuse* appear as a veritable turning point in both his public and his private life. To emphasize the writer's disinterestedness, his self-sacrifice even, Dieterle invents a scene in which Zola reads a letter from the poet François Coppée telling him that his lifelong dream would soon be realized and he would be elected to the

Académie Française.[20] A few hours later, when Zola decides to enter the fray and to write *J'Accuse*, he tears up the letter lying on his desk: he has sacrificed the Académie to his passion for truth.

It is worth noting that Dieterle omits, in his *Life of Zola*, any mention of Jeanne Rozerot, the young woman who became Zola's mistress and the mother of his two children a few years before the affair. Evidently, in a Hollywood film in 1937, one could not show a sublime intellectual who was not also perfectly virtuous in his private life.

Finally, Dieterle also realizes what may be called the "timeliness factor" of the myth: toward the end of the film, we see Zola making an impassioned plea for world peace. The war that looms on the horizon, he says, can be avoided, if only there's the will. Zola supposedly pronounces those words in 1900, but their raison d'être in Dieterle's film obviously is more closely linked to the situation of Europe in 1937, when the Spanish Civil War already was raging. It is understandable why an anti-Nazi German filmmaker at that time felt drawn to the sublime archetype. And it is also understandable that his film could be made only in the United States. The story of a heroic, successful fight against intolerance and anti-Semitism was too incendiary for the European mass media of the time, and not only in the fascist countries.[21]

Unlike Dieterle's Hollywood "biopic," Stellio Lorenzi's eight-hour telefilm, *Zola ou la conscience humaine* (shown on French television in four installments in the spring of 1978) aims for documentary accuracy. The scenario, written by Lorenzi and by Zola's biographer Armand Lanoux, is scrupulous in its respect for details, both as concerns Zola's private life (thus, Jeanne Rozerot and her children play a big role) and as concerns public events. The trials, both those involving Zola (1898) and Dreyfus's retrial in Rennes (1899), are represented in great detail, based on the official court records. Given its desire for historical accuracy, it is all the more interesting to note that Lorenzi's film also conforms to the sublime paradigm as far as the representation of Zola is concerned. The actor who plays Zola (Jean Topart) emphasizes his passionate, combative side, rather than his modesty, but that's a minor variation. All the personal character traits as well as all the narrative elements of the myth are present. Take the heroic choice, for example: unlike the earlier film, this narrative shows

Zola's involvement in the affair and the articles that precede *J'Accuse*. Other details are also accurate—thus, no letter from Coppée arrives announcing Zola's imminent election to the Académie. But as I mentioned earlier, Lorenzi inserts a scene in which Zola takes down a volume of Voltaire and reads it just before sitting down to write *J'Accuse*, thus reinforcing the sublime paradigm. And Lorenzi imagines another scene as well, which corresponds to the renunciation of the Académie in Dieterle's film: Madame Zola (he never married Jeanne Rozerot) enters Zola's study in the middle of night, dressed in her nightgown. When he tells her what he is doing, she tries to dissuade him: "Think about it. . . . You think this is how you're going to get into the Académie ?" He replies: "I don't give a damn about the Académie. It's over, I'm not going to try to get elected again." Then, when she insists and accuses him of insincerity, he gets angry: "If you don't understand, well, too bad. What! They want to murder an innocent man, crush democracy, overturn the Republic! And this is the moment you choose to pick a fight with me!" Madame Zola asks him to forgive her for having misunderstood him. We're up to our ears in the sublime.[22]

And Now?

It's time to return to the questions with which we began. What is the fate, and role, of intellectuals in the postmodern world? Does Zola (the sublime Zola) have something to teach us on that subject?

Let us return for a moment to Lorenzi's film. What accounts for its appeal (or even for the fact of its having been made) in 1978? The pragmatic explanation is that it was made then because it couldn't be made earlier. According to the film historian John Frazer, "until 1950 no film concerning the Dreyfus Affair could be shown in France and it was not until 1974 that the ban on making a film on the affair was lifted by President Giscard d'Estaing."[23] Indeed, Lorenzi's film had to wait a long time before being made: the biography on which it was based, Lanoux's *Bonjour monsieur Zola*, had been published in 1954. The directors seized the first opportunity they had, we might argue. But this explanation, although not wrong on the factual/pragmatic level, does not go very far on the theoretical/cul-

tural level. What, if any, ideological or cultural/mythical function was fulfilled by this film watched by millions of television viewers in France in
1978? Did its success disprove Foucault's contention that the myth of the
"great writer as universal intellectual" had waned long ago in the Western world? Or, on the contrary, did it prove that very notion by serving
up a moment and a figure of the past forever gone—a great pot of cultural
nostalgia? Was it, perhaps, a ploy on the Socialists' part to revive a glorious moment of the Left's past in preparation for its electoral victory at the
polls three years later? (The 1981 elections gave the Socialists a majority
in the Assembly and put François Mitterrand into the presidency). If so,
there is a definite irony in the fact that less than two years after that victory, *Le monde* launched an *enquête* on why there were so few traditional
left-wing intellectuals in France. How was one to explain, the venerable
daily wondered, "the silence of the intellectuals of the Left"?

These questions have become all the more pertinent after the war in
Bosnia—a war that elicited surprisingly little reaction from intellectuals,
despite the atrocities and human rights violations it produced. In ap-
proaching an answer, it may be useful to evoke once again Sartre's double
discourse of fifty years ago, as well as Blanchot's later one. At the very
height of his theory of *engagement* (in my terms, it was a theory of sublime engagement), Sartre was already aware of the parodic potential of the
myth he was promoting—as if every sublime gesture was haunted by its
grotesque simulacrum. Right after his remark that "it's not bad to start
one's life like Rimbaud, to begin a Goethean return to order in one's thirties, to throw oneself at fifty, like Zola, into a public debate," Sartre added:
"Naturally, it will not be a matter of realizing each episode in all its violence, but rather of *indicating* it, the way a serious tailor indicates the current fashion without servility."[24]

An astonishing image: cultural myths can be tried on and discarded like
so many jackets or neckties. Today, this idea does not shock us, we who
have read Roland Barthes's *Mythologies* and Guy Debord's *La société du
spectacle*. Obviously, Sartre, too, knew something about postmodernity
before the term became fashionable. Sartre saw himself both as an actor
on the stage of history (the sublime writer as man of action) and, simultaneously, as a comedian in the "society of the spectacle" (a parody and sim-

ulation of the sublime, and of action). As for Blanchot, he occupies almost the opposite place, but he too has a doubled vision. Blanchot had read Foucault when he wrote his essay on intellectuals, and indeed quotes him. He also had read Lyotard's essay on "the tomb of the intellectual," bidding a permanent farewell to the figure of sublime engagement.[25] Blanchot agrees with Foucault that the time is over for sublime intellectual heroes who purport to speak in the name of all humanity and rise above the crowd. And yet (this is the other side of his vision), he also affirms, more than once and without the slightest trace of irony, that on certain occasions, intellectuals will be impelled to respond to "moral demands, at once obscure and imperious": "It is anti-Semitism (together with racism and xenophobia) that reveals the intellectual most strongly to himself . . . it is in that form that a concern for others impels him (or not) out of his creative solitude."[26]

Since racism and xenophobia have not disappeared (and this is even more true today than in 1984, when Blanchot was writing), Blanchot concludes that it would be a mistake to try to bury the "universal intellectual." Personally, I agree—with the proviso that women too can embody the universal. In fact it was a woman intellectual, Susan Sontag, who recently deplored the absence of action on the part of intellectuals in protesting the Bosnian war.[27] But whether the mantle of ethical behavior is worn by a man or a woman is less important than that it should be worn—even if only provisionally, or (in Richard Rorty's sense) ironically.

Zola is dead. Today we may no longer be able to accomplish sublime gestures without a sense of parodic repetition. But does an ironic self-consciousness necessarily impede action? Or have we become truly indifferent?

Intellectuel(le) universel(le) pas mort(e). Lettre suit.[28]

MAURICE GODELIER

Is the West the Universal Model for Humanity?
The Baruya of New Guinea Between
Change and Decay

As an anthropologist specializing in the study of societies that are literally on the other side of the world from the West, in Oceania, I have had the opportunity since 1967 of observing the changing lifestyle and thinking of a tribe in New Guinea, one of those societies we refer to as "primitive," the Baruya, who were discovered in 1951 and subjected to Australian colonial rule in 1960. In 1975, the country became independent, and the Baruya were transformed into citizens of a new state that was a member of the United Nations, furnishing one further proof of the West's advance in that part of the world.

But since November 9, 1989, the date when the Berlin Wall came down, it surely would be true to say that the process of Westernization has resumed inside Europe itself. The West, which for several decades was divided between the two Europes, is being unified and tomorrow will exert an even stronger influence on the world's destiny, shaping it in its own image and in accordance with its own interests. Nevertheless, we should note that Westernization no longer is an accomplishment of the Western peoples alone. It has also become a product of the East, of Japan and the four or five "little dragons." But in these cases, Westernization no longer is just the expansion of the West, since it is an achievement of societies that have retained their political sovereignty and preserved their cultural identity, of which one major component is certainly Buddhism. Westernization is spreading, but not every aspect of the West—or at least not with the same degree of success as previously.

What is the West today? What are its essential components? Components that occur in association in the West may be dissociated and appear in combination with different social and cultural components in other parts of the world. In my view, the West is a blend of the real and the imaginary, of achievements and standards, of modes of behavior and ways of thinking that today make up a sort of ball of energy that either attracts or repels. It revolves around three axes, three sets of institutions, each with its own logic, symbols, and values: capitalism, parliamentary democracy, and Christianity.

Capitalism is the most developed form of market economy that has ever existed. Parliamentary democracy is a system of government that, no matter whether it takes the form of a republic or a constitutional monarchy, entrusts power to representatives elected by universal suffrage and recognizes that all citizens have, in principle, equal rights and equal duties in the eyes of the law. And Christianity is a religion that emphasizes the sins and salvation of the individual and also preaches that one should love one's neighbor as oneself and should render to Caesar the things that are Caesar's, and to God the things that are God's.

In short, the West today derives its strength from a combination of components that emerged at different points in its history and that only lately have come together and fused. Christianity has exerted its influence for two thousand years and antedates the appearance of capitalism by many centuries. Capitalism first developed before the sixteenth century within the feudal and monarchical societies. Originally, therefore, it had nothing in common with democracy. Indeed, as late as 1906, Max Weber wondered whether there was any necessary link between capitalism and democracy. Taiwan and South Africa currently prompt the same question. But South Africa is Christian, whereas Taiwan is not.

These unfavorable examples remind us that there is also a darker side to the West: the conquering, colonial, despotic West that draws its wealth from the resources of the rest of the world, closing its eyes whenever convenient to the lack of freedom and rights accorded by the regimes that serve it or are associated with it, encouraging not only individualism, but also egoism. Such denunciations do not come only from the Third World:

in the West, equal rights coexist, sometimes successfully and sometimes not, with what are at times enormous disparities in standards of living, and there are still those who believe that the accumulation of capital depends in part on the legal exploitation of labor.

In short, the West is not a flawless or stainless model, but is still today a source of attraction, rather than repulsion. At the same time, like any historical phenomenon, it runs the risk of being demolished sooner or later by history itself as a result of its contradictions and ambiguities. But since the events in Berlin and Bucharest, that day would seem to have been postponed for several decades, or even several centuries.

Having defined the West in these terms, I will now proceed to consider the Westernization of pre-industrial societies, but will confine my remarks to tribal societies, which are still major components of many nations in Africa, Asia, America, and Oceania.

But, first of all, what is a tribe? A tribe is a local society composed of a set of kinship groups, united by the same principles of social organization and ways of thinking, interconnected by repeated marriages, and cooperating in the defense of a common territory and the exploitation of its resources. Several tribes may share the same language and the same principles of social organization. What distinguishes them, then is the control of a part of nature, a territory.

Thus, tribal identity is a composite reality consisting of a cultural and social framework and identification with a territory that has been conquered or inherited from the tribal ancestors and that must be passed on to future generations. Tribal societies always have been highly diverse. In general, however, they may be classified on the basis of two criteria: whether they are sovereign in their own territory or already integrated in a precolonial state governed, in most cases, by the members of a dominant tribe, and whether power within the tribe is shared more or less equally between all groups or is concentrated in the hands of a few at the top of a hierarchy, hereditary or otherwise. In 1951, the Baruya of New Guinea provided an example of a tribal society with its own sovereign territory in which ritual and political power was held largely by a number of families descended from conquering groups. I will analyze the forms taken by the processes of Westernization in that tribal society and the stages through which those processes passed. I will proceed not by making comparisons, but by drawing general conclusions from the processes I will show to have operated among the Baruya—processes that, as will readily be seen, also have occurred and recurred elsewhere.

Who are the Baruya? A society living in two high valleys (at an altitude of two thousand meters) in a chain of mountains in the interior of New Guinea. They were discovered in 1951 by an Australian officer who had heard of the Batiya, renowned as salt producers, and who organized a military expedition to locate them. In 1951, New Guinea was divided into three colonial regions: Irian-Jaya, controlled by the Netherlands, New Guinea, a former German colony placed under Australian trusteeship after World War I by the League of Nations, and Papua, a former British colony "given" by Great Britain to Australia in 1904.

In 1951, the Baruya population amounted to some eighteen hundred people living in roughly a dozen small villages. The society was made up of fifteen clans, eight of which had been formed by invaders who had conquered local groups. The economy was based primarily on a form of extensive slash-and-burn agriculture (*Brandwirtschaft*), but the Baruya also practiced more intensive techniques, growing irrigated crops on terraces. Pig breeding was mainly women's work, and hunting, which was an exclusive preserve of the men, had a chiefly ritual significance and contributed to the assertion of male superiority. At the beginning of the twentieth century, the tools were still made of stone, bone, or wood, but the Baruya had no good stone on their territory to manufacture their tools. They obtained it by trading in salt, which they produced from the ashes of a plant.

The organization of society was based on the interplay of kinship relations and the general subordination of women to men. Lineage was patrilinear and women were prohibited from owning land, bearing arms, and possessing the magic and ritual objects that, according to the Baruya, ensure children's growth. Marriage involved a direct exchange of women among the men. Every three years, great male initiation ceremonies were held, and the entire tribe, with all the villages and lineages taking part, built a large ceremonial house the Baruya described as a gigantic "body." Each vertical post represented one of the tribe's young men who was to be initiated.

What we have here is an example of a small, local society, politically independent, with a partly autarkic economy, able to maintain itself, but dependent on the salt trade for the acquisition of tools, weapons, ritual objects, and other items—in short, for its means of production, destruction, and other objects essential for its reproduction. It was a classless society, but not an egalitarian one. There were various kinds of inequality: a general inequality between men and women, and another kind that set "big men" apart from others. These "big men" were great by virtue of either their function or their merit. They were either masters of rituals who had inherited from their ancestors the sacred objects necessary for children's growth or the struggle against evil spirits, or else they were great warriors who had killed many enemies or were hunters of cassowaries. The cassowary for them is not only a type of game, it is a wild woman who wanders in the forests of New Guinea. As for the universe, the Baruya had no concept of the creation of the world. They believed that after a period when sky and earth were one and when animals and human beings lived together and spoke the same language, the present order of the world was born: the sun and moon broke away from the earth and rose above it, pushing the sky before them. For the Baruya, the sun and the moon are powers of remote deities whose actions are beneficial. For example, the sun acts in women's wombs together with male sperm to produce children. What concerns and scares the Baruya are the evil spirits of the forest and the caves, especially the spirits of the dead.

We should note that in Baruya society there is no direct link between economics and kinship, between the production of wealth and the reproduction of life: a woman can be exchanged only for another woman. In many other societies in New Guinea and in Africa, a woman is exchanged for wealth (bridewealth), and contact with the West rapidly has led to an enormous inflation in dowries. This draws our attention to the great variety characterizing the societies on which the West has acted.

The Westernization of the Baruya took place in four stages under the influence of various forces that acted either separately, one after the other, or jointly. The meeting of the two worlds took place in 1951, but by that time the West already had transformed the lives of the Baruya, although no European had appeared in the region. During the previous twenty years preceding this contact, the Baruya, through their salt trading, had obtained steel axes and machetes made in Sheffield and Solingen, in an industrial Europe of whose very existence they were unaware. Seeing the effectiveness of these new tools, they threw their traditional stone tools away in the forest. With their more effective steel tools they saved time, which they spent either fighting or doing nothing. But they were obliged to produce more salt in order to acquire them. The women, who were excluded by tradition from the work of tree felling, continued to make use of their wooden tools, and, inasmuch as the Baruya started to clear larger gardens and raise more pigs, the introduction of the white men's tools meant that the women had more work to do. Thus, by abandoning their old stone tools, the Baruya already had placed themselves without realizing it in a position of material and economic dependence on the West. But other surprising events occurred during the years that led up to the arrival of the whites. One day the Baruya saw in the sky two large birds chasing each other and spitting fire. They were terrified. This was an episode in World War II, an air battle between Japanese and Australians that probably took place in 1943. Sometime later a Baruya named Dawatnie, who had gone to trade in salt among the Watchakes, a tribe living far to the north of the Baruya, was led by his hosts to the top of a mountain, from where he was shown in the valley below several of these large birds. Beings of human form were entering the stomachs of these birds. On returning home he related what he had seen, and thus, even though they had never seen any Europeans, the Baruya discovered the existence of supernatural beings of human form and with light skin who lived in large firebirds.

In 1951, the first white man, Jim Sinclair, arrived at the head of a column of soldiers and bearers. The Baruya were then at war with their neighbors, whose fortified villages were positioned on top of the mountains on the other side of the valley. The white man set up a camp, and in the center he erected a pole on which he hoisted the Australian flag. He drew up his men and ordered them to present arms to the flag. The Baruya were dazzled by the flashing bayonets, and when the flag was raised the following morning, a warrior named Bwarinmax fell into a trance. He believed he had been possessed by the white man's power, which had revealed itself in the flashing bayonets. At that point, the Baruya decided to kill the white man and massacre his troops. But Jim Sinclair, who was completely unaware of their intentions, asked for a dozen very thick shields to be brought and invited some powerful warriors to fire arrows at them. He then drew up a platoon of soldiers and told them to open fire. The shields shattered. This demonstration of force impressed the Baruya, who abandoned their plans for a massacre. Thus, in 1951, another dimension was added to the Baruya's material dependence on Western tools: their military subordination.

Thirty years later, after independence, things would no longer be the same when the Baruya and neighboring tribes resumed their warfare. The government sent an officer and a few soldiers to arrest the "ringleaders," and the officer made as if to order his men to open fire on the crowd. The Baruya explained to him that they were not afraid: he would not be able to kill all of them, as they were too numerous, and in any case he and his soldiers rapidly would be overwhelmed.

But let us return to 1951. The first sight of a white man in the flesh produced a great change in the Baruya. They soon discovered that he was a man like themselves and not a supernatural being, a man who was superior, but certainly not a spirit or a god.

Several years went by, during which no other whites appeared. Then, suddenly, in 1960, an impressive column of soldiers and bearers emerged into the Wonenara Valley, on the border between the Baruya and their enemies. This was a flat area where the tribes traditionally gave battle, and because it was flat, the white men decided to build a landing strip there. A patrol post was set up at the end of the strip, and some of the soldiers went off to identify the tribes and inform them that they no longer had the right to fight each other. The officer in charge of establishing the administration later summoned representatives of the various tribes to explain the new order of things and sent them home after appointing them "chiefs" of their villages on behalf of Her Majesty, Queen Elizabeth of England. Unfortunately, one of these men was attacked on the way home by some warriors of the Yunduye tribe, with which his own tribe had been at war when the whites had arrived. He was killed, and his body was fed to the dogs.

On hearing this news, the officer organized a punitive expedition, and three people subsequently were killed, including a woman. A column of prisoners was brought back to the post. One of the prisoners, a great shaman, believed that he could escape from the white men by flying away, since the spirit of the shamans is a bird, and he therefore threw himself—in handcuffs—from the top of a cliff. He crashed to the ground, but did not die, and has been terribly disabled ever since.

Another incident, this time among the Baruya, gave the local tribes a fresh opportunity to gauge the white men's strength and determination. Following the suicide of a woman, a battle had broken out between the inhabitants of her village and those of her husband's village. When the officer was informed, he burned the village of the people he believed to have been responsible for the battle, the dead woman's village. Unfortunately for the Baruya, two sacred objects disappeared in this fire: the dried fingers of a great warrior who had led their ancestors in the conquest of the territory and, much more seriously, the flints used to rekindle the sacred flame during initiation ceremonies, which disintegrated in the heat of the fire. The officer never knew anything of these losses.

Thus, very quickly, within the first months of being colonized, the local tribes lost a major attribute of their existence: the right to lead their own lives and the right to apply their laws on their own territory. In short, they lost at one and the same time what we would call political sovereignty and cultural autonomy.

A comprehensive census of the population was begun at that time, because a state can exercise its authority only over a registered population. Peace was imposed and the villages were relocated on the valley floor for census purposes and ease of control. The people were obliged to cooperate in the census and to submit to the law. They were prohibited from taking the law into their own hands. The Baruya had just come into contact with an institution that has played a great role in the development of humankind and is an indicator of civilization: the state. Of course, the state that had discovered them was colonial and authoritarian, but it was seen by the Europeans as representing a necessary stage in progress toward the democratic, parliamentary state that would replace it after independence.

In 1966, another component of the West, Christianity, entered the field in force. Lutheran missionaries came to settle near the patrol post and built both a mission and a school. They brought with them evangelists from the coastal tribes, which had been converted to Christianity long before, and they placed one in each village to preach the word of the Lord. They preached in pidgin English, the language taught in school together with the rudiments of arithmetic and writing. The Baruya and the neighboring tribes welcomed this move, and soon more than one hundred children were attending the school. Two years later, the best pupils were sent to a mission secondary school in a town of the interior. One of the boys in this first class later became a forestry engineer, another a mathematics teacher, and a third, a policeman. One even became a minister.

Throughout their stay at college, the missionaries forbade them to return to their tribe to take part in initiation ceremonies. They were told that their ancestors had worshipped false gods and that they and their parents previously had been living in sin without knowing it. A split developed between most of the boys, who were to remain "bush Kanaka" like their parents, and the minority, the "schoolboys," who had begun to "evolve." Some of the latter declared at that time that the customs of their ancestors should be abandoned and that they "spat on the loin cloths" of their fathers. Fifteen years later, however, nearly all of them returned of their own accord to take part in the great initiation ceremonies. Before we are done, we will see why.

"Kanaka" comes from the word "canaque," which the French use to refer to the tribes of New Caledonia. This term had been taken over by the Australian administration to refer to the scarcely pacified bush tribes. The Baruya therefore had become bush Kanaka, primitive people living in the forests.

But it was these same bush Kanaka who so quickly had decided to send some of their children to school. That decision demonstrated a determination to integrate to some extent in the new world that had been imposed on them or offered to them, a world that, as they quickly realized, they could no longer escape. The soldiers, evangelists, and bearers, black like themselves and coming from unknown tribes, were proof of that. They therefore sent their boys to school either without initiating them or with their initiation limited to several hours and a few rites, whereas tradition demanded that boys be separated from their mothers and the world of women by the age of nine and that they should live in the house of men up to the age of twenty, when they would marry.

This did not prevent the Baruya's leading shaman from sending his son to school. Twenty years later, it was this son who returned to his tribe a minister and became deputy to the German missionary in charge of the Lutheran mission. At the time, two Baruya clans had decided, with government encouragement, to establish a sort of sales and purchasing cooperative, and they entrusted its management to him. He was expelled from the mission, however, for making his wife's mother pregnant. He later gave up his other position on suspicion of having misappropriated the shop's funds. Today, having taken a second wife, he lives in his village and still enjoys undoubted power.

In 1965, the administration began to recruit up to 30 percent of the men in certain villages for work in the coastal plantations. Many Baruya who wanted to travel volunteered for this work and went off for a period of two years. At the time, the administration did not allow natives to renew their contracts because it was afraid they would begin to form organizations if they remained for too long at the same plantation. The men were housed in barracks, fed, and paid a few dollars a week. At the end of their contract they were given roughly two hundred Australian dollars each, which they could spend as they wished. Most of them spent part of this sum on tools, blankets, and umbrellas, which they distributed when they got back to the village. The Baruya thus became wage earners who freely had sold their labor.

In fact, the money they earned and the food rations they received were not the equivalent of real wages. They had experienced the discipline of continuous piecework under the supervision of foremen, an experience that was completely foreign to their traditional labors. They had encountered the sea (of whose existence they had not dreamed), and ships and aircraft. But on their return in 1967, many declared that they would not leave again, even if asked.

In 1967, following the soldiers, the missionaries, and the civil servants, an academic anthropologist arrived: myself, bringing the Western presence up to full strength. Following Western forms of authority, there was now a Western form of knowledge. After a few months, I was asked by the officer in charge of the post to tell him who the true fight leaders were, since it was obvious that the Baruya had put forward men without importance as their village chiefs. The missionaries, for their part, would have liked to know what went on during the shamanist ceremonies and who the "sorcerers" were. Like any doctor, I then invoked professional ethics to justify my silence.

In 1968, the administration, in its concern for development, organized huge campaigns to encourage the tribes to plant coffee and distributed thousands of coffee plants free of charge. Agronomists came to explain what types of soil were suitable for the crop and what exposure they required. At the time, coffee fetched a good price because Brazil was going through a production crisis, something of which the Baruya were completely unaware. As producers of salt, they knew what it meant to produce for exchange or sale. But their salt was at one and the same time a commodity and their currency. Coffee was a commodity that they produced, but did not consume themselves, and the currency they received for it was made and controlled by others.

The Baruya set to planting coffee trees in the belief that they would be able to make money without leaving their valleys and without subjecting themselves to the discipline of plantation work. But a problem soon arose: certain families had good ground for coffee and others did not. Initially, the old rule of reciprocity between families allied by marriage applied, and those who had a large area of good land allowed their brothers-in-law to plant coffee trees on that land. But a coffee tree has a life of some twenty years. Allowing someone to use one's land to plant coffee therefore was entirely different from allowing him to plant sweet potatoes or vegetables, which are harvested at the end of a single season. Economic differentiation began to develop between families and between individuals, a phenomenon that had not applied to subsistence agriculture, although it already had existed for salt-producing land. In short, the Baruya began to *makim bisnis,* to do business in the way the administration did, which was widely used in those regions that had been colonized for a long time. But *makim bisnis* meant selling to the whites, not—yet—to one's brother, to a member of one's tribe, to a Baruya.

That threshold was crossed on the day the Baruya decided to sell the meat of a pig they had killed. Among the Baruya, pigs always had been exchanged as gifts between relatives, allies, initiates, and so on. The selling of pig meat meant changing a gift into a commodity and accepting the idea that anyone with money could apply to purchase that commodity, even though he had no personal link with the pig's owner. Impersonal commodities and an abstract *Homo economicus* had just made their appearance in a society that traditionally had functioned on the basis of personal relationships.

At the end of 1968, Australia decided to organize elections throughout the country in order to establish an assembly of representatives from the various regions, the first step toward the parliamentary democracy that was designed to replace the colonial administration after independence. Parties already existed in the country, including the PANGU Party, which was demanding independence and whose secretary, Michael Somare of the Sepik, was to become prime minister of the first government of the independent state of Papua New Guinea. But in 1968, the Baruya were entirely unaware of these parties and of the significance of the elections. By chance, I was present when the elections took place.

The various tribes of the region were assembled at several points in the mountains that were within easy reach. A European officer arrived with his interpreters and set up a polling station in a tent. He explained that all the registered adults should vote and that by so doing they would send to the capital people who would speak up for them to the government. Then, because hardly anyone could read and therefore choose between ballot papers, the crowd was shown posters with the pictures of nine candidates, black and white, who were unknown to the tribes. The officer provided some information about the candidates and their programs. Each man and woman was then called by name and asked to point to one of the photos. Even the men were shy—and the women were terrified. For example, one of them who placed her finger between two photos was shouted at. She then pointed to one photo at random. She had "voted."

Such were the first steps in learning about a parliamentary government. Since then, the Baruya have come to be perfectly well aware of the importance of having their own representative in the National Parliament. But they have encountered two problems that they have not yet solved. It is essential for their families to agree on a single candidate and that other tribes be prepared to back that candidate. But each tribe wants to be represented by one of its own members, and each family would prefer to choose the representative from within its own ranks.

In 1975, the Baruya became, without asking or wanting to be, citizens of an independent nation that immediately became a member of the United Nations. This was the period of decolonization, and independence had been granted to them by Australia, which was then governed by the Labor Party. The colonial period had been extremely short, just fifteen years. A further fifteen years now have passed since independence. What has happened to them in the interval?

Several months before the proclamation of independence, Dick Lloyd, a missionary from the Summer Institute of Linguistics who at the end of 1951 had been the first European to live continuously among the Baruya and learn their language, returned with the first book printed in that language, a remarkable translation of the book of Genesis. At the time, only two of the small number of Baruya who knew how to read and write had become Christians, since in order to be baptized it was necessary for polygamous men to repudiate all but one wife. But repudiating a woman meant breaking an alliance with people to whom a man had given his own sister. It also changed drastically the status of the children of the woman concerned. The Baruya found this too difficult. They also did not really understand why the white missionaries from the various Protestant sects—the Seventh-Day Adventists, the Lutherans, and the New Tribes Mission—fought among themselves to recruit them.

At that time, the Lutheran mission, led by a German who had escaped from the German Democratic Republic, opened a trading post beside the mission. Two hundred dollars was invested to purchase the usual range of goods: knives, rice, umbrellas, and so on. When this first batch was sold, the money was reinvested to buy a second batch. At the end of the year, the missionary had fourteen thousand dollars worth of cash and stock. The American missionary from the New Tribes Mission, who boasted of living in poverty, criticized him for running this flourishing business. The rate of profit was quite appreciable, but nothing compared with that of the large Australian commercial companies in the towns, Burns Philips and Steamships.

Fresh elections were held to elect the first parliament of the independent New Guinea. The Baruya voted successfully for a brilliant young man, "Peter," a medical assistant who was a member of a traditionally hostile tribe, the Andje. At the same time, they also provided him with a wife. Unfortunately, Peter was killed three years later in an air crash, and his successor came from a tribe with which the Baruya had little contact.

After independence, increasing numbers of children were sent to the school, including girls, who, for the first time in the history of the Baruya, competed directly with the boys in learning to read, write, count, and even run. Many young men went off to work in the plantations or looked for employment in the towns. The older men remained in the village and continued to plant coffee. But much was now changing in the country. Many of the coastal plantations had been sold by their European owners, who were wary of the consequences of independence and who left the country en masse. The plantations had been bought up by the "big men" of the local tribes. The number of Europeans actually living in the country was dwindling. In the towns, insecurity and delinquency increased. Alcohol, which formerly had been reserved for the consumption of whites or for the few natives allowed to enter their pubs, now was freely on sale.

The initiation ceremonies—which never had been discontinued among the Baruya during the colonial period, but which merely had been held far from the gaze of the missionaries and the soldiers—now increased in scale, albeit still with rituals associated with war, which was now forbidden, and with homosexual relations between the initiates, which were on the decline. It was at that time that some Baruya who had studied and become policemen, nurses, and teachers returned to take part in the initiation ceremonies. These were the same people who twenty years previously had scorned the customs of their ancestors. And it was one of them who in 1979 supplied the reason for their return. He publicly explained to all the men of the tribe and young initiates that the initiations had to be continued because strength was needed to resist the life of the towns and the lack of work or money. People had to depend on themselves. But there was a central paradox in his explanation. In my presence he shouted "We must find strength in our customs; we must base ourselves on what the whites call culture."

Things continued to develop in this contradictory fashion, with the Baruya drawing on certain elements of their culture and abandoning others. They began to combine what they retained with ideas and practices from the West. Thus, in 1980, the Baruya decided to initiate new shamans and organize grand ceremonies, which are usually held every eight or ten years. There were few volunteers, since a person who becomes a shaman among the Baruya must remain in the tribe to protect it against the attacks of evil spirits and to conduct a struggle every night against the witch doctors of neighboring tribes, who seek to lead the spirits of the Baruya astray or to devour their livers. The young men preferred to travel or else had less confidence than their elders in the powers of their shamans. The elders in turn admitted that their powers had not been the same since the whites had come. And yet a compromise was reached with the medical knowledge of the Europeans. People attended the small medical post for the treatment of fractures, wounds, and infections. The shaman was consulted for internal pains, which were signs of poisoning by means of sorcery.

That was the situation in 1986, when a problem unresolved during the colonial period suddenly reemerged, a problem concerning good coffee-growing land lying along a river. The Yuwarrunatche, neighbors and enemies of the Baruya, who had lost a war and the land in question just before Jim Sinclair arrived, decided to recover it by force of arms once they realized that the new state lacked the strength of the colonial administration. War broke out again. The enemy tribe burned the Baruya village nearest to their border and fired arrows into a Baruya warrior, telling him to return to the land of his ancestors, who had taken the land away from them. All the schools closed down and the villages were reestablished on the mountaintops, protected by impenetrable stockades. The hospital and the airstrip no longer could be reached by the Baruya because of the proximity of their enemies, who maintained a permanent presence in the area. No aircraft would agree to land to load the Baruya's coffee. The road that the colonial administration had built with the labor of the Baruya and their neighbors was cut by the latter and the bridges destroyed. The road became unusable after the first rainy season. A kind of regression then set in and continued up until 1988.

Six or seven of the Baruya were killed in various battles, and four of their enemies were killed, including their great fight leader. But it was not the same kind of war as in the old days. Women and children no longer were killed because that usually led to police intervention. Indeed, the police came on two occasions by helicopter to arrest the "ringleaders," but each time the villages were empty and the police merely burned down a few houses.

At length, in 1988, a long truce was established, but without a genuine peace. The airstrip became accessible again, but the Baruya had drawn a lesson from the war and had started to build their own landing strip in 1987 in the neighborhood of the village farthest away from their enemies, on a high mountain terrace. This strip was operational in 1990. In short, life began again, and the changes briefly interrupted by the war resumed with a new momentum. I will now mention some of these further changes.

The Baruya planted increasing amounts of coffee, which is men's work. But the bulk of the subsequent work—harvesting, drying, and hulling the coffee cherries—is done by the women and young girls. Some men also perform this work, however—those for whom coffee production and moneymaking have become a sort of passion. Several of them already have managed to save the equivalent of five hundred to one thousand dollars. They have learned to sell at the right time and to use transistor radios to keep in touch with the coffee prices in Goroka, a town that is half an hour away by air. Up until now they have done practically nothing with their money. In order to prevent it being stolen, the administration has advised them to place it in savings books, which it supplies. The money is then taken to the town.

The Baruya continue to open small shops, several individuals banding together in order to do so, in which they resell at extremely high prices the usual range of goods—rice, soap, kerosene, and matches—that they have flown in on the mission aircraft. But these businesses often go bankrupt, because the people working in the shops help themselves or give presents for which they do not pay. Increasingly, the Baruya kill pigs in order to sell the meat at extremely high prices. The rule is to make as much money as possible, *makim bisnis*. The women also have entered the market economy. Almost every day one hundred or so of them come to sit near the medical center, laying out in front of them several kilos of sweet potatoes and bananas and exchanging recent gossip while waiting for customers. Toward midday, they return to their villages, most having sold nothing. They then eat what they had come to sell—which had not, in any case, been produced for sale. Economically, these exchanges are marginal, but at the social and psychological level they demonstrate a desire to imitate the Western world and even to become a part of it, if only in symbolic rather than real terms.

It is this same desire to integrate that, I believe, explains a new phenomenon of major importance. It will be remembered that in 1975, no more than two Baruya had been baptized. Since 1988, however, although there are no more European missionaries in the region, churches made of wood and thatch, *Haus Lotu*, have been built in nearly all the villages. Many young people and some old women gather in these churches on Sundays. Someone who can read pidgin English "recites" the Bible, and people sing in pidgin English or in Baruya, thanking God for having brought light and life and asking Him to forgive the sins of His creatures. In 1988, I was shown long lists of the names of Baruya who were preparing to be baptized. Most of them wish to join the Lutheran Church, but some want to belong to an American sect, The Church of Christ, which recently has arrived in the country. Among these recruits were many polygamous men. When I expressed astonishment, I was told that polygamists now could be baptized. I do not believe this is so, but the Baruya themselves think so, and it seems to make their conversion to Christianity somewhat easier.

What is the explanation of this increasing desire for baptism? I am not very sure. The Baruya do not seem to understand the concept of sin, and their new Christian feelings do not prevent them from applauding when their enemies are killed, their foes' villages burned, or their adversaries' pigs stolen. I see in this another aspect of their wish to become part of the Western world, the world of their time. It is perhaps significant that the Baruya put on European dress when they go to pray and that the women cover up their breasts. Those preparing for baptism give much thought to the Christian name they are to receive: John, Samuel, Mary, and so on.

What certainly has changed most among the Baruya are relations between men and women and between generations. Although the boys who remain in the village still are initiated and live in the house of the men, which they should only leave to go into the forest, avoiding all contact with women, they now can be seen crossing the village and talking to the girls. Remarkably, the girls in one village even have set up a basketball team like the boys have done and are practicing on the same playground at the edge of the village. Jokes and glances are exchanged freely, something that would have been impossible five years ago.

That is the situation in which the Baruya find themselves 40 years after the day when a white man at the head of a column of soldiers and bearers appeared on one of their mountain tops and planted his flag in the middle of their valley. Their society has not collapsed: it is still there, and the Baruya have even increased in number. But their lifestyle and ways of thinking have been transformed, turned upside down—and the process is irreversible. The Baruya have not accepted these changes passively, but have been partly responsible for them, both the great shaman who sent his son to school and the orphan who became a mathematics teacher at the University of Port Moresby after being sent by the Australians to study in Sydney, Melbourne, and Auckland. But although they know how to adapt and thus to "create" a society, the Baruya no longer control the development of their own society. It is now subject to enormous external forces that have penetrated and direct it, forces that all have come from the West and that already have made the small society a part of the West's ever-expanding process of development. In the Pacific, the West is not identical with Europe: half the goods sold in New Guinea come from Japan.

Let us briefly recapitulate the various aspects of these now irreversible processes, submission to the West and integration with it. The Baruya no longer produce their own tools and no longer would be able to make or use the old stone tools. They have need of a currency that is not their own and must either become unskilled and poorly paid wage earners or become small-scale producers of coffee, which they do not consume and which others export to the world market.

The Baruya have become citizens of a state whose principles and models are of Western origin. Indeed, it was the West that introduced them before granting independence to this artificial nation. Since independence, Australia has continued to provide one-third of the budget of the new state, but this does not mean that the latter simply takes orders from its former colonial master. All this is still way over the heads of the Baruya.

We should note in passing that it is probably the existence of over seven hundred and fifty tribes of different sizes and of many different languages that has made it possible to establish and maintain a form of parliamentary democracy. In a country of mountains and jungles where travel always has been extremely difficult, no tribe ever has been able to establish its hegemony even over several others. Elsewhere, in Africa and Asia, in places where one ethnic group wielded power over others before or after the period of European colonization, many one-party states and puppet parliaments were established after independence.

But the very factors that facilitated the introduction of parliamentary democracy in New Guinea have reduced its effectiveness. The postcolonial state does not have the material and human resources necessary to maintain a universal presence and to enforce its laws. The tribes quickly realized this and have returned to the use of violence in settling their problems with their neighbors, as in the good old days. The war between the Baruya and the Yuwarrunatche is an example of this general trend. The state is seen both as an abstract and far-off power that is best avoided and as a mysterious, nearly inexhaustible source of money and various forms of assistance that should be exploited as much as possible. Each tribe invokes its right to obtain as much as the others, and each attempts to obtain more than the others. The Baruya also have learned the rules of this game.

They are culturally subject to the West, as well as being subordinate to it in economic and political terms. They have learned to read and write in pidgin English, a colonial language composed of broken English and Malay similar to the French and English Creole spoken today by the black populations of the West Indies. Those who receive secondary or higher education must learn English, the only language that enables them—as it does us—to communicate with the rest of the world. But the most important change is the general erosion and dismantling of the Baruya's innermost culture and the irremediable destruction of some of its components. And this has happened in spite of the fact that, as we have seen, many Baruya are proud of their customs and have not reacted passively or with indifference to their disappearance. But of all the forces acting on their society two make direct attacks on their culture: the state, which prohibits war and assumes the right to dispense justice, and Christianity, which asserts that the sun and the moon are false gods, that the true religion is the religion of Christ, and that men live in sin, especially if they are unaware that Christ died on the cross to redeem the sins of men of all races and all colors. Like Islam and Buddhism, Christianity is a religion that seeks converts, and the Baruya probably all will be Christian in a few generations, espousing a form of Third World Christianity that may differ considerably from European Christianity, but that still draws its inspiration from the latter's great visions and symbols.

Some of these changes are welcomed by the Baruya themselves. They do not wish to see the reappearance of constant, endemic warfare between them and their neighbors. But if war no longer is seen as a normal necessity for men, for which they must be prepared when they are very young, and as an opportunity to become a "big man," this means the collapse of some traditional values and of the traditional social hierarchy.

In addition, the Baruya men no longer like to spend their entire lives in the two valleys where their ancestors lived and in the four or five others they visited at the risk of their lives. They like to travel by air, to stay away for several years, to play cards, to drive trucks. One of them even joined a Japanese factory ship. Two or three have married women from the coast, announcing that they would not be returning to the village and that the women who had been promised to them could be married off to other men.

But, most importantly, there has been a major change in the deepest structure of Baruya society, the relations between men and women, a movement away from the traditional denial of women and affirmation of male dominance. Not that these changes have been accepted without violence. Seven or eight women were beaten to death or executed by husbands who could not tolerate the fact that they no longer were shown the obedience and submission to which tradition entitled them. But the men today are less afraid of women's uncleanness and the women less afraid of the symbols of male superiority. Young fathers now can be seen playing with their babies, even when those babies are girls. Previously, the very idea would have made them spit in disgust and shame. One thing has not changed, however: marriage, which is still based on the direct exchange of sisters between two men and two families. But the girls increasingly have a say, and they are not forced to marry against their will.

That is my view of the forms and mechanisms involved in the West-ernization of a tribal society. For the Baruya, a white person is no longer a supernatural being, but does remain a superior being, albeit one from whom since decolonization they no longer will accept orders or kicks. But in one sense, it is the whites themselves who, by granting independence, have denied themselves such liberties. And, on a higher level, it is the whites' religion that asserts that all men are equal before God.

Will these processes continue? Yes. Are they irreversible? Yes. Will they spread throughout the entire world? Probably, but here we must return to the idea that Westernization will spread, but that its present three com-ponents will not spread with the same degree of success. Japan is today the most dynamic capitalist country, but it has become so without losing ei-ther its political independence or the basis of its cultural identity. Indeed, Japan never was a colony, and Christianity has not long been allowed to vie with Buddhism there. But the tiny society of the Baruya is as nothing alongside Japan, and there are hundreds of such societies.

The West's first triumph will be in Europe, where it will finally conquer Eastern Europe, a task begun in the sixteenth century, well before the ad-vent of communist regimes. It will also spread in the Orient, even if the West is not synonymous there with Europe. Must we join in the applause or tiptoe off the stage? Leaving aside the people of the Third World, why should silence be required of those in the West who continue to believe that Christianity is not the only true religion and that there is indeed no true religion, those who see that political democracy does exist and wel-come it, but know that there is much to be done to extend social democ-racy and that nearly everything remains to be done to ensure that the economy and the wealth produced by capitalism or appropriated by it are shared out more fairly in the West itself and elsewhere? Why should we refuse to see these bad aspects, which are there and do affect our lives? What reason could there be for putting up with them? Could it really be because the end of history has arrived and we are at last living in the best of all possible worlds?

Reference Matter

Notes

Cassin, Speak, If You Are a Man

This text recapitulates in part a talk given at the colloquium "Common Non-sense" organized by Jean-François Lyotard at Urbino in July 1987. The epigraph is from Aristotle, *Topics*, trans. W. A. Pickard-Cambridge, in *The Complete Works of Aristotle*, ed. Jonathan Barnes, 2 vols. (Princeton: Princeton University Press, 1984), 1: 174.

1. Translator's note: The French word "sens," used throughout Cassin's essay to resonate with the term "consensus," is here translated variously as "meaning" and "sense."

2. Aristotle, *Metaphysics*, trans. Christopher Kirwan (London: Clarendon Press, 1971), *Gamma* 3, 1005 b 13–14. All subsequent in-text citations are based on modifications of this edition.

3. Ibid., translation modified.

4. Ibid., translation modified.

5. Nietzsche, quoted by Martin Heidegger in *Nietzsche*, ed. and rev. David Farrell Krell, trans. Joan Stambaugh (San Francisco: Harper, 1987), vol. 3, *The Will to Power as Knowledge and Metaphysics*, p. 111.

6. Heidegger, ibid., pp. 111–12.

7. Ibid., p. 112.

8. Martin Heidegger, *History of the Concept of Time: Prolegomena*, trans. Theodore Kisel (Bloomington: Indiana University Press, 1985), pp. 272–73.

9. Karl-Otto Apel, "Rekonstruktion der Vernunft durch Transformation der Transzendentalphilosophie," interview in *Concordia* 10 (1986): 3.

10. Karl-Otto Apel, "The *A Priori* of the Communication Community and the Foundations of Ethics: The Problem of a Rational Foundation of Ethics in the Scientific Age," in *Towards a Transformation of Philosophy*, trans. Glyn Adey and David Frisby (London: Routledge and Kegan Paul, 1980), p. 260.

11. Karl-Otto Apel, "La question d'une formation ultime de la raison," trans. S. Foisy and Jacques Poulain, *Critique* 15 (October 1981): 899.

12. Translations modified.

13. Apel, "The *A Priori*," pp. 261, 262.

14. Translations modified.

15. Apel, "La question," p. 926.

16. Gilles Deleuze, *The Logic of Sense*, trans. Mark Lester with Charles Stivale (New York: Columbia University Press, 1990), p. 68.

17. Jürgen Habermas, *Moral Consciousness and Communicative Action*, trans. Christian Lenhardt and Shierry Weber Nicholsen (Cambridge, Mass.: MIT Press, 1990), pp. 99 (original emphasis),100.

18. Ibid.

19. Richard Rorty, "Pragmatism, Relativism, Irrationalism," in *Consequences of Pragmatism (Essays: 1972–1980)* (Minneapolis: University of Minnesota Press, 1982), p. 165.

20. Ibid., pp. 166–67.

21. Ibid., p. 170.

22. Jacques Poulain, "Richard Rorty ou la boite blanche de la communication," *Critique* 417 (February 1982): 149.

23. Rorty, "Pragmatism, Relativism, Irrationalism," p. 167.

24. Gorgias, 82B23D.K.

25. Rorty, "Pragmatism, Relativism, Irrationalism," p. 172.

Goux, Subversion and Consensus

1. See Karl Polyani, *The Great Transformation* (1944; Boston: Beacon Press, 1957); Jean-Joseph Goux, "Remarques sur le mode symboliser capitaliste," in *Psychanalyse et politique* (Paris: Seuil, 1974); René Dumont, *Homo aequalis: Genèse et épanouissement de l'idéologie economique* (Paris: Gallimard, 1977); Pierre Rosanvallon, *Le liberalisme économique: Histoire de l'idée de marché* (Paris: Seuil, 1979).

2. Aristotle, *Nicomachean Ethics*, book 5, chapter 8.

3. Pierre-Joseph Proudhon, *De la capacité des classes ouvrières* (1865), book 2, chapter 14.

4. Because the English translation of Marx's *Grundrisse*, ed. and trans. David McLellan (New York: Harper & Row, 1972), is incomplete, I cite the German and French editions: *Grundrisse der Kritik der politischen Okonomie* (1850–59; Berlin: Dietz, 1953), p. 85; *Fondemonts de la critique de l'économie politique*, vol. 1 (Paris: Anthropos, 1967), p. 106.

5. Karl Marx, *A Contribution to the Critique of Political Economy*, trans. N. I. Stone (New York: International Library, 1904), p. 166.

NOTES TO PAGES 40–66

6. Gianni Vattimo, *La fin de la modernité* (Paris: Seuil, 1987), p. 25.

7. Auguste Comte, *Plan des travaux scientifiques necessaires pour réorganiser la société*, (1822; Paris: Aubier-Montaigne, 1970).

8. Auguste Comte, *Discours sur l'ensemble du positivisme* (1848), §64. My translations.

9. Ibid. "Préambule général."

10. Ibid.

11. The structural solidarity between these registers is shown in my essay "Numismatics," in *Symbolic Economies: After Marx and Freud*, trans. Jennifer Curtiss Gage, (Ithaca, N.Y.: Cornell University Press, 1990), pp. 9–63.

12. See Jean-Joseph Goux, *Les iconoclastes* (Paris: Seuil, 1978), chapter 2, "Le temple d'Utopie," 31–35, translated in *Symbolic Economies*, pp.151–67.

13. 50–56; translated as *The Coiners of Language*, trans. Jennifer Curtiss Gage (Norman: University of Oklahoma Press, 1994), chapter 4. See also idem, "Catégories de l'échange: Idéalité, symbolicité, réalité," in *Encyclopédie philosophique universelle*, vol. 1 (Paris: Presses Universitaires de France, 1989), pp. 227–33.

14. Marx, *Grundrisse*, German ed., p. 160; French trans., p. 194.

15. Jacques Lacan, *Le Séminaire*, book 1, *Les écrits techniques de Freud* (Paris: Seuil, 1975), pp. 178, 220, 178, 179, 220.

16. Auguste Comte, *Système de politique positive* (1851), book 2, chapter 2.

Augé, End or Continuation?

1. *Le genre humain*, no. 22 (1990).

2. Alain-Gérard Slama, *L'angélisme exterminateur* (Paris: Grasset, 1993).

3. Emmanuel Terray, "Le consensus français sur la réforme," *Le genre humain*, no. 22 (1990): 173–98.

4. François Furet, Jacques Julliard, and Pierre Rosanvallon, *La république du centre: La fin de l'exception française* (Paris: Fondation Saint-Simon, 1988).

5. Marcel Gauchet, "Conflits et partages," in *Lieux de mémoire*, ed. Pierre Nora, vol. 3, *La France*, (Paris: Gallimard, 1993), p. 459.

6. Gérard Althabe, "La construction de l'étranger dans la France urbaine d'aujourd'hui," in *L'Europe entre culture et nation*, ed. Daniel Fabre (Paris: Editions de la Maison des Sciences de l'Homme, 1996), pp. 215, 225.

Gaillard, Terror of Consensus

1. François Furet, Jacques Julliard, and Pierre Rosanvallon, *La république du centre: La fin de l'exception française* (Paris: Fondation Saint-Simon, 1988), p. 10.

2. Jacques Rancière, "La democratie corrigée," *Le genre humaine,* November 1990, p. 66.

3. I do not have space here to deal with the third perverse effect of consensus, which is the return of the archaic in the form of the prepolitical passion that is hatred. What is hatred? Nothing if not the pure rejection of the other. Hatred is everywhere therefore when there no longer is any political management of alterity. Current events bring to our attention every day painful proofs of the influence of the mounting tide of hatred. Only utter naïveté could allow us to think that consensus would be a remedy for hatred. By dismantling the political rostrum, where hatred found an outlet and a potential for rational transformation, consensus instead made hatred more at home. How can we expect the cure from the very vector that provoked the disease? Instead, as suggested by the title of the November 1990 issue of the review *Le genre humain* frequently cited here, "Le consensus, nouvel opium du peuple," consensus has become our new opium.

4. The affair of the contaminated blood supply in France involved establishing the responsibility of members of the government for the transmission of AIDS to hemophiliacs and other patients as a consequence of blood transfusions. It is the perfect example of the consensual crusades on which the several media concentrate today because it appealed to mere emotion, if not to the irrational, giving rise to archaic and strictly prepolitical forms of behavior such as the search for scapegoats.

5. Serge Moscovici and Willem Doise, "Du consensus dans les sociétés modernes," *Le genre humain,* November 1990, p. 15.

6. Annie Frénaux, *Le journal du dehors* (Paris: Gallimard, 1990), p. 99

7. Alain Touraine, *Critique de la modernité* (Paris: Fayard, 1992), p. 385.

Wood, "Democracy" and "Totalitarianism"

1. Victor Farias, *Heidegger et le nazisme* (Paris: Verdieu, 1987).

2. See my "French Thought under Mitterrand: The Social, Economic, and Political Context for the Return of the Subject and Ethics, for the Heidegger Scandal and for the Demise of the Critical Intellectual," *Contemporary French Civilization* 15, no. 2 (summer/fall 1991): 244–67.

3. For a representative example, see Nancy Hartsock, "Foucault on Power: A Theory for Women?" in *Feminism/Postmodernism,* ed. Linda Nicholson (New York: Routledge, 1990), especially p. 163.

4. For example, see Jacques Derrida, "'Eating Well,' or The Calculation of the Subject: An Interview with Jacques Derrida," in *Who Comes After the Subject?* ed. Eduardo Cadava, Peter Connor, and Jean-Luc Nancy (New York: Routledge, 1991); Gilles Deleuze, *Pourparlers* (Paris: Minuit, 1990).

5. Unfortunately, I have no room here to engage with Habermas and Frank in the detail they deserve. The following will suffice, however, to neutralize their attacks. Habermas commits the following two fundamental errors. First, he conflates Derrida with structuralism. Thus Saussurian difference is seen as the model for the *différance* that is at the basis of archewriting. See Jurgen Habermas, *The Philosophical Discourse of Modernity* (Cambridge, Mass.: MIT Press, 1987), p. 180. However, difference for Saussure—like difference for Hegel, who is Derrida's real point of departure in this matter, within whose text Saussure, unwittingly, was writing—is what is knowable by a subject (as in, for example, what Saussure calls "synchronic" linguistics in part 2 of the *Cours de linguistique générale*). Archewriting or *différance* "precede" this difference and, if one is to insist on a connection with Saussure, constitute a radicalization of Saussurian difference that alters the fundamentals of these questions beyond recognition (see below). This conflation of Derrida with Saussure is a frequent error among commentators.

Second, again like many other commentators, Habermas attributes semiotic idealism to Derrida: "The presence of whatever shows itself in actual intuition becomes directly dependent on the representative power of the sign" (p. 178). This is the familiar misreading of "There is no outside to the text." But "text" never meant "writing" or "language" in the colloquial senses of these terms. (I discuss these issues in some detail in the text.) Manfred Frank, whose philosophical erudition and acumen are superior to those of Habermas, has made an extraordinarily conscientious, painstaking, and honest attempt to understand Derrida—and has failed. (Lest these remarks appear condescending, let me add that I do not believe this to be a matter of "intelligence.") The core of his misunderstanding is located in his failure to detect the crucial distinction between Hegelian difference and Derridean *différance*: Frank does not see why "Derrida comes to a halt at that which Hegel calls 'difference' and does not proceed onward to that self-sublation that takes place in 'contradiction.'" See Manfred Frank, *What is Neostructuralism?* (Minneapolis: University of Minnesota Press, 1989), p. 274. Here I can do no more than point to my pages below on *différance*, which try to make vivid the distinction between Hegel and Derrida on this fundamental point. One might add that it is not enough to counter Derrida's objections to the Hegelian Absolute with the plea that "Hegel's variant of metaphysics does not take a principal presence or positivity as its point of departure, but rather . . . it leads up to it" (ibid.). Hegel's system can work only because it assumes from the outset that difference can be turned into "contradiction": that is to say, something that falls within the purview of a subject, can be represented, sublated, and thereby known. (Again, see below.)

6. François Furet, Jacques Julliard, and Pierre Rosanvallon, *La république du centre: La fin de l'exception française* (Paris: Calmann-Lévy, 1988).

7. Martin Heidegger, *Nietzsche*, vol. 4, trans. Frank A. Capuzzi (New York: Harper & Row, 1982), 96. Although it is significantly related to them, this objec-

tion to the *sub-iectum* in Nietzsche should not be assimilated indiscriminately to the earlier objections in *Being and Time* to positing an "I" or subject "as that which is proximally given," as something substantial or present at hand, an idea that "still posits the subjectum (*hypokeimenon*) along with it." *Being and Time*, trans. John Macquarrie and Edward Robinson (Oxford: Blackwell, 1973), p. 72. See also pp. 150, 367.

8. Jacques Derrida, *De l'esprit: Heidegger et la question* (Paris: Galilée, 1987).

9. Luc Ferry and Alain Renaut, *Heidegger et les modernes* (Paris: Grasset, 1988), 10. All translations from French texts are my own.

10. Ibid., pp. 42–43.

11. It is true that all these words—"emotion," "perception," and so on—have a history and so do not always mean the same thing at different times and in different places, and while the claim would be problematic that there is some stratum of universal meaning that is common to all these histories such that we can make general assertions about them, I would hold, nonetheless, that my last sentence still can be written without running counter to these qualifications.

12. Martin Heidegger, *Introduction to Metaphysics*, trans. Ralph Manheim (New Haven: Yale University Press, 1959), p. 45.

13. In what follows, I will limit the discussion to this text because of limits of space, because it gives rise to all the questions we need to broach, since with *Being and Time* it is Heidegger's most important work, and because it is in this text that one can trace the important *Kehre* or turning in Heidegger's thought.

14. Heidegger, *Nietzsche*, 4: 86.

15. Ibid.

16. Ibid., 4: 119.

17. The case of Foucault is somewhat different and cannot be treated here.

18. Heidegger, *Nietzsche*, 4: 93–94.

19. Ferry and Renaut, *Heidegger et les modernes*, pp. 160–171.

20. For the reader who is not closely familiar with Heidegger's work, what he means by Being is very hard to explain in a matter of a few lines. Suffice it to say that Being is something like what an earlier philosophical tradition would have called the "condition of possibility" of singular beings or entities. Except that—and this is what makes for the extreme difficulty of Heidegger's treatment of the notion—Heidegger is acutely concerned to exclude any suggestion that while distinguishable from beings, Being might precede beings as an origin, or that it might be separate from them. (The difficulties entailed by these demands will become apparent shortly in my discussion of *différance*.) Crucially, Being—like Freud's unconscious, or the ramifications of the "mode of production" in Marxism that constitute a "political unconscious," in Jameson's felicitous phrase—is "forgotten," necessarily, for singular entities or beings to emerge for Dasein, with dire consequences.

21. In what follows, I adopt the translator's usage of the term "man" for what contemporary sensibilities might generally prefer to see named as "humanity." I do this for a number of reasons, the most important being that it seems to me that, from a feminist point of view, it might be important not to forget this usage—rather than edulcorating it in order to avoid giving offense. Furthermore, from this point on in this text, I will not place the term "man" in quotation marks, in order not to give the erroneous impression that we can distance ourselves from the term.

22. Ferry and Renaut, *Heidegger et les modernes*, pp. 166–69. I confess that I find the account of the second alternative somewhat unclear.

23. Ibid., pp. 220–21.

24. See, for example, the essay "Nihilism and the History of Being," in *Nietzsche*, 4: 199–250.

25. Heidegger, *Nietzsche*, 4: 216.

26. Ibid., 4: 217.

27. Ibid., 4: 218.

28. Ibid.

29. Martin Heidegger, *Poetry, Language, Thought*, trans. Albert Hofstadter (New York: Harper & Row, 1971), p. 179.

30. Jacques Derrida, "Différance," in *Margins of Philosophy*, trans. Alan Bass (Chicago: University of Chicago Press, 1982), p. 14. "*Différance* (at a point of almost absolute proximity to Hegel . . .) must sign the point at which one breaks with the system of the *Aufhebung* and with speculative dialectics." Jacques Derrida, *Positions*, trans. Alan Bass (Chicago: University of Chicago Press, 1981), p. 44.

31. Georg Wilhelm Friedrich Hegel, *The Science of Logic*, trans. A. V. Miller (New York: Humanities Press, 1989), pp. 414–16.

32. Ibid., p. 415.

33. Heidegger, *Nietzsche*, 4: 208–9.

34. Georg Wilhelm Friedrich Hegel, *Lectures on the Philosophy of Religion*, trans. E. B. Speirs and J. Burdon Sanderson (New York: Humanities Press, 1974), p. 200.

35. Georg Wilhelm Friedrich Hegel, *Differenz des Fichteshen und Schellingshen Systems*, in *Sämtliche Werke*, 20 vols., ed. Georg Lasson (Leipzig: Felix Meiner, 1928), 1: 17. My translation.

36. Ibid., 1: 17–18.

37. Hegel, *Science of Logic*, p. 68.

38. Ibid., p. 841.

39. Derrida, "Différance," p. 26 n. 26.

40. Jacques Derrida, "Structure, Sign, and Play in the Discourse of the Human Sciences," in *Writing and Difference*, trans. Alan Bass (Chicago: University of Chicago Press, 1978), p. 280.

41. Derrida, *Positions*, p. 66.

42. Jean Baudrillard, *La société de consommation* (Paris, Denoël, 1970).

43. See Heidegger, *Nietzsche*, 4: 197–250, especially 203–5.

44. Jean-Paul Sartre, *L'Etre et le néant* (Paris: Gallimard, 1943), pp. 136–38.

45. Derrida, "Différance," pp. 3–4. Translation modified.

46. It is true that Derrida himself has not developed his own notion of *différance* along these lines. I will not speculate here regarding his grounds for not doing so. At this time, however, I see no reasons for anyone else to practice similar restraint.

47. For a useful introductory discussion of the issues—to which I am indebted in what follows—see Roger R. Jackson, "Matching Concepts: Deconstructive and Foundationalist Tendencies in Buddhist Thought," *Journal of the American Academy of Religion* 63, no. 3: 561–89. For more substantive studies, see Robert Magliola, *Derrida on the Mend* (West Lafayette, Ind.: Purdue University Press, 1984); David Loy, *Nonduality: A Study in Comparative Philosophy* (New Haven: Yale University Press, 1988); and Harold Coward, *Derrida and Indian Philosophy* (Albany: State University of New York Press, 1990).

48. "When emptiness 'works,' then everything in existence 'works.'" *Mulamadhyamakakarikas* 24: 14, in Kenneth K. Inada, *Nagarjuna: A Translation of his Mulamadhyamakakarika, with an Introductory Essay* (Tokyo: The Hokuseido Press, 1970). I am indebted to Roger R. Jackson for the interpretation of this line.

49. Theodor W. Adorno, *The Jargon of Authenticity*, trans. Knut Tarnowski and Frederic Will (Evanston, Ill.,: Northwestern University Press, 1973), pp. 112–13.

50. The key German sentences in question actually read as follows: "Die Neugier ist überall und nirgends. Dieser Modus des In-der-Welt-seins enthüllt eine neue Seinsart des alltäglichen Daseins, in der es sich ständig entwurzelt" (Curiosity is everywhere and nowhere. This manner of being-in-the-world discloses a new mode of being on the part of everyday Dasein, in which it is constantly uprooting itself). Martin Heidegger, *Sein und Zeit* (Tubingen: Neomarius Verlag, 1949), p. 173. I have modified the standard translation.

51. I am not sure how necessary it is to point this out, but it should not be forgotten that racism does not necessarily entail totalitarianism (in the strictly historical sense of the term, as it was originally applied to the authoritarian regimes of the 1930's) and that liberal democracies like the United States and Great Britain—two countries whose endemic racism is surpassed only by that of South Africa—have shown themselves to be quite comfortable with it for long periods of time. One can certainly make the argument that the liberal democracies are totalitarian in ways more sophisticated than Fascist and Communist regimes of the past, and that the racism of these societies reflects this. But that is another issue.

52. In the recent stampede in the United States away from the work of Derrida and toward that of Deleuze, originally motivated principally by a desire to be post-structuralist without being sullied by the Heidegger and de Man scandals, it is often forgotten how important Heidegger was for Deleuze. See, in particular, the importance of Heidegger's ontological difference in *Différence et répétition* (Paris: Presses Universitaires de France, 1968), explicitly mentioned at pp. 1 and 89–91.

53. Benjamin's thesis is often forgotten by those, like Paul de Man, who have sought to use his work in textual exegesis that strenuously occludes politics. The sentence in question—an exemplary dictum in this era of sententiousness and shameless maneuvering for the moral high ground—reads as follows: "There is no document of civilization which is not at the same time a document of barbarism." Walter Benjamin, *Illuminations*, trans. Harry Zohn (Glasgow: Fontana/Collins, 1973), p. 258.

54. Derrida's recent work has begun to fill in some of the gaps here. See especially Jacques Derrida and Gianni Vattimo, eds., *La religion* (Paris: Editions du Seuil, 1996).

55. I share the view of Heidegger, Baudrillard, Immanuel Wallerstein, and many others that, deadly rivalries notwithstanding, capitalist and communist regimes shared a common metaphysical space and constituted one geopolitical order in which the antagonists had a common interest. The Russian and Chinese Revolutions, in other words, were simply the means whereby feudal societies industrialized and Westernized in order to survive in a planetary regime the parameters of which had been dictated by the West.

Poster, *The Lyotard-Habermas Debate*

1. Jean-François Lyotard, *The Postmodern Condition: A Report on Knowledge*, trans. Geoff Bennington and Brian Massumi. Theory and History of Literature 10 (Minneapolis: University of Minnesota Press, 1984), p.15.

2. Jürgen Habermas, *The Philosophical Discourse of Modernity: Twelve Lectures*, trans. Frederick Lawrence (Cambridge, Mass.: MIT Press, 1987).

3. Ibid., p. 296.

4. Manfred Frank, in a seminar at University of California, Irvine, 1988.

5. Lyotard, *The Postmodern Condition*, p. 82. Philippe Lacoue-Labarthe refers to Habermas as a "dinosaur from the *Aufklärung*," "Talks," *Diacritics* 14, no. 3 (fall 1984): 25.

6. Seyla Benhabib, "Epistemologies of Postmodernism: A Rejoinder to Jean-François Lyotard," in *Feminism/Postmodernism*, ed. Linda Nicholson (New York: Routledge, 1990), pp. 107–30.

7. Jürgen Habermas, "Taking Aim at the Heart of the Present," in *The New*

Conservatism: Cultural Criticism and the Historians' Debate, trans. Shierry Weber Nicholsen (Cambridge, Mass.: MIT Press, 1989), pp. 173–79.

8. Jürgen Habermas, "Modernity, An Incomplete Project," in *The Anti-Aesthetic: Essays in Postmodern Culture,* ed. Hal Foster (Port Townsend, Wash.: Bay Press, 1983), p. 8.

9. This position is fully developed in Habermas's magnum opus, *The Theory of Communicative Action,* vol. 1, *Reason and the Rationalization of Society,* trans. Thomas McMarthy (Boston: Beacon Press, 1984), and vol. 2, *Lifeworld and System: A Critique of Functionalist Reason,* trans. Thomas McCarthy (Boston: Beacon Press, 1987).

10. Jürgen Habermas, *The Structural Transformation of the Public Sphere: An Inquiry into a Category of Bourgeois Society,* trans. Thomas Burger (1962; Cambridge, Mass.: MIT Press, 1989), p. 163.

11. Arjun Appadurai, "Disjuncture and Difference in the Global Cultural Economy," *Public Culture* 2, no. 2 (spring 1990): 10.

12. Habermas, *The Structural Transformation of the Public Sphere,* pp. 170–71, 175, 179, 164.

13. Mark Poster, *The Mode of Information: Poststructuralism and Social Context* (Chicago: University of Chicago Press, 1990).

14. On this question, see Peter Miller, *Domination and Power* (London: Routledge and Kegan Paul, 1987).

15. Benhabib, "Epistemologies of Postmodernism," pp. 107–30.

16. See Linda Nicholson, ed., *Feminism/Postmodernism* (New York: Routledge, 1990).

17. For example, see Meaghan Morris, "Postmodernity and Lyotard's Sublime," in *The Pirate's Fiancée: Feminism, Reading Postmodernism* (New York: Verso, 1988), pp. 223–40. For a positive view of the same position, see John Hinkson, "Postmodernism and Structural Change," *Public Culture* 2, no. 2 (spring 1990): 84.

18. Dick Hebdige characterizes these standard themes as totalization, telos, and utopia in *Hiding in the Light: On Images and Things* (New York: Routledge, 1988), pp. 186–98.

19. Ernest Laclau and Chantal Mouffe, *Hegemony and Socialist Strategy: Towards a Radical Democratic Politics,* trans. Winston Moore and Paul Cammack (London: Verso, 1985), chapter 3.

20. In this connection, see Jean-François Lyotard, "The Sublime and the Avant-Garde," trans. Lisa Liebman, *Paragraph* 6, no. 2 (1985): 1–18, and "Sensus Communis," trans. Marian Hobson and Geoff Bennington, *Paragraph* 11, no. 1 (1988): 1–23.

21. Jean-François Lyotard, *The Differend: Phrases in Dispute,* trans. Georges van den Abbeele (Minneapolis: University of Minnesota Press, 1988), presents a minimalist argument for critique.

22. Jean-François Lyotard, *The Inhuman: Reflections on Time*, trans. Geoffrey Bennington and Rachel Bowlby (Stanford, Calif.: Stanford University Press 1991) especially chapters 5, 7, 8. See also his "The Wall, The Gulf, and the Sun: A Fable," in *Politics, Theory and Contemporary Culture*, ed. Mark Poster (New York: Columbia University Press, 1993), pp. 261–75.

23. Donna Haraway, *Simians, Cyborgs, and Women: The Re-Invention of Nature* (New York: Routledge, 1991).

24. Tom Bridges, "Multiculturalism as a Postmodernist Project," *Postmodern Culture*. This journal is distributed electronically and may be received by pointing to http://jefferson.village.virginia.edu/pmc/ on the World Wide Web. The filename is bridges-essay-1.

25. Michel Foucault, "Two Lectures," in *Power/Knowledge*, ed. Colin Gordon, trans. Colin Gordon et al. (New York: Pantheon, 1980), p. 83.

26. I am referring to the important collection edited by Lawrence Grossberg, Cary Nelson, and Paula Treicher simply entitled *Cultural Studies* (New York: Routledge, 1992). Most of the essays confront the issue of essentialist agency in the context of multiculturalism, though that term is not often used. See for example, Tony Bennett, "Putting Policy into Cultural Studies," p. 31; Homi Bhabha, "Postcolonial Authority and Postmodern Guilt," p. 57; Angie Chabram-Dernersesian, "I Throw Punches for My Race . . . ," p. 85.

27. Homi Bhabha has articulated most fully the dilemma of minority subject positions. He writes, for example, that "the marginal or 'minority' is not the space of a celebratory, or utopian, self-marginalization." "Introduction," in *Nation and Narration*, ed. Homi Bhabha (New York: Routledge, 1990), p. 4. His concept of hybridity is an effort to expose the complexity of non-Western (and Western) subject positions.

Lionnet, Universalism and Diversity

I wish to thank John McCumber for his comments on early versions of this paper, as well as the friends and colleagues in my Northwestern University reading groups who generously provided extensive reactions to it. I also benefited greatly from my participation in 1991–92 in the minority discourse research group of the University of California Humanities Research Institute at Irvine.

1. Pierre Bourdieu, *La Distinction: Critique sociale du jugement* (Paris: Minuit, 1979).

2. See David Beriss, "High Folklore: Challenges to the French Cultural World Order," *Social Analysis* 33 (September 1993): 106. Beriss goes on to add in a footnote that "in a striking example of this logic, *Libération* (July 14, 1989, pp. 6–7) ran an article summarizing the human rights violations in each of the coun-

tries whose leaders were present in Paris [for the celebration of the Bicentennial]. Only one country escaped their largely negative review: France" (p. 124n7).

3. See, for example, Françoise Lionnet, "Identity, Sexuality, and Criminality: 'Universal Rights' and the Debate around the Practice of Female Excision in France," *Contemporary French Civilization* 26, no. 2 (summer/fall 1992): 294–307.

4. *L'Evénement du jeudi*, November 14–20, 1991, p. 60.

5. The reality represented in the movie *La haine* and the movie's enormous success in 1995 actually belies the idea that such "consensus" is developing in France.

6. Arjun Appadurai, "Disjuncture and Difference in the Global Cultural Economy," *Public Culture* 2, no. 2 (spring 1990): 10–11.

7. Hélène Cixous, "Sorties: Out and Out: Attacks/Ways Out/Forays," in Catherine Clément and Hélène Cixous, *The Newly Born Woman*, trans. Betsy Wing (Minneapolis: University of Minnesota Press, 1986), p. 71.

8. For a discussion of these circumstances in the *départments d'Outre-Mer*, see Françoise Lionnet, "*Créolité* in the Indian Ocean: Two Models of Cultural Diversity," *Yale French Studies* 82 (1993). Circumstances quite unlike those helped put Bill and Hillary Clinton in the White House (and I specify "Bill and Hillary" because of the obvious symbolic importance of that coupling for American institutional practices as these take their cues from the so-called "White House politics of inclusion"). The irony, however, is the speed with which symbolic gains by women have been contained in the United States. As Susan Estrich writes in "The Last Victim: The White Man Lashes Back," *New York Times Magazine*, Sunday, December 18, 1994, p. 55: "The new men's movement isn't about hating blacks and women or wanting to reverse our national commitment to equality. But it is about scapegoating, with men as the new victims. No one has been blamed more effectively than Hillary Clinton. . . . The most prominent woman in America has become the Wicked Witch of the West Wing, the embodiment, the caricature, of what angry white men are angry about. She has been demonized as the power-hungry, lesbian, arrogant, liberal, secretive, affirmative-action-loving, unfaithful First Lady who hates baking cookies. Repetition of rumors, lies and innuendo have magnified her mistakes beyond proportion. This was an organized campaign of vilification, and it worked." This situation does not invalidate my point. Quite the contrary: it seems that Hillary Clinton has suffered the same fate in the public sphere as "French thought" has in conservative academic circles.

9. Naomi Schor, "The Righting of French Studies: Homosociality and the Killing of 'La pensée '68,'" *Profession* 92 (New York: Modern Language Association, 1992): 32.

10. See, for example, Carmen Bernand-Nuñoz and Serge Gruzinski, *Histoire*

du nouveau monde, vol. 2, *Les métissages (1540–1620)* (Paris: Fayard, 1993). The term "hexagon" is a well-known shorthand for metropolitan France (derived from its geographic shape), not including its colonies and overseas departments.

11. Cixous, "Sorties," p. 71.

12. Elaine Marks and Isabelle de Courtivron, eds., *New French Feminisms, An Anthology* (Amherst: University of Massachusetts Press, 1980).

13. Leïla Sebbar, *Shérazade* (Paris: Stock, 1982), and *Les carnets de Shérazade* (Paris: Stock, 1985).

14. See Dorothy Blair, "Introduction," to her translation of *Sherazade* (London: Quartet, 1991).

15. Abdelkebir Khatibi, *Maghreb pluriel* (Paris: Denoël, 1983), pp. 17, 18.

16. Edouard Glissant, *Poétique de la relation* (Paris: Gallimard, 1990), pp. 165–66.

17. Edouard Glissant, *Tout-Monde* (Paris: Gallimard, 1993).

18. Henri Giordan, "Langue française et néo-jacobinisme," *Libération,* August 4, 1992, p. 5

19. Cited in ibid., p. 5.

20. Herman Lebovics, *True France: The Wars Over Cultural Identity, 1900–1945* (Ithaca: Cornell University Press, 1992), 9.

21. Ibid., pp. 9–10.

22. "Franco-French" may seem an odd term to American readers, the equivalent of saying "U.S.-American." However, it has a specific meaning in France: it refers to the "authentic," true-born, even blue-blood French, as opposed to the descendants of immigrants. The Unites States, a country of immigrants, does not have a strictly comparable group.

23. Gérard Noiriel, *Le creuset français: Histoire de l'immigration XIXe-XXe siècle* (Paris: Points, 1988), p. 61.

24. Ibid., p. 136.

25. For a discussion of some of these issues see Françoise Lionnet, "Immigration, Poster Art, and Transgressive Citizenship: France 1968–1988," *Substance* 76/77 (1995): 93–108.

26. In this regard, see Gerald Graff's admonition embodied in his title: "Teach the Conflicts," *South Atlantic Quarterly* 89, no. 1 (winter 1990): 51–67.

27. Noiriel, *Le creuset français,* p. 327.

28. Ibid., p. 358. See also Simone Bonnafous, "Dire et penser l'autre en France et aux Etats-Unis," in *L'Immigration américaine: Exemple ou contre-exemple pour la France,* ed. Sylvia Ullmo (Paris: L'Harmattan, 1994), pp. 65–70.

29. David Lloyd and Abdul JanMohamed, "Introduction: Toward a Theory of Minority Discourse. What Is To Be Done," *The Nature and Context of Minority Discourse* (New York: Oxford University Press, 1990), pp. 1–2.

30. David Lloyd, "Ethnic Cultures, Minority Discourse, and the State," unpublished manuscript, p. 8, cited in Hillis Miller, *Illustration* (Cambridge, Mass.: Harvard University Press, 1992), p. 152 n. 7.

31. J. L. Austin, *How To Do Things with Words* (New York: Oxford University Press, 1965).

32. Appadurai, "Disjuncture and Difference," pp. 10–11.

Apostolidès, Theater and Terror

1. I understand here the word "spectacle" in its Situationist signification. See Guy Debord, *Society of the Spectacle*, trans. Donald Nicholson-Smith (New York: Zone Books, 1994).

2. Charles-Guillaume Etienne and Alphonse Martainville, *Histoire du théâtre français depuis le commencement de la Révolution jusqu'à la réunion générale*, 4 vols. (Paris: Barba, Year X–1802). See 3: 43–64.

3. Ibid., 3: 66–67. In July 1793, this same theater presented an even more outrageous play, *La liberté des femmes*, which was canceled after its second performance.

4. Etienne and Martainville affirm that the actors from the Théâtre de la République were in part responsible for the arrest of their rivals. See ibid., 3: 105–6.

5. This information is borrowed from an important study by Maurice Dommanget, *Sylvain Maréchal, l'egalitaire* (Paris: Spartacus, 1950), pp. 260–65.

6. Sylvain Maréchal, *Le jugement dernier des rois*, in *Théâtre du XVIIIᵉ siècle*, ed. Jacques Truchet, vol. 2 (Paris: Gallimard, 1974). See p. 1321. All the following quotations refer to this edition.

7. Quoted by Annie Le Brun in *Petits et grands théâtres du marquis de Sade*, (Paris: Art Center, 1989), p. 237.

8. Marquis de Sade, *Oeuvres complétes*, 9 vols. (Paris: Cercle du Livre Précieux, 1966). See 7: 45.

9. Annie Le Brun, *Perspective dépravée* (Brussels: La Lettre Volée, 1991).

10. Quoted by Alphonse de Lamartine, *Histoire des Girondins*, 4 vols. (Paris, 1884), 3: 382.

11. Regarding the importance of the guillotine in the French imagination, see Marie Hélène Huet, *Rehearsing the Revolution* (Berkeley: University of California Press, 1982); Daniel Arasse, *La guillotine et l'imaginaire de la Terreur* (Paris: Flammarion, 1987); Daniel Gerould, *Guillotine, Its Legend and Lore* (New York: Blast Books, 1992).

12. See. p. 1307. In the first draft of Maréchal's text, the general upheaval against European monarchies took place on the day of Saturnalia.

13. Antonin Artaud, *The Theatre and Its Double* (New York: Grove Weiden-feld, 1958.

14. See Mona Ozouf, *La fête révolutionnaire* (Paris: Gallimard, 1976).

15. See my article "*La guillotine littéraire,*" *The French Review* 62, no. 6 (May 1989): 985–96.

16. Etienne and Martainville, *Histoire du théâtre français,* 3: 117–18.

Saint-Amand, Hostile Enlightenment

1. Ernst Cassirer, *The Philosophy of the Enlightenment,* trans. Fritz C. A. Koelln and James P. Pettegrove (Princeton: Princeton University Press, 1951), p. 234. On this question, see also Bronislaw Baczko, "Retour aux origines," in *Rousseau: Solitude et communauté* (Paris: Mouton, 1974), pp. 60–70.

2. See Michel Foucault, *Language, Counter-Memory, Practice* (Ithaca: Cornell University Press, 1977), p. 151.

3. Marshall Sahlins, *Stone Age Economics* (Chicago: Aldine Atherton, 1972), p. 173.

4. Gilles Lipovetsky, *L'Ere du vide* (Paris: Gallimard, 1983), p. 247.

5. Quoted in Peter Gay, *The Enlightenment: An Interpretation,* vol. 2, *The Science of Freedom* (New York: Norton, 1969), p. 29.

6. The authorship of this article is uncertain. Diderot attributed it to Nicolas Boulanger, but it has also been attributed to Diderot himself. See Paul Sadrin, *Nicolas-Antoine Boulanger ou avant nous le déluge,* Studies on Voltaire and the Eighteenth Century, no. 240 (Oxford: Voltaire Foundation, 1986), pp. 40–41.

7. S.v. "Société," in *Encyclopédie* (Neuchâtel: 1765), vol. 15.

8. Jean-Jacques Rousseau, *Emile,* trans. Allan Bloom (New York: Basic Books, 1979), p. 189.

9. Marcel Mauss, *The Gift,* trans. Ian Cunnison (New York: Norton, 1967).

10. Mary Douglas, Foreword to Marcel Mauss, *The Gift* (New York: London, 1990), p. ix.

11. Pierre Clastres, *Recherches d'anthropologie politique* (Paris: Seuil, 1980), p. 200.

12. Gay, *The Enlightenment: An Interpretation,* 2: 397–407.

13. Susan Jacoby, *Wild Justice* (New York: Harper & Row, 1983), p. 137.

14. See Roger Chartier, *The Cultural Origins of the French Revolution,* trans. Lydia G. Cochrane (Durham, N.C.: Duke University Press, 1991), pp. 233–39. Unable to make sense of this violence, to give it a symbolic interpretation, Robert Darnton simply finds it mysterious: "It would be nice if we could associate the Revolution exclusively with the Declaration of the Rights of the Citizen, but it was born in violence and it stamped its principles on a violent world." He simply

declares: "The violence remains a mystery." *What Was Revolutionary About the French Revolution?* (Waco, Tx.: Baylor University Press, 1990), p. 13, 16.

15. Philippe Godard, "Eloge de la vengeance," *Digraphe* 62 (1992): 44.

16. S.v. "Société," in *Encyclopédie* (Neuchâtel: 1765) vol. 15.

17. Montesquieu, *The Spirit of the Laws*, trans. Thomas Nugent (New York: Hafner, 1949), p. 4.

18. Louis Althusser, *Montesquieu, Rousseau, Marx: Politics and History*, trans. Ben Brewster (London: Verso, 1982), p. 80.

19. "There remain few important subjects for dispute. . . . In this age of enlightenment, everyone knows how to calculate to the penny the worth of his honor and his life." *The Letter to M. d'Alembert on the Theatre*, in *Politics and the Arts*, trans. Allan Bloom (Ithaca: Cornell University Press, 1960), p. 71.

20. Jean-Jacques Rousseau, *La nouvelle Héloïse*, (Paris: Garnier-Flammarion, 1967), p. 102.

21. Ibid., p. 103.

22. Marcel Hénaff, *Sade: L'Invention du corps libertin* (Paris: Presses Universitaires de France, 1978), p. 256.

23. Roland Barthes, *Sade, Fourier, Loyola*, trans. Richard Miller (Berkeley: University of California Press, 1989), p. 165.

24. Montesquieu, *Persian Letters*, trans. C. J. Betts (Harmondsworth: Penguin), letter 83, pp. 162–63.

25. Ibid., p. 166.

26. Ibid., p. 162.

27. For an optimistic analysis of this letter and the unconditional affirmation of the transcendence of justice, see Dena Goodman, *Criticism in Action* (Ithaca: Cornell University Press, 1989), pp. 79–104.

28. Montesquieu, *Persian Letters*, p. 163.

29. Marquis de Sade, *Juliette*, trans. Austryn Wainhouse (New York: Grove Press, 1968), p. 606.

30. Ibid., pp. 732, 78.

31. Friedrich Nietzsche, *On the Genealogy of Morals*, trans. Walter Kaufmann (New York: Vintage, 1967), third essay, section 9, p. 114.

32. Maurice Blanchot, *La Communauté inavouable* (Paris: Minuit, 1983), p. 81.

33. Simon-Nicolas-Henri Linguet, *Théorie des lois civiles* (Paris: Fayard, 1984), p. 127.

34. Adam Ferguson, *An Essay on the History of Civil Society* (New Brunswick, N.J.,: Transaction Books, 1980), section 4, p. 20, section 3, p. 16.

35. Immanuel Kant, "To Perpetual Peace: A Philosophical Sketch," in *Perpetual Peace and Other Essays*, trans. Ted Humphrey (Indianapolis: Hackett, 1983), p. 124.

NOTES TO PAGES 157–64   213

36. Claude Lefort, *Ecrire: A l'épreuve du politique* (Paris: Calmann-Lévy, 1992), p. 246.

37. See Dorinda Outram, *The Body in the French Revolution* (New Haven: Yale University Press, 1989), pp. 12–15, where she compares Schmitt's vision with the progressive anthropology of Norbert Elias.

38. Carl Schmitt, *The Concept of the Political*, trans. George Schwab (New Brunswick, N.J.: Rutgers University Press, 1976), p. 68.

Suleiman, Intellectual Sublime

An earlier version of this essay appeared, in French, in *Les cahiers naturalistes*, no. 67 (1993).

1. Jean-Paul Sartre, "Situation of the Writer in 1947," trans. Bernard Frechtman, in *What Is Literature? and Other Essays* (Cambridge, Mass: Harvard University Press, 1988), pp. 144–45 (translation slightly modified).

2. Jean-Paul Sartre, "Introducing *Les Temps modernes*," trans. Jeffrey Mehlman, in *What Is Literature? and Other Essays*, p. 252.

3. Michel Foucault, "Truth and Power," in *Power/Knowledge: Selected Interviews and Other Writings*, ed. Colin Gordon (New York: Pantheon Books, 1980), p. 129.

4. Anatole France, funeral oration for Emile Zola, quoted in Armand Lanoux and Stellio Lorenzi, *Zola ou la conscience humaine* (Paris: Atelier Marcel Jullian, 1978), pp. 308–11. Unless otherwise stated, all translations from the French are my own.

5. In fact, *J'Accuse* was one of a series of polemical articles in favor of Dreyfus that Zola published between 1897 and 1900, collected in 1901 under the title *La vérité en marche*. For a detailed analysis of *J'Accuse* and its immediate consequences, see the excellent study by Alain Pagès, *Emile Zola, un intellectuel dans l'affaire Dreyfus* (Paris: Librairie Séguier, 1991).

6. Maurice Blanchot, "Les intellectuels en question," *Le débat* 29 (March 1984): 17. This article was written in response to Jean-Denis Bredin's *L'Affaire* (Paris: Julliard, 1983), a scrupulously researched account of the Dreyfus affair that was a best-seller in France.

7. Blanchot, ibid., p. 25.

8. In fact, the postcards alone devoted to Zola could be the subject of a whole separate study. According to the catalogue assembled by Xavier Granoux in *"L'Affaire Dreyfus," catalogue descriptif des cartes postales ilustrées* (Paris: H. Daragon, 1903), among the thousands of postcards devoted to the affair, those representing Zola in a variety of heroic poses were by far the most numerous. Besides various portraits (sometimes he is shown wearing a laurel wreath),

Zola is represented as Saint George slaying the dragon, as Christ entering Jerusalem seated on a donkey, as a dignitary leading the triumphal chariot of Justice, and so on. Obviously, one also can find a great many negative cartoons and drawings of Zola, published for the most part in the anti-Dreyfusard press. Among the postcards, however, the heroic representations predominate. I wish to thank Naomi Schor for having told me about Granoux's catalogue.

9. Here is a small sampling of works I consulted, by genre. Biographies: see note 13. Personal testimonies: Alfred Bruneau, *A l'ombre d'un grand coeur: Souvenirs d'une collaboration* (1931; Geneva: Slatkine Reprints, 1980); Denise Le Blond-Zola, *Emile Zola raconté par sa fille* (Fasquelle, 1931); E. A. Vizetelly, *With Zola in England: A Story of Exile* (London: Chatto, 1899). Eyewitness accounts of the trials: see note 11. Homages: *Livre d'hommages des lettres françaises à Emile Zola* (Société Libre d'Editions des Gens de Lettres, 1898); Louis-Ferdinand Céline, "Hommage à Emile Zola," in Robert Denoël, *Apologie de "Mort à Credit" suivi de "Hommage à Emile Zola" par L.-F. Céline* (Paris: Denoël & Steele, 1936), *discours de Médan* of 1933, in which Céline doesn't mention the affair; Jules Romains, *L'exemple de Zola* (Flammarion, 1937), *discours de Médan* of 1935, which devotes considerable space to Zola's role in the affair. Films: William Dieterle, *The Life of Emile Zola*, United States, 1937; José Ferrer, *I Accuse*, United States, 1957; Stellio Lorenzi, *Zola ou la conscience humaine*, France, 1978. Plays: Hans J. Rehfisch and Wilhelm Herzog, *L'Affaire Dreyfus*, French version in three acts and ten tableaux by Jacques Richepin (Albin Michel, 1931). Fiction: Roger Martin du Gard, *Jean Barois* (Gallimard, 1913). For a detailed discussion of *Jean Barois* and other fictional representations of the Dreyfus affair, see my essay "The Literary Significance of the Dreyfus Affair," in *The Dreyfus Affair: Art, Truth, and Justice*, ed. Norman Kleeblatt (Berkeley: University of California Press, 1987), a volume accompanying the 1987 exhibition at the Jewish Museum in New York.

10. Séverine, *Vers la lumière . . . Impressions vécues* (Paris: Stock, 1900). Besides reports on the Zola trials of February and May 1898, the book includes some earlier articles about Zola, as well as reports on Dreyfus's trial in Rennes (August 7 to September 9, 1899). See also, in a similar vein, the much less successful book by Alfred Berl, *Le procès Zola: Impressions d'audience* (Paris: Aux Bureaux du Journal *Le siècle*, 1898).

11. Séverine, *Vers la lumière*, pp. 49, 51.

12. Ibid., pp. 91, 169.

13. For detailed accounts of the scandals created by Zola's writings before 1898, see Frederick Brown's excellent biography, *Zola: A Life* (New York: Farrar, Straus & Giroux, 1995).

14. For a sampling of vicious caricatures of Zola, see Kleeblatt, ed., *The Dreyfus Affair*.

15. Maurice Barrès, *Scènes et doctrines du nationalisme* (Paris: Félix Juven,

1901), p. 41. In 1908, Barrès used the same argument to deny any value whatsoever to Zola's work and to oppose the transfer of Zola's ashes to the Panthéon. (Zola's ashes were transferred nonetheless, in June 1908.)

16. Among the negative portraits of Zola, the one by Léon Daudet (a rightwing publicist, son of the novelist Alphonse Daudet), published years after the affair, stands out by its viciousness: "The basic character trait of that unhappy megalomaniac, an impure mix of French and Italian, of imagination and stupidity, was envy. . . . He had a taste for dishonor, decay, and the death of his fellowman." *Au temps de Judas: Souvenirs des milieux politiques, littéraires, artistiques et médicaux de 1880 à 1908* (Paris: Nouvelle Librairie Nationale, 1920), pp. 56–64.

17. Christophe Charle, *Naissance des "intellectuels," 1880–1900* (Paris: Minuit, 1990), p. 160. Brunetière's famous critique of intellectuals who engage in politics is in his article "Après le procès," published soon after the first Zola trial in *La revue des deux mondes* and then republished separately (Paris: Perrin, 1898). Barrès's critique, where he rejects the notion that intellectuals must defend universal values, is in *Scènes et doctrines du nationalisme*, chapters 2 and 3.

18. One problem with this myth, despite its attractiveness in some ways, is that it appears to make a "natural" connection between sublime engagement and a masculine hero (the "great writer"). Theoretically, the hero could be a woman— but historically and linguistically, the "great writer" has been coded as male. Even more importantly, the philosophical tradition (including Sartrean existentialism) always has identified the universal with the masculine, women being "particular."

19. Jean Fréville, *Zola semeur d'orages* (Paris: Editions Sociales, 1952), pp. 147, 156. Among the many other heroic biographies that appeared between Zola's death and 1960, one can cite Paul Brulat, *Histoire populaire d'Emile Zola* (Paris: La Librairie Mondiale, 1906); Matthew Josephson, *Zola and His Time* (New York: Macaulay, 1928), which served as the basis for William Dieterle's film, *The Life of Emile Zola* (1937); Alexandre Zévaès, *Zola* (Paris: Nouvelle Revue Critique, 1945); Armand Lanoux, *Bonjour monsieur Zola* (Paris: Amiot-Dumont, 1954), which served as the basis for Stellio Lorenzi's telefilm, *Zola ou la conscience humaine* (1978); Henri Guillemin, *Zola, légende ou verité?* (Paris: Julliard, 1960).

20. In fact, although he had tried several times to be elected, by 1898 Zola had very small chance of entering the Académie. Nor would Coppée have supported him, since he was a staunch anti-Dreyfusard. See Brown, *Zola: A Life*, pp. 611, 697.

21. The film was forbidden in France for fifteen years, being shown for the first time in 1952—and then in a single theater in Paris, in a heavily cut version (twenty minutes were cut from the scenes of the Zola trial, on grounds of "insult to the army"). Furthermore, the film was preceded by a warning about its

historical inaccuracies, which appeared just before the opening credits. For details about the film's vicissitudes in obtaining a permit, see *Les cahiers du cinéma*, no. 18 (December 1952): 56–58.

22. As this scene shows, the "sublime effect" can very well coincide with the "ordinary everyday." Except for the rhetorical phrasing of the sentence about "murdering an innocent man . . . overthrowing the Republic," the scene is linguistically in the "everyday" mode, like Madame Zola's nightgown and robe. But the lighting, the actors' facial expressions, and the movement of the camera (which shows several profiles of Zola bent over his desk, writing) produce a solemn, elevated mood.

23. John Frazer, *Artificially Arranged Scenes: The Films of Georges Méliès* (Boston: G. K. Hall, 1979), p. 80. The film that lifted the ban was a documentary by Jean Chérasse, *Dreyfus ou l'intolérable vérité*. Méliès had made a film about the affair in 1899, but it caused such an uproar that it was not allowed to be shown in France. Two other early films titled *L'Affaire Dreyfus*, by Ferdinand Zecca (1899) and Lucien Nonguet (1907), suffered similar fates. After that, there was nothing in France until Chérasse's film, then Lorenzi's dramatization. Thus, for almost three-quarters of a century, no French filmmaker was able to make a film about the Dreyfus affair in France. It strikes one as hard to believe.

24. Sartre, "Situation of the Writer in 1947," p. 145, translation slightly modified.

25. Jean-François Lyotard, "Le tombeau de l'intellectuel," *Le monde*, October 8, 1983.

26. Blanchot, "Les intellectuels en question," p. 25. I note with some regret that Blanchot's vision of the intellectual is exclusively male, like that of Sartre, Foucault, and just about every other male theorist. For the elaboration of a different view inspired by (but also somewhat critical of) Richard Rorty's figure of the ironist, see my "Epilogue: The Politics of Postmodernism after the Wall; or, What Do We Do When the Ethnic Cleansing Starts?" in *Risking Who One Is: Encounters with Contemporary Art and Literature* (Cambridge, Mass.: Harvard University Press, 1994). See also Toril Moi, *Simone de Beauvoir—The Making of an Intellectual Woman* (Oxford: Blackwells, 1994).

27. Susan Sontag, "'There' and 'Here': A Lament for Bosnia," *The Nation*, December 25, 1995, pp. 818–20. Sontag evokes, with a touch of nostalgia, the 1930's and 1960's, when intellectuals still felt a sense of international (that is, universal) responsibility: "If the intellectuals of the 1930's and the 1960's often showed themselves too gullible, too prone to appeals to idealism to take in what was really happening in certain beleaguered, newly radicalized societies that they may or may not have visited (briefly), the morosely depoliticized intellectuals of today, with their cynicism always at the ready, their addiction to entertainment, their reluctance to inconvenience themselves for any cause, their de-

votion to personal safety, seem at least equally deplorable" (p. 820). Like Blanchot's, her argument moves toward the necessity of reviving the "universal intellectual."

28. "Universal intellectual not dead. Letter follows." This is a take-off on a
famous telegram sent by one of Zola's disciples, Paul Alexis, to a reporter who
was doing an *enquête* on naturalism as a literary school. Alexis wrote: "Naturalism not dead. Letter follows." Note that in my rewriting, "intellectuel" also can
be a feminine noun.

Index of Names

In this index, "f" after a number indicates a separate reference on the next page, and "ff" indicates separate references on the next two pages. A continuous discussion over two or more pages is indicated by a span of page numbers, e.g., "57–59." *Passim* is used for a cluster of references in close but not consecutive sequence.

Library of Congress Cataloging-in-Publication Data

Terror and consensus : vicissitudes of French thought / edited by
Jean-Joseph Goux and Philip R. Wood.
    p.   cm.
  "The papers assembled here comprise contributions to a conference
entitled 'Terror and Consensus: The Cultural Singularity of French
Thought?' held at Rice University in 1993, the bicentenary of the
Great Terror of the French Revolution, and other contributions
solicited subsequently"—Introd.
  Includes bibliographical references and index.
  ISBN 0-8047-2969-7 (cloth). — ISBN 0-8047-2970-0 (pbk.).
  1. France—Intellectual life—19th century—Congresses. 2. France—
Intellectual life—20th century—Congresses. 3. Philosophy, French—
19th century—Congresses. 4. Philosophy, French—20th century—
Congresses. 5. Political science—France—History—19th century—
Congresses. 6. Political science—Philosophy—Congresses.
7. Political science—France—History—20th century—Congresses.
8. France—Politics and government—1789—Congresses.
I. Goux, Jean-Joseph II. Wood, Philip R.
B2185.T47 1998
944.08—dc21   97-44523
                                           CIP
                                         Rev.

∞ This book is printed on acid-free, recycled paper.

Original printing 1998
Last figure below indicates year of this printing:
07 06 05 04 03 02 01 00 99 98